SAP R/3 Admi...
For Dumm...

M000239014

Transaction Code

Transaction Code	Menu Path	Function
PFCG	Tools⇨Administration⇨Maintain Users⇨Activity Groups	Activity Groups
SA38	System⇨ABAP/4 Reporting	ABAP/4 Reporting
SCC3	Tools⇨Administration⇨Administration⇨Client Admin⇨ Copy Logs	Copy Logs
SCC4	Tools⇨Administration⇨Administration⇨Client Admin⇨ Client Maintenance	Client Administration
SCCL	Tools⇨Administration⇨Administration⇨Client Admin⇨ Client Copy⇨Local Client Copy	Local Client Copy
SE09	Tools⇨ABAP/4 Workbench⇨Overview⇨ Workbench Organizer	Workbench Organizer
SE16	Tools⇨ABAP/4 Workbench⇨Overview⇨Data Browser	Data Browser
SM02	Tools⇨Administration⇨Administration⇨System Messages	System Messages
SM04	Tools⇨Administration⇨Monitoring⇨User Overview	User Overview
SM12	Tools⇨Administration⇨Monitoring⇨Lock Entries	Display and Delete Locks
SM13	Tools⇨Administration⇨Monitoring⇨Update	Display Update Records
SM21	Tools⇨ABAP/4 Workbench⇨Tests⇨System Log	System Log
SM28	Tools⇨Administration⇨Administration⇨Installation Check	Installation Check
SM36	Tools⇨Administration⇨Jobs⇨Define Job	Define Background Job
SM37	Tools⇨Administration⇨Jobs⇨Job Overview	Background Job Overview
SM59	Tools⇨Administration⇨Administration⇨Network⇨ RFC Destination	RFC Destinations (Display/Maintain)
SMLT	Tools⇨Administration⇨Administration⇨ Language Transport	Language Transport Utility
SPAD	Tools⇨Administration⇨Spool⇨Spool Administration	Spool Administration
SPAM	Tools⇨ABAP/4 Workbench⇨Utilities⇨Maintenance⇨Patches (SPAM)	SAP Patch Manager
SPRO	Tools⇨Business Engineering⇨Customizing	IMG
ST01	Tools⇨Administration⇨Monitoring⇨Traces⇨System Trace	System Trace
ST02	Tools⇨Administration⇨Monitoring⇨Performance⇨ Setup/Buffers⇨Buffers	Setups/Tune Buffers Tune Buffers
ST03	Tools⇨Administration⇨Monitoring⇨Performance⇨ Workload⇨Analysis	Performance, SAP Statistics, Workload
ST04	Tools⇨Administration⇨Monitoring⇨Performance⇨ Database⇨Activity	Select DB Activities
ST05	Tools⇨Administration⇨Monitoring⇨Traces⇨SQL Trace	SQL Trace
ST22	Tools⇨Administration⇨Monitoring⇨Dump Analysis	ABAP/4 Runtime Error Analysis
SU01	Tools⇨Administration⇨Maintain Users⇨Users	Maintain User
SU02	Tools⇨Administration⇨Maintain Users⇨Profiles	Maintain Authorization Profiles
SU03	Tools⇨Administration⇨Maintain Users⇨Authorizations	Maintain Authorizations
SU53	System⇨Utilities⇨Disp. Auth. Check	Display Check Values

SAP R/3 Administration For Dummies®

Cheat Sheet

tp Unconditional Code Values

Code	Export	Import
0	N/A	Do not delete from bufffer of target system after import. U1 is set in request buffer.
1	Ignore incorrect status	Request can be imported again.
2	N/A	Original objects in target system can be rewritten.
3	N/A	System dependent objects in target system can be rewritten.
4	N/A	Ignore that request was addressed for another system.
5	N/A	Object can originate from any system.
6	N/A	Unconfirmed repairs can be rewritten.
8	N/A	Ignore limits to table classsfification.
9	N/A	Ignore locks for transport types.

Saprouter Command Line Flags

Command	Function
-r	Run SAProuter
-s	Stop SAProuter
-l	List all connections on SAProuter
-c <id>	Terminate connection
-n	Reread routing table
-t	Write to logfile
-T	Write to named logfile
-d	Write technical information to logfile
-R	Explicit path to SAProutab
-G	Name of logfile
-S	Service name
-H	Hostname
-P	Password for information requests

User Information System Reports Run by SA38 or SE38

Command	Report
RSUSR020	Displays users with specific authorizations
RSUSR025	Deletes users who have not logged on in X days
RSUSR030	Deletes users expanded selection
RSUSR000	Displays current active users
RSUSR002	Displays users based on selection criteria
RSUSR003	Checks password for SAP* and DDIC users in all clients
RSUSR005	Displays list of users with critical authorizations
RSUSR006	Displays a list of users who are locked

...For Dummies®: Bestselling Book Series for Beginners

TM

References for the Rest of Us!®

BESTSELLING BOOK SERIES

Are you intimidated and confused by computers? Do you find that traditional manuals are overloaded with technical details you'll never use? Do your friends and family always call you to fix simple problems on their PCs? Then the *...For Dummies*® computer book series from IDG Books Worldwide is for you.

...For Dummies books are written for those frustrated computer users who know they aren't really dumb but find that PC hardware, software, and indeed the unique vocabulary of computing make them feel helpless. *...For Dummies* books use a lighthearted approach, a down-to-earth style, and even cartoons and humorous icons to dispel computer novices' fears and build their confidence. Lighthearted but not lightweight, these books are a perfect survival guide for anyone forced to use a computer.

> *"I like my copy so much I told friends; now they bought copies."*
>
> — Irene C., Orwell, Ohio

> *"Quick, concise, nontechnical, and humorous."*
>
> — Jay A., Elburn, Illinois

> *"Thanks, I needed this book. Now I can sleep at night."*
>
> — Robin F., British Columbia, Canada

Already, millions of satisfied readers agree. They have made *...For Dummies* books the #1 introductory level computer book series and have written asking for more. So, if you're looking for the most fun and easy way to learn about computers, look to *...For Dummies* books to give you a helping hand.

IDG
BOOKS
WORLDWIDE®

SAP R/3
ADMINISTRATION
FOR
DUMMIES®

SAP R/3 ADMINISTRATION FOR DUMMIES®

by Joey Hirao and Jim Meade

IDG Books Worldwide, Inc.
An International Data Group Company

Foster City, CA ◆ Chicago, IL ◆ Indianapolis, IN ◆ New York, NY

SAP R/3 Administration For Dummies®

Published by
IDG Books Worldwide, Inc.
An International Data Group Company
919 E. Hillsdale Blvd.
Suite 400
Foster City, CA 94404
www.idgbooks.com (IDG Books Worldwide Web site)
www.dummies.com (Dummies Press Web site)

Library of Congress Catalog Card No.: 99-61340

ISBN: 0-7645-0375-8

Printed in the United States of America

10 9 8 7 6 5 4 3 2 1

1O/QR/QU/ZZ/IN

Distributed in the United States by IDG Books Worldwide, Inc.

Distributed by CDG Books Canada Inc. for Canada; by Transworld Publishers Limited in the United Kingdom; by IDG Norge Books for Norway; by IDG Sweden Books for Sweden; by Woodslane Pty. Ltd. for Australia; by Woodslane (NZ) Ltd. for New Zealand; by TransQuest Publishers Pte Ltd. for Singapore, Malaysia, Thailand, Indonesia, and Hong Kong; by ICG Muse, Inc. for Japan; by Norma Comunicaciones S.A. for Colombia; by Intersoft for South Africa; by Le Monde en Tique for France; by International Thomson Publishing for Germany, Austria and Switzerland; by Distribuidora Cuspide for Argentina; by Livraria Cultura for Brazil; by Ediciones ZETA S.C.R. Ltda. for Peru; by WS Computer Publishing Corporation, Inc., for the Philippines; by Contemporanea de Ediciones for Venezuela; by Express Computer Distributors for the Caribbean and West Indies; by Micronesia Media Distributor, Inc. for Micronesia; by Grupo Editorial Norma S.A. for Guatemala; by Chips Computadoras S.A. de C.V. for Mexico; by Editorial Norma de Panama S.A. for Panama; by American Bookshops for Finland. Authorized Sales Agent: Anthony Rudkin Associates for the Middle East and North Africa.

For general information on IDG Books Worldwide's books in the U.S., please call our Consumer Customer Service department at 800-762-2974. For reseller information, including discounts and premium sales, please call our Reseller Customer Service department at 800-434-3422.

For information on where to purchase IDG Books Worldwide's books outside the U.S., please contact our International Sales department at 317-596-5530 or fax 317-596-5692.

For consumer information on foreign language translations, please contact our Customer Service department at 1-800-434-3422, fax 317-596-5692, or e-mail rights@idgbooks.com.

For information on licensing foreign or domestic rights, please phone +1-650-655-3109.

For sales inquiries and special prices for bulk quantities, please contact our Sales department at 650-655-3200 or write to the address above.

For information on using IDG Books Worldwide's books in the classroom or for ordering examination copies, please contact our Educational Sales department at 800-434-2086 or fax 317-596-5499.

For press review copies, author interviews, or other publicity information, please contact our Public Relations department at 650-655-3000 or fax 650-655-3299.

For authorization to photocopy items for corporate, personal, or educational use, please contact Copyright Clearance Center, 222 Rosewood Drive, Danvers, MA 01923, or fax 978-750-4470.

is a registered trademark or trademark under exclusive license to IDG Books Worldwide, Inc. from International Data Group, Inc. in the United States and/or other countries.

About the Authors

Joey Hirao: An SAP consultant, currently working for Arthur Anderson Consulting. He has also worked as a Basis Team Leader and as a technical trainer for several companies. Joey has a BA in Economics/Business from UCLA. When the bugs are gone, Joey goes surfing.

Jim Meade: A professional writer of computer books, ranging from large systems to books on PCs. Among others, he has authored *LotusScript For Dummies* and *Dynamic HTML Explorer*. Jim has a Ph.D. in English from Northwestern University.

ABOUT IDG BOOKS WORLDWIDE

Welcome to the world of IDG Books Worldwide.

IDG Books Worldwide, Inc., is a subsidiary of International Data Group, the world's largest publisher of computer-related information and the leading global provider of information services on information technology. IDG was founded more than 30 years ago by Patrick J. McGovern and now employs more than 9,000 people worldwide. IDG publishes more than 290 computer publications in over 75 countries. More than 90 million people read one or more IDG publications each month.

Launched in 1990, IDG Books Worldwide is today the #1 publisher of best-selling computer books in the United States. We are proud to have received eight awards from the Computer Press Association in recognition of editorial excellence and three from Computer Currents' First Annual Readers' Choice Awards. Our best-selling *...For Dummies®* series has more than 50 million copies in print with translations in 31 languages. IDG Books Worldwide, through a joint venture with IDG's Hi-Tech Beijing, became the first U.S. publisher to publish a computer book in the People's Republic of China. In record time, IDG Books Worldwide has become the first choice for millions of readers around the world who want to learn how to better manage their businesses.

Our mission is simple: Every one of our books is designed to bring extra value and skill-building instructions to the reader. Our books are written by experts who understand and care about our readers. The knowledge base of our editorial staff comes from years of experience in publishing, education, and journalism — experience we use to produce books to carry us into the new millennium. In short, we care about books, so we attract the best people. We devote special attention to details such as audience, interior design, use of icons, and illustrations. And because we use an efficient process of authoring, editing, and desktop publishing our books electronically, we can spend more time ensuring superior content and less time on the technicalities of making books.

You can count on our commitment to deliver high-quality books at competitive prices on topics you want to read about. At IDG Books Worldwide, we continue in the IDG tradition of delivering quality for more than 30 years. You'll find no better book on a subject than one from IDG Books Worldwide.

John Kilcullen
Chairman and CEO
IDG Books Worldwide, Inc.

Steven Berkowitz
President and Publisher
IDG Books Worldwide, Inc.

Eighth Annual Computer Press Awards ≥1992

Ninth Annual Computer Press Awards ≥1993

Tenth Annual Computer Press Awards ≥1994

Eleventh Annual Computer Press Awards ≥1995

IDG is the world's leading IT media, research and exposition company. Founded in 1964, IDG had 1997 revenues of $2.05 billion and has more than 9,000 employees worldwide. IDG offers the widest range of media options that reach IT buyers in 75 countries representing 95% of worldwide IT spending. IDG's diverse product and services portfolio spans six key areas including print publishing, online publishing, expositions and conferences, market research, education and training, and global marketing services. More than 90 million people read one or more of IDG's 290 magazines and newspapers, including IDG's leading global brands — Computerworld, PC World, Network World, Macworld and the Channel World family of publications. IDG Books Worldwide is one of the fastest-growing computer book publishers in the world, with more than 700 titles in 36 languages. The "...For Dummies®" series alone has more than 50 million copies in print. IDG offers online users the largest network of technology-specific Web sites around the world through IDG.net (http://www.idg.net), which comprises more than 225 targeted Web sites in 55 countries worldwide. International Data Corporation (IDC) is the world's largest provider of information technology data, analysis and consulting, with research centers in over 41 countries and more than 400 research analysts worldwide. IDG World Expo is a leading producer of more than 168 globally branded conferences and expositions in 35 countries including E3 (Electronic Entertainment Expo), Macworld Expo, ComNet, Windows World Expo, ICE (Internet Commerce Expo), Agenda, DEMO, and Spotlight. IDG's training subsidiary, ExecuTrain, is the world's largest computer training company, with more than 230 locations worldwide and 785 training courses. IDG Marketing Services helps industry-leading IT companies build international brand recognition by developing global integrated marketing programs via IDG's print, online and exposition products worldwide. Further information about the company can be found at www.idg.com.
1/24/99

Dedication

I dedicate this book to my mom, Hisayo Hirao, who always believed in me and my dad, Osatake Hirao, who gave me my strength. I thank my sister, Risa Hirao, for her wisdom and my girlfriend, Jeanmarie Nowlan, for giving me the courage to continue. — Joey

To my lovely wife, Nina, and her mom and dad, Dr. Solbert Permutt and Loretta Permutt (who are showing signs of beginning to accept me). — Jim Meade

Acknowledgments

First of all, we'd really, really like to thank our Acquisitions Editor, Sherri Morningstar, for her vision in putting this project together and for getting us together as authors.

We also really appreciate the contribution of our tech editor, Matt Franklin, Director of SAP Integration Services at Promenix, Inc. in Chadds Ford, PA, an integration firm specializing in SAP Enterprise Application Integration. Check out its Web site at www.promenix.com.

Thanks to our totally proficient, exacting Project Editor, Pat O'Brien, who kept us on time, on target, and on task. And much appreciation to Christine Beck, our skilled copy editor.

We'd like to thank all the others at IDG who worked with us. (You'll see their names in the Publisher's Acknowledgments.)

Thanks to the folks in management, too, with special mention to Steve Berkowitz, John Kilkullen, Mary Bednarek, and Leah Cameron. And here's a special nod to the sales force, who give IDG Books Worldwide its vivacity and market presence. Without them, even the greatest book doesn't get its due.

And I'd like to thank my family — Nina, Molly, Ben, and Josh — who seem to think it's their mission in life to keep me from becoming too much of a nerd. — Jim

Publisher's Acknowledgements

We're proud of this book; please register your comments throught our IDG books Worldwide Online Registration Form located at `http://my2cents.dummies.com`.

Some of the people who helped bring this book to marke include the following:

Acquisitions, Editorial, and Media Development

Project Editor: Pat O'Brien

Acquisitions Editor: Sherri Morningstar

Copy Editor: Christine Beck

Technical Editor: Matt Franklin

Associate Permissions Editor: Carmen Krikorian

Editorial Manager: Mary C. Corder

Editorial Assistant: Alison Walthall

Production

Project Coordinator: Tom Missler

Layout and Graphics: Linda M. Boyer, Angela F. Hunckler, Brent Savage, Janet Seib, Kathie Schutte

Proofreaders: Christine Berman, Nancy Price, Kathleen Sparrow, Ethel M. Winslow, Janet M. Withers

Indexer: Sherry Massey

General and Administrative

IDG Books Worldwide, Inc: John Kilcullen, CEO; Steven Berkowitz, President and Publisher

IDG Books Technology Publishing: Brenda McLaughlin, Senior Vice President and Group Pubisher

Dummies Technology Press and Dummies Editorial: Diane Graves Steele, Vice President and Associate Publisher, Mary Bednarek, Director of Acquisitions and Product Development; Kristin A. Cocks, Editorial Director

Dummies Trade Press: Kathleen A. Welton, Vice President and Publisher; Kevin Thornton, Acquisitions Manager

IDG Books Production for Dummies Press: Michael R. Britton, Vice President of Production and Creative Services; Cindy L. Phipps, Manager of Project Coordination, Production Proofreading, and Indexing, Kathie S. Schutte, Supervisor of Page Layout; Shelley Lea, Supervisor of Graphics and Design; Debbie J. Gates, Production Systems Specialist; Robert Springer, Supervisor of Proofreading, Debbie Stailey, Special Projects Coordinator; Tony Augsburger, Supervisor of Reprints and Bluelines

Dummies Packaging and Book Design: Patty Page, Manager, Promotions Marketing

◆

The publisher would like to give special thanks to Patrick J. McGovern, without whom this book would not have been possible

◆

Contents at a Glance

Cartoons at a Glance

By Rich Tennant

The 5th Wave By Rich Tennant

"I asked for software that would biodegrade after it was thrown out, not while it was running."

page 71

The 5th Wave By Rich Tennant

"I ran Thompson's numbers. Either he's our top sales rep or the next Emperor of Japan."

page 7

The 5th Wave By Rich Tennant

HMM—NICE TREE STRUCTURE.

page 31

The 5th Wave By Rich Tennant

"Your database is beyond repair, but before I tell you our backup recommendation, let me ask you a question. How many index cards do you think will fit on the walls of your computer room?"

page 225

The 5th Wave By Rich Tennant

"OH YEAH, AND TRY NOT TO ENTER THE WRONG PASSWORD."

page 147

The 5th Wave By Rich Tennant

Rags wondered whether he'd said all he wanted to in his report to the CEO.

ARF! ARF! Nrooof arf!

Arf, arf, arf.

page 299

The 5th Wave By Rich Tennant

5th Wave Power Tip: To increase application speed, punch the Command Key over and over and over as rapidly as possible. The computer will sense your impatience and move your data along quicker than if you just sat and waited. Hint: This also works on elevator buttons and cross walk signals.

page 279

Fax: 978-546-7747 • E-mail: the5wave@tiac.net

Table of Contents

· ·

Part III: Doing Everyday Stuff 71

Chapter 7: (SA)People Skills 73

Chapter 8: You Ain't Got a Thing If You Ain't Got Printing 115

Introduction

*P*eople look at you funny when you say you're writing *SAP R/3 Administration For Dummies*. "You may as well write *Rocket Science For Dummies,*" they say.

Admittedly, it is a bit of an oxymoron to write about an ambitious topic like SAP R/3 administration in a modest book like this *...For Dummies* book. But we think we're aware of the challenges:

- ✔ Making this a *...For Dummies* book that satisfies real R/3 administrators.
- ✔ Making this an R/3 book that satisfies loyal *...For Dummies* readers.

We're willing to face these challenges and write a book that is helpful to real R/3 administrators without being frustrating to ordinary people. It's our objective here to do just that — basically, to give you real information in a way that you can understand.

About This Book

This book, as we see it, is a readable book about technical stuff (an oxymoron).

As we see it, books fall into two categories — technical documentation and books that are fun to read. Technical documentation you use as a reference, looking only for what you need and ignoring the rest. Books that are fun to read — novels, humor books, travel nonfiction — you read to get your mind off the serious matters in life.

This book is replete with technical information — no doubt about that. Heady stuff is in here. You can use this book as a reference if you want, and we encourage you to do so. In here you can find out how to

- ✔ Configure systems
- ✔ Monitor performance
- ✔ Update source code

But this book is also readable. If you're curious about something like Enterprise Resource Planning or SAP System Landscape, you can read about it here in a way that you can understand. If you want a definition of, say, Online Service System (OSS) that doesn't leave you so confused that you're sorry you asked, you can find it here.

How to Use This Book

After you have the book, we can't say much about how you're going to use it, can we? We *can* tell you what we have in mind, though.

First of all, sure, you can use *SAP R/3 Administration For Dummies* as a reference. That is, you can look up how to do something like set up users with passwords and privileges, and we walk you through the whole process step by step.

Also, we hope that you think of this book as a reference to the most important things you want to do as an R/3 administrator. As we cover possible administration tasks, we talk about the ones we think you find most common, most useful, and most in demand by your company. (If you master the tasks outlined in this book, you probably know enough to work your way through many others on your own anyway.)

Because we have selected the most valuable things for you to do as an SAP administrator, you may choose to do some general reading in the book as well. "Hey, I'm curious about CCMS," you may say to yourself, and you can get a nice, solid, readable introduction in here.

Those three possibilities are the main ways we think of for using this book, but you can do whatever you want. In this book, you can jump around at random. You can spread the book open like a cookbook and go step by step, and you can read for your general edification. We're just happy you're here.

Who Do We Think You Are?

You may think we've answered the question in this heading quite clearly in our title — *SAP R/3 Administration For Dummies*. That is, we must think you are an R/3 administrator.

Well, we do, but the boundaries around such a classification can be a little blurry.

First of all, you may be a new R/3 administrator — the obvious target for a *...For Dummies* book. Certainly we want to be helpful to people first taking responsibility for configuring systems, managing memory, setting security privileges, getting online Help, and all the other things that R/3 administrators do. We like to make things simple for such people and go step by step.

Or you may be a would-be R/3 administrator, and we certainly want to meet the needs of such people — those who aren't yet R/3 administrators but have the attitude that "I could do that." This book is a great place to start.

Or you may be a presently-working R/3 administrator. If you can do administrator tasks already, do you have any use for this book? Certainly — whenever you have to do something you haven't taken on before, such as configure systems with Workbench Organizer. Perhaps at times you don't remember how you did something a few months or a year ago, and you need a refresher. And admit it — haven't you had times when, even though nobody else is aware of it, you know that you're faking it a little bit, and you'd like to know more? Or maybe sometimes you wonder whether you ought to be doing some key activities that you're currently overlooking. In any of these scenarios, you can pick up this book and get a little assistance.

You may even be someone who just uses R/3 but would like to understand the environment you work in when you run your HR or accounting application. Want to know what you can ask your administrator to do? This book gives you the vocabulary.

This book, then, is for anyone who administers SAP R/3 at any level, and even for people who have something else to do with SAP R/3 but don't administer it. If you don't have anything at all to do with SAP R/3, well, this book may not be directly for you. But nobody says you can't read it if you want.

How This Book Is Organized

We see the chapters here as a series of mountain peaks in the world of information that any R/3 administrator may encounter.

We did follow a certain plan in putting the chapters together, even though you don't have to follow our plan in using the chapters.

In general, we move from introductory to advanced topics. In the early part of the book, we introduce concepts we think you'll find helpful in the rest of the book — the technical environment, Team Basis, the system landscape, and things like that. Pretty soon, we get into the hands-on administration you're probably looking for. At the end, we have some key lists in the part of tens and a really great glossary that can bail you out when you're not sure about a topic. For the curious, here's a quick look at what you can find in the parts of this book.

Part I: The World According to SAP

SAP is so comprehensive, so ambitious, so *big,* that you can't work in it efficiently without a sense of the big picture. Also, until you get a sense of the overall workings of SAP R/3, you may be tempted just to turn tail and run. Here you get an introduction to open systems, database independence, Enterprise Resource Planning, and Team Basis.

Part II: Checking Out the (SA) Parts

Jumbo jets taxi a little before they take off, and we offer you the same opportunity before you take off for real as an R/3 administrator. In this part you find out about functional modules, look over the setup of the system you administer, and gain extremely useful information about navigating in R/3 and getting help.

Part III: Doing Everyday Stuff

Your users may take printing as a basic right, but printing from within R/3 isn't necessarily trivial. Here you get your feet wet (your hands inky?) by setting up R/3 printing. You also see how to set up users with proper security and how to schedule jobs to run in the background (so they don't annoy people who are running jobs in the foreground).

Part IV: Somebody's Gotta Do It: R/3 Tuning and Maintenance

The rubber definitely meets the road in this part. Start here first only if you have R/3 experience or just like to torture yourself. Here you schedule operation modes, copy and transport clients, start and stop R/3, and fine-tune the performance of the operating system, networks, databases, and R/3 itself.

Part V: Being a Hero: Deployment and Troubleshooting

This section acts as a bit of a mop-up for things that may happen to you as you work in previous parts. You find out about using the Workbench Organizer to coordinate development (and avoid mistakes). You see how to apply SAP patches to fix errors in the code. And you find out some of the intricacies of the Online Service System — that sophisticated vehicle for getting all kinds of up-to-date help, some of it directly from SAP experts.

Part VI: The Part of Tens

Administrators love lists. You can use them to guide you, or you can use them just to check off that you've done everything. Here, in the Part of Tens, you get useful lists like Ten Daily, Grief-Saving SAP Housekeeping Tasks. We also provide a Glossary that's kind of a safety net for any time you start to get lost.

Part VII: Appendixes

In this part, we've listed common SAP terminology and transaction codes in handy alphabetical order. When you're stumped, start here.

Icons Used in This Book

Icons are cool. They break up the monotony, and they call your attention to things in special ways. Here are the ones we used:

Sometimes we tell you something elsewhere and don't want to seem like we're repeating ourselves, but we think a helpful reminder in a certain spot might be useful. The Remember icon lets you know that this information appears somewhere else, too, alongside some other topic where it is also relevant.

In paragraphs marked with Technical Stuff icons, we get into some pretty nitty-gritty stuff, maybe start throwing around codes and tables and things. If you're just getting a feel for things in general, you may want to skip these. If you're a techie, you may choose to read only these.

Sometimes we want to throw in a little bit of extra, practical advice — a shortcut, a way to save some time or trouble, or something particularly interesting. Look to Tip icons for that kind of information.

We can't anticipate all the pitfalls you may run into, but we like to alert you to risks whenever we can. Warning icons mark information about potential trouble spots.

What Now?

Go to the coffee pot and get a fresh cup. Then go over and turn off the TV. But don't put this book down.

Let's go!

Part I
The World According to SAP

The 5th Wave · By Rich Tennant

"I ran Thompson's numbers. Either he's our top sales rep or the next Emperor of Japan."

In this part . . .

SAP is so big (really, really big) and the activity of the administrator is so focused that we thought you might want to get a feel for the whole before plunging into the parts of SAP in later sections.

Here, we introduce you to open systems, database independence, Enterprise Resource Planning, and Team Basis itself. This part is designed to get you oriented and to help get you familiar with the kinds of things your users are concerned with.

Chapter 1

What's the Big Deal?

. . . .

In This Chapter

▶ Crossing boundaries in hardware and operating systems

▶ Pulling data from once-impossible places

▶ Putting the data together into once-impossible reports

▶ Taking a quick look at the big picture — Enterprise Resource Planning

. . . .

*T*ell people that you've been reading *SAP R/3 Administration For Dummies*, and they probably shake their heads in disbelief. A *...For Dummies* book on R/3 administration seems impossible, because SAP R/3 is just so big and does so much that's so complicated.

Actually, people do R/3 administration every day, and later chapters of this book show you how. This particular chapter, though, shows you the big picture of that worldwide, ambitious, complex system that you administer.

Most of the time, you work with the parts of the system — getting printing to work, setting up new users, and things like that. But someone with so much responsibility for the parts may want to have some sense of the whole of what SAP is about.

So the truth is that you may skip this chapter or just skim it before turning to something hardcore like client copies in Chapter 11. But sometime you may want to take a few minutes to get familiar with the big picture that you're a part of as you administer.

In this chapter, you take a look at the SAP open systems, find out about database independence, and get a brief glimpse at the very big subject of Enterprise Resource Planning.

Bursting Open Your Systems

Hardware makers all used to compete with each other. Competition was probably healthy for the time. Hewlett-Packard, Digital, IBM, Compaq, Bull/Zenith, you name it — hardware vendors all developed proprietary systems. Companies contributed to the proliferation of systems by buying from the multiple vendors. The old adage "Nobody ever got fired for buying IBM" wasn't enough to keep lots of people from buying hardware and software from lots of vendors.

Sometimes different divisions of the same company have the freedom to choose their own operating systems and platforms, and the different divisions choose different systems. What happens, too, after an acquisition, when a large company suddenly wants to integrate hardware and software from, say, both IBM and Bull/Zenith? Acquisition or not, what happens when a company matures and wants to integrate all its departments?

What often happens, as you probably well know as an SAP administrator, is that the company adopts SAP to integrate the different systems. SAP is *open,* which means that it runs on the hardware platforms of all those giants — IBM, Compaq, Hewlett-Packard, and others.

Of course, multiple platforms doesn't just mean multiple hardware platforms; it means multiple operating systems. Windows NT may be taking over the world, but it hasn't done it yet. UNIX and its different flavors continue as major players. Look around, and you can find AIX, Digital Unix, HP-UX, SINUX, and Solaris.

SAP R/3 runs on various operating systems as well as various hardware platforms. Some folks suggest that the term *middleware* appropriately describes SAP R/3. Thanks to its open architecture, you can use R/3 in all kinds of software and hardware environments without losing any of the R/3 capabilities. The SAP middleware offers interfaces to system software so that R/3 can readily run on many different systems.

R/3 is not only an open system but is also integrated software that performs virtually every aspect of business management (human resources, finance, logistics, production, distribution, and so on.) Therefore, an even better name for it than *middleware* is *Enterprise Resource Planning* software, a concept that we talk about more later in this chapter.

According to the literature, at least, R/3 makes all but obsolete the very question of technological platform. Whatever combination of computing engines and operating systems your planning geniuses have put into place at your company, SAP can supposedly run on it. (It may be your job as administrator to help turn the *supposedly* into *truly.*)

SAP is one of those sets of initials — like AT&T or IBM — that just exists on its own. You hear people say "AT&T" all the time, but when do you ever hear "American Telephone and Telegraph"? Nevertheless, it's nice to know what the initials stand for. SAP, in German, stands for *Systeme, Anwendungen, Produkte in der Datenverarbeitung.* Luckily, the initials carry over nicely to English, where SAP means *Systems, Applications, and Products in Data Processing.* You heard it here first (unless you've already heard it somewhere else).

Pulling Data from Everywhere

Hardware platforms and operating systems are a good enough thing, we suppose, but nobody would go around installing these megamillion-dollar hardware setups just for the challenge of getting them installed. People put them in to get at data. We say more about the data question in the section "Planning the Resources of the Enterprise," later in this chapter.

But the heart of the data question is database systems. You've heard of them: Adabas D, Microsoft SQL Server, Oracle. Database systems collect the huge mounds of data that your company piles up on a daily basis and allow you to report on that data in ways that sometimes may be halfway meaningful to some people.

But SQL Server and Oracle, for just two examples, developed quite independently from each other and probably secretly hate each other. They're rivals. They probably never intended to work together.

In the modern enterprise, though, someone or something has to step forward to make them work together. SAP does that (assisted by you, the R/3 administrator). Nowadays, the HR department wants to include data in its reports from — oh, I don't know — the manufacturing department. Sales wants financial information from the controller. Anybody can want information from anybody, and it just doesn't cut it any more to go to a group of people and say, "Sorry, you can't get to their information. They're running on Windows NT, and you have an Oracle database."

When you integrate hardware, operating system, and database, you have to have a way for the user to get at all that nicely integrated information. The way to do it is with an interface — SAPGUI in the world of SAP. And you have to run on a network — TCP/IP networks for the world of SAP.

SAP does the gargantuan task of integrating platforms, operating systems, databases, user interfaces, and applications. Just the thought of integrating so many hardware and software systems can be a little bewildering. A table showing all of them may be a little bewildering, too, but at least Table 1-1 shows in one place the various systems that SAP pulls together into one. If it seems ambitious to list everything in one table like this, imagine what it's like to get everything working in one integrated system, the way you do as administrator.

Table 1-1		SAP Open Systems		
Hardware	*Operating System*	*Database*	*SAPGUI*	*Network*
AT&T, Bull/Zenith, Compaq, Data General, Digital, HP, IBM, Sequent, SNI	Windows NT	Adabas D, SQL Server Oracle	Windows 3.1, Windows 95, Windows NT, OSF/Motif, Presentation Manager, Macintosh, OS/2	TCP/IP
Bull/Zenith, Digital, HP, IBM, SNI, SUN	AIX Digital Unix HP-UX SINUX Solaris	Adabas D, DB2 for AIX, Informix, Oracle	Windows 3.1, Windows 95, Windows NT, OSF/Motif, Presentation Manager, Macintosh OS/2	TCP/IP
AS400	OS/400	DB2/400	Windows 3.1, Windows 95, Windows NT, OSF/Motif, Presentation Manager, Macintosh, OS/2	TCP/IP

To get their business information, people run applications software. SAP, which runs on top of the databases, computers, and operating systems, provides software for doing business — accounting software, manufacturing software, human resources software, sales software, plant maintenance software, and others. Chapter 4 introduces the various *business modules* of software and shows how they work together.

The point here is that the software modules *do* all work together.

If the current modules don't provide what you may need, you can use the SAP R/3 programming language — ABAP — to develop what you need. And to complete the picture, R/3 allows software from all kinds of other companies — from so-called *third-party* companies like Microsoft and IBM — to operate together with SAP.

Trying Out Operating System Independence

The openness of SAP enables you to move objects from one system to another, such as moving an HP-UX operating system and an Oracle database to a system using Windows NT and SQL Server 6.5. You can try out a short example of this openness in a situation that's similar to one you're likely to run into often as a Basis Administrator.

Here's the setup: The customer wants the SAP preconfigured client (PCC) on its system. SAP provides the customer with a *transport* (a transport is the SAP way of moving objects). The only constraint of this transport is that PCC runs on HP-UX and Oracle, but the customer wants to use it on SQL Server 6.5 and Windows NT. Take the following steps to move the object from one system to another:

1. **Download the compressed file from the SAP Web site.**

   The SAP Web site is shown in Figure 1-1.

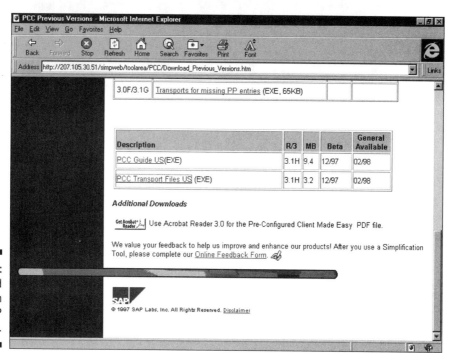

Figure 1-1:
Download
PCC from
the SAP
Web site.

2. **Uncompress the file and move it to the SAP application server.**

3. **Move all K**** files to** \USR\SAP\TRANS\COFILES**.**

4. **Move all R*** and D*** to files to** \USR\SAP\TRANS\DATA**.**

5. **Log on to the Windows NT server as** <sid>adm **and go to a DOS prompt.**

6. **Change directories to** \USR\SAP\TRANS\BIN**.**

7. **For each transport, enter the following two commands.**

```
tp addtobuffer <SAPsystemID>K<IdentificationNumber>
     <TargetSID>
```

The first command, shown in Figure 1-2, puts the transport into the buffer.

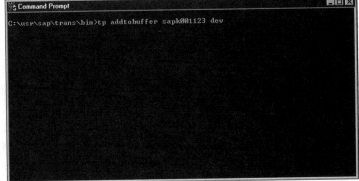

Figure 1-2:
Put the
transport
into the
buffer.

```
tp import <SAPsystemID>K<IdentificationNumber> <TargetSID>
     client=<TargetClient>
```

The second command, shown in Figure 1-3, imports the transport into your system's client.

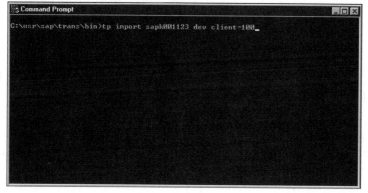

Figure 1-3:
Import the
transport
into your
system's
client.

Openness, then, isn't pure theory; it's a reality that you have to contend with every day as administrator. Openness has its value in the business end of the company, which we talk about in the next section.

Planning the Resources of the Enterprise

What's the big advantage of openness? Only one thing would justify all that goes into creating openness — namely, the ability to make more money. Hardware independence, flexibility with operating systems, and freedom across databases mean that SAP can increase company revenues.

How? By letting people do business better than before. Not only can departments get information they couldn't get before, but they can also manipulate it into all kinds of reports that help them make good decisions and manage the company.

With the SAP software modules in every department of the company, executives can bark really unreasonable commands at people and get an answer. "How much of our sales revenue gets funneled back into materials management?" "For all our employees in all our divisions, what is our daily operating cost?" "How many bananas do we have to buy to keep our second-level manufacturing reps from going out and buying their own?"

Anything one department of the company does affects the rest of the company, and the company needs to track what's going on. Suppose, for example, that your wholesale distributor in Taiwan takes in a major customer order. That order affects the finance department, because it means money for the company. It affects sales, who make projections based on such information. It affects manufacturing, who, after all, have to produce the materials to fulfill the order. It may affect human resources, who may have to adjust upward their plans for downsizing because of the magnitude of the order.

Any activity anywhere in the company can affect anything else. Those far-reaching effects have always been there, but now, with SAP, companies have half a chance of beginning to track those effects and plan accordingly.

People used to pretend to do research on the sweeping questions and then make up answers. Now, they can run SAP before making up their answers. SAP makes for much more convincing fiction in answering those tough, sweeping executive questions (and some of the answers may even be more than just fiction).

The name for this new kind of planning, which becomes possible when you can suck in data from all your business applications and prepare reports on them, is Enterprise Resource Planning, or simply ERP.

When you work as administrator and you do something like give a manager access to SAP or get a report to work or make data available, you may feel as if you're just getting rid of some headache or other. Actually, though, you're contributing to Enterprise Resource Planning and helping your company do its business more effectively (and, thereby, make more money).

What so much openness and integration means to you as system administrator, of course, is a lot of status around the company. Think about it — nobody else wants to touch the inner workings of a system that runs on Windows NT or UNIX; operates on a TCP/IP network; runs modules for human resources, materials management, sales, and more; and draws upon SQL Server, Oracle, and Informix databases. No way.

Plenty of people stare under the hood of a car and don't want to disconnect even one wire for fear of what they might do to everything else. As system Administrator, you're supposed to connect, disconnect, reconnect, configure, reconfigure, and solve a system that makes a car engine look about as complicated as a stone.

Being R/3 administrator brings you a huge amount of respectability. Of course, some of that respectability is earned, because you really do have to do some tuning of that worldwide, integrated, open system. This book gives you a little assistance in that monumental task. In the next chapter, you find out about real-world advantages that you bring your people as they use R/3.

Chapter 2

Why Make the Switch?

In This Chapter

▶ Ignoring the Y2K panic

▶ Seeing the scope of R/3 in the real world

▶ Taking a terrifying glimpse at the coming deluge of innovations

*I*n Part II and all the rest of this book, you find yourself immersed in the bowels of R/3 administration and nothing else. You probably love that anyway (and you may find *bowels* kind of a crude term for where you work in those chapters).

To feel at home working on the innards of a system, though, you may want to have some feel for the scope of the whole thing. For example, a school custodian really ought to go outside sometimes, climb a hill, and just look at the sweet institution he's cleaning day after day. Or to choose a more uplifting example, a traffic cop shouldn't spend eight hours a day at some mad intersection trying to keep people from running into each other and trying *not* to read the lips of irate motorists going by. Such a public servant ought to climb a skyscraper and watch the meaningful flow of humanity in all that traffic that she directs each day.

As an R/3 administrator, you, too, ought to have some feel for what your activity is contributing to the living, working world around you. This chapter explains contributions that R/3 is making to the world. It gives you the big picture so that you can better appreciate your contribution as a traffic cop for the whole thing.

This chapter discusses the "why" of SAP as it relates to the technical material in Chapter 1, showing administrators key advantages that they can bring to their users by using SAP.

Dodging Y2K Problems

If the rest of the world weren't facing such a big deal about Year 2000 compliance, we wouldn't have much to say about SAP's compliance. Dates would be in the same category as the fact that SAP starts up when you log in, that its screens display stuff on them, and that you can use it in color. You can take it for granted that SAP will still work right when you round the corner into the year 2000.

SAP, very simply, supports four-digit year codes instead of the two-digit codes that are causing such nightmares for so many. Figure 2-1, for example, shows a typical date in SAP. If you click on the selection arrow next to the year field in the SAP calendar, you get your choice of years going well beyond 2000.

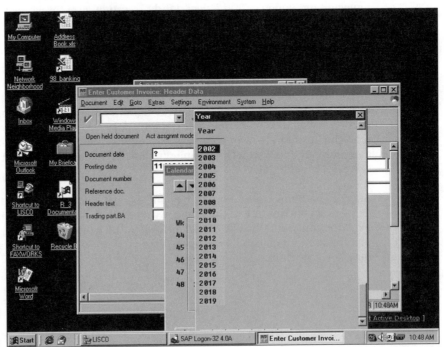

Figure 2-1:
SAP
supports
four-digit
year codes.

The risks of Y2K noncompliance

Y2K compliance would be nothing special for SAP except for one thing: A big portion of the rest of the programming world is going nuts without it. Consider, just for the sake of contrast, some problems that other systems are running into:

☛ Paying tons of $200-an-hour programmers to change over old systems so that they do support Year 2000

☛ Finding embedded date codes in existing systems (as in, "What if there's an embedded date code that will shut down the electricity at the turn of the millennium?")

☛ Potentially losing business when they don't find embedded date codes and their computers crash, causing impatient customers to shop elsewhere

We don't want to be "the sky is falling" type of guys about Y2K. You can take it for granted that R/3 is compliant if you want to. You may as well. But simply being Y2K-compliant for so many applications across the company is a pretty big deal, even if it is pretty much invisible.

Madly Automating Everything

Automating has been going on in business for some time. Even computer automation has been going on for some time. *Enterprise Resource Planning*, though, is a term that SAP has brought into the mainstream in business around the world. ERP automates more aspects of a business in more ways than almost anyone is used to. The next section talks a bit about what R/3 offers retail stores as one example of automating business. Later on, we look in detail at other kinds of businesses that R/3 automates.

Making purchasing and retail work better

To get an idea of what R/3 does for business, consider two quick examples of the many business solutions that R/3 offers — purchasing and retail sales. (Later on in this chapter, you get a glimpse of some of the other areas of business that SAP automates as well.)

Putting power in purchasing

Unless you happen to be in the purchasing department yourself, that particular cost-control organization may not be your favorite bureaucratic group in your company. Those are the folks who hold you up as you await approval of, say, the Ferrari you need for business trips. And they're the ones who sometimes give you a flat "No" to absolute necessities (like the chair you need because your old one is broken).

The purchasing department, though, is one of those unfortunate necessities in life — like taxes, police departments, speed limits, and children. SAP offers a capability called *Integrated Flow* that lets you live with it.

Thanks to Integrated Flow, you can purchase stuff over the Internet from your own desk, without needing the purchasing department to do it for you. You can check prices, availability, and delivery time. You can even check out the supplier's catalog.

Of course, that department can still veto a purchase and still tracks what's going on. (You just can't have everybody going hog-wild and buying everything.) SAP refers to its purchasing solution as a *Business-to-Business Procurement Solution*, and it's one example of the way that SAP actually automates real business.

Revving up retailing

SAP also has a special business-to-business component aimed especially at retail stores. Using a browser, stores can order shelves full of stuffed rabbits, glass beads, and tons of other stuff that you, as a consumer, later go in and buy.

Using the SAP retail component is not like picking up the phone and ordering blind, the way stores used to have to do. A manager can quickly find out about many more potential products than before, compare them, analyze market conditions, choose the best supplier, and put in the order. According to the SAP literature, everything happens so fast and efficiently that administrative costs stay low. The manager or employees can check out inventory, too. ("Let's see. We only have five piles of beads in the warehouse. We better order some more.")

Using SAP, a process that was once much more guesswork than many folks involved in it even realized becomes much more systematic. (Of course, some guesswork is still involved, but isn't that part of the fun?)

Meeting the needs of just about everybody else

R/3 has taken into account what you might call the wondrous diversity of the world of business, and it tailors its solutions to the needs of just about anybody.

With a cute little program called *Solution Maps,* SAP can set out a complete solution for your business, including the requirements for your business and the processes you should follow. Most of us never get that organized in our own lives, but when your company gets big enough, you just gotta get organized. SAP is there to do it for you.

Here's a quick list of some of the industry solutions that SAP now provides. (And some of these industries, in our jaded opinion, could really use a good solution for their situations.) By the way, you can download all of these maps from the SAP Web site at www.sap.com/.

- ✔ Aerospace & Defense
- ✔ Automotive
- ✔ Banking
- ✔ Chemicals
- ✔ Consumer Products
- ✔ Engineering & Construction
- ✔ Healthcare
- ✔ High Tech
- ✔ Insurance
- ✔ Knowledge Management
- ✔ Media
- ✔ Metal, Paper & Wood
- ✔ Oil & Gas
- ✔ Pharmaceuticals
- ✔ Public Sector
- ✔ Real Estate
- ✔ Retail Service Provider
- ✔ Telecommunications
- ✔ Transportation
- ✔ Utilities

Gosh, the world of SAP can be a little on the staggering side, if you stand back and look at the whole thing. What if you had to administer R/3 for some massive conglomerate that ran R/3 in all those areas? If you had to know everything about all of those areas, the task would be rather challenging. You don't, of course. You just have to know how to administer.

Moving Recklessly into the Future

Depending on how you look at it, SAP is "ambitious," "relentless," or just "totally committed." It's planning to offer even more capabilities for you to manage than the ones already outlined in this and Chapter 1. The next sections describe some of what you can look forward to in upcoming releases.

SAP Business Information Warehouse

Providing access to data is a strength of R/3, and it's your responsibility as an administrator. SAP Business Information Warehouse (BW) will enable companies to aggregate external and internal data, convert it into information, and respond with speed and accuracy to market changes. The SAP BW solution will combine state-of-the-art data warehousing technologies with SAP business expertise to create an end-to-end solution. The SAP data warehouse solution will provide users with a comprehensive view of data across the organization, including SAP R/3 and non-SAP data.

SAP Human Resources System Release 4.0

Human resources, too, is going more global than ever. The SAP Human Resources System helps give managers direct access to personnel information such as benefits, work schedules, and payroll. Most importantly, it helps managers deploy their workforce more effectively (which we hope doesn't mean that it helps in downsizing and restructuring, but it probably does).

SAP Euro functionality

The SAP software keeps up-to-date with current global economic issues like the Euro. Starting with Release 3.1I, SAP addresses the Euro currency. Currency tables enable accurate money valuation and conversion. You can also do things like convert an existing price list to a Euro price list.

SAP Strategic Enterprise Management (SAP SEM)

What will the head honchos be able to do? Things like advanced simulation and scenario modeling. Cynics may say, "Oh, great, we'll have the managers playing video games all day." But that's not it. These activities help management protect the value of the company for stockholders.

SAP Ready-to-Run

Everybody talks about how long it takes to implement SAP R/3. People measure implementation in months and years rather than days and weeks, as for most implementations . Talk about a concern for the administrator — slow implementation probably heads the list.

Responding to the concern, SAP announced its SAP Ready-to-Run R/3 (SAP RRR) solution, which gives you a baseline system configuration, thereby getting you off to a running start in implementation.

That head start may make life easier for you as you implement. The solution has bundled server and network hardware systems, a preinstalled and pre-configured R/3 system, an operating system, and a database. Tinkering with something that's already configured is much better than having to do the whole setup from scratch.

In Part IV of this book, you find out about tuning and managing R/3. SAP RRR means that you can quickly get into a position where you have something to tune and manage.

All in all, SAP is an ambitious program. It's global. It automates just about everything in a business. It automates just about any business. When it automates, it does so with such thoroughness that you're likely to say, "Where does a person begin here?" And besides all that, SAP keeps changing and making itself better.

All the SAP capabilities can drive you nuts as an administrator if you think about them too much. Knowing that they exist is good, though, and this chapter gives you a sense of what capabilities are available.

Chapter 3

Our Starting Lineup: Team Basis

In This Chapter

▶ Getting a feel for the sweeping role of the Basis Administrator

▶ Reviewing the special responsibilities of the System Administrator

▶ Looking over the areas of concern of the Database Administrator

▶ Sharing (momentarily) the worries of the Security Administrator

*S*AP R/3 is pretty big. If you haven't seen that for yourself already, you can gather as much from a quick glimpse at Chapters 1 and 2. Such size makes for an horrendous amount of administering, and you shouldn't have to do all the administration by yourself.

R/3 administration gets into enough technical areas to demand not just an expert but a team of experts. This chapter shows you some precedents as to how you can assign the various administration tasks to your team. These aren't hard-and-fast roles, of course. You can have people do whatever you want. You can put the System Administrator in charge of the coffee machine if you like. (Many times, that's a good idea, because System Administrators drink a lot of coffee. It can be a bad idea, though, because System Administrators will drink anything that's called coffee, including mud, and may not maintain your quality control.)

Typically, you set up your team of experts like this:

 ✔ **Basis Administrator:** For responsibilities that have to do with the over-all working of the system, you put the Basis Administrator in charge.

 ✔ **System Administrator:** For activities closely tied to the operating system, have someone who supposedly knows a lot about the operating system — the System Administrator — in charge.

✔ **Database Administrator:** The database is a separate concern. As we explain in Chapter 1, SAP draws on a company-wide database that may include more than one database system (like SQL Server, Oracle, and things like that). Database Administrators are a special breed — not like other programmers, not like administrators either, and you probably want to have a Database Administrator to deal with hassles related to the working of the database.

✔ **Security Administrator:** Security can be a separate area of responsibility, too, even though it overlaps with all the others. Crooks might break into databases; they might make their way though the operating system; they might do just about anything. (They're crooks, after all. They make it their style to be unpredictable.) You may want to have one person or a group of specialists take responsibility for security as the Security Administrator.

The Basis Administrator should share responsibilities with the System Administrator, the Database Administrator, and the Security Administrator. Contrary to popular belief, not every problem that comes up in R/3 is a problem for the Basis Administrator.

Keeping Everything Working: The Basis Administrator

Basis is the technical infrastructure of your SAP implementation, including matters pertaining to the system, to databases, to functional modules, to Enterprise Resource Planning itself, and to anything else that can somehow fall through the cracks.

Basis is an actual SAP system with its own components. Table 3-1 lists the Basis components — not for you to memorize them, but so that you can see how Basis affects almost every part of R/3.

Table 3-1	Basis Components
Component	*Description*
BC-KERN	Kernel Components
BC-SRV	Basis Services
BC-ADM	System Administration
BC-OP	Operating System Platforms
BC-DB	Database Interface, Database Platforms

Component	Description
BC-FES	Front-end Services
BC-FEP	Front-end Platforms
BC-DWB	ABAP Development Workbench
BC-BEW	Business Engineering Workbench

The Basis Administrator is the go-to person, the fall person, and the overall whipping person whenever something doesn't go as expected in SAP (or doesn't go at all, in which case the whippings are even worse).

The Basis Administrator really ought to know a little bit about all the other areas — system administration, database administration, and security administration. In fact, he or she ought to know a lot about those areas, because the Basis Administrator can get involved in any one of them at any time.

As the overall know-it-all, the Basis Administrator particularly ought to understand issues that arise where the other areas overlap. For example, when the database doesn't work right, the Database Administrator should be able to assess the situation and say, "The database works fine; the operating system is the problem." Then the Basis Administrator can bring in the System Administrator to solve the problem. If the System Administrator accuses the database, though, and the Database Administrator accuses the operating system, who has to try to work things out? The Basis Administrator, of course.

The Basis Administrator is the first person people go to when they need help and aren't sure where to get it, and he or she is the last person they go to when all other help fails. Basis Administrator is not always the world's most comfortable position, but the pay is good, so people are willing to do it.

Here is a summary of the responsibilities of the Basis Administrator:

- ✔ **SAP R/3 administration:** R/3 is the overall installed version of SAP at your company. All of Part III in this book talks about R/3 administration. But, as Basis Administrator, don't overlook Part IV or Part V. You may have to administer anything to do with R/3.

- ✔ **Correction and transport:** In a *correction,* you fix something. In SAP administration, you may want to renew or replace data in a second system by transporting from a first. *Transporting* is transferring objects from a source system to the database of a target system. Transporting involves both the operating system and databases of participating systems. It crosses lines between traditional responsibilities and is, ergo, the responsibility of the Basis Administrator. Chapter 12 shows you how to do transports.

✔ **Client copy and export:** Clients, in SAP, are separate, logical systems. They have databases, and they reside on the operating system. Thanks to their position spanning both databases and operating systems, they naturally become the responsibility of the Basis Administrator.

✔ **OSS notes fixes:** OSS (Online Service System) contains error reports, notes on problems, requests for development, and stuff like that from users. Did someone mention the word *problem?* Customer problems can cover a broad range, so OSS is a natural bailiwick for the Basis Administrator.

Doing Techie, OS Stuff: The System Administrator

System Administrator is a mainstream computer term. The System Administrator worries about stuff that has to do with the system, especially with the operating system and the network. The System Administrator is a true techie — maybe more of a techie than the Basis Administrator, who has to know a little bit about everything.

Here are the main responsibilities of the System Administrator:

✔ **Operating system backup/recovery:** Whether the operating system is Windows NT, some flavor of UNIX, or one of the other operating systems we mention in Chapter 1, the System Administrator is in charge of backing up the system and, in the unlikely event that it fails, restoring that puppy to working order again.

✔ **SAP printing:** As you find out in Chapter 8, R/3 pretty much leaves printing up to the operating system. All R/3 does is provide what it hopes to be a seamless interface to the operating system.

Because printing is the responsibility of the operating system, it is likewise the responsibility of the lucky person responsible for the operating system — the System Administrator. If printing isn't working, after all, chances are the problem lies not with SAP, not with Basis, not with the database system, but with the operating system.

✔ **Operating system security:** A Security Administrator worries about user security, as you find out a bit later in this chapter. How much does that Security Administrator know about that most technical of technical areas — the operating system? Probably not enough, so responsibility for operating system security falls upon the System Administrator.

✔ **OSS connectivity:** As a repository of fascinating information (complaints, broken things, fixes), OSS can be important to any of the administrators mentioned in this chapter. Certainly the Basis Administrator accesses OSS and responds to users through it. (Chapter 17 talks about OSS in more detail.)

✔ **Other stuff:** The System Administrator ends up digging into all kinds of things that normal humans wouldn't begin to touch, such as network administration, using the Computing Center Management System to monitor the system (see Chapter 12), startup and shutdown (see Chapter 13), managing the print spool, and archiving.

Dealing with Data: The Database Administrator

Databases are a world of their own. As we mention in Chapter 1, databases in SAP can be any of those giants you've heard about — Adabas D, Microsoft SQL Server, Oracle, DB2 , or Informix, among others.

The database person can get involved at the beginning — setting up the database system and doing things like getting the database configured. (If you're not a Database Administrator, try thinking about the relationships in a relational database. Just thinking gives you a headache. If you want to configure a database, figure on taking some training or finding a friend who's already done that.)

As the Database Administrator, you can work with SAP utilities that help you administer your database and see information like what actions it has been up to. You can start and stop the database system (which isn't the same as starting and stopping R/3). You can even get involved in database reorganization, though you may as well face the fact that you're likely to have better luck in getting a Rubik's Cube put together than in getting your database successfully reorganized.

The main concerns of the Database Administrator in R/3, though, are these:

✔ **Database backup/recovery:** Any crash is an unpleasant thing. Given the complexity of a database, though, a crash is particularly nightmarish. Therefore, the Database Administrator has to be adept at backing up the data files and the control file for the database. SAPDBA comes in pretty handy for that.

✔ **Database monitoring and tuning:** You wouldn't want to go in and reorganize your database altogether, as we just mentioned. Keeping it running smoothly is a good idea, though, so the administrator should make sure that the database is using its space efficiently and should make little adjustments to it as necessary.

Worrying a Lot: The Security Administrator

Security is just too important to be left to chance. Every other administrator has to have some concern about security, but the company also needs to have someone who makes security his or her primary focus. Here are the main concerns of the Security Administrator:

✔ **SAP user administration:** The Security Administrator's biggest concerns don't have to do with people from outside the company breaking into things. The biggest concern is everyday users. You have to keep them organized and give them the proper privileges so that they only go in and mess up the files they're supposed to mess up, not files anywhere else on SAP.

Chapter 7 talks about defining users, putting constraints on them, giving them passwords, and things like that. You want a person focusing on just those things on your technical team.

✔ **SAP security authorization:** You may set up users initially with standard authorizations, but you can do plenty to change those standard authorizations in various ways. In fact, tinkering with authorizations is a separate responsibility of the administrator. Find out about it in Chapter 7.

✔ **OSS security:** The online service system is a repository of all kinds of complaints, weaknesses, tips, and just general grumblings about your R/3 installation. It's pretty sensitive stuff, and you don't want the wrong people getting access to the wrong things. So OSS security is also a primary concern of the Security Administrator.

Part II
Checking Out the (SA)Parts

The 5th Wave   By Rich Tennant

HMM — NICE TREE STRUCTURE.

In this part . . .

*1*n SAP, you have the *really* big picture, which you can find
out about in Part I. Then you have the somewhat smaller
big picture, which you find out about in this part. You get an
introduction to all those functional modules your users have
their hands on (even though you don't so much *use* them as
administer them). You find out about the setup of development, database, and application servers (which you have to
understand when you administer R/3). And you finally get
your hands on R/3 itself as you find out secrets for navigating
R/3 speedily and efficiently.

Chapter 4

Who SD PS IS Hard?

*A*s much as you have to worry about as an SAP administrator, there is, fortunately, a whole bunch more that you can pretty much ignore — namely, the SAP functional modules. You have to keep them working, but you don't have to know all that much about them.

It's helpful, though, to have some basic knowledge of the business activity that's going on thanks to your activities with the innards of SAP. In this chapter, you take a really, really quick tour through the so-called *functional modules* — financial, logistics, human resources, and common systems. Basically, you use this chapter if you suddenly have to talk with somebody in a functional area and you don't want to appear completely stupid. You want to be able to say, "Oh, sure, I'm quite familiar with materials requirements planning." You won't be, not from this chapter, but you will at least know what the initials stand for. (We suppose that should be "for what the initials stand.") That means you can skip this chapter until you need it, or if you're curious, you can skim it really quickly now.

Checking Out the Functional Modules

Business users have to do the financial accounting, the materials management, the enterprise controlling, and all the other business activities of your company. For your part, as administrator, you just want to know that the activity exists and that it's working okay. You don't have to become an accounting, manufacturing, engineering, or human resources expert.

Table 4-1 summarizes the modules and lists those mysterious acronyms that you see all the time when people talk about SAP. Initials like that can be a little annoying. Everybody knows what the initials mean for the module they use all the time, but nobody else does. A manufacturing person knows that PM stands for Plant Maintenance. Anybody else thinks it means *post meridiem.* Memorize all the acronyms for a quiz tomorrow morning.

Table 4-1	SAP Functional Modules
SAP Grouping	*Modules*
Financials	Financial Accounting (FI)
	Controlling (CO)
	Asset Management (AM)
	Project Systems (PS)
Logistics	Plant Maintenance (PM)
	Quality Management (QM)
	Production Planning (PP)
	Materials Management (MM)
	Sales and Distribution (SD)
Human Resources	Human Resources (HR)
Common Systems	Workflow (WF)
	Industry Solutions (IS)

The following sections briefly explain each of the groupings.

Thinking Money: Financial Modules

Money is power. SAP is well aware of that truism and packs plenty of power into its own financial modules — for accounting, controlling, and other financial matters. (The power, though, is especially in the accounting and controlling.) In the following sections, we talk about financial modules.

Financial Accounting

"If FI is for Financial Accounting," you may aptly wonder, "why isn't it FA?" Well, as close as we can tell, the I is for Information. Financial Accounting draws on a database that collects all the accounting data within your company. FI evaluates the information in various ways and displays it on the screen.

Users, of course, can configure the modules to their needs. (What good is an expensive general ledger module, for example, that only describes somebody else's company?) SAP also includes "best-practice" processes for managing financial needs. For example, you can configure the aging rules for your accounts receivable (meaning that you can set up stuff like when to bill again and when just to give up because the deadbeat is never going to pay).

Here are the modules in FI:

- General ledger
- Accounts receivable
- Accounts payable
- Treasury functions
- Other sub-ledger accounts
- Consolidations
- Management reporting

Controlling

Controlling (CO) is a module that appeals to many Type A personalities and other control freaks, because they just have to be in charge. Controlling deals with stuff like overhead — costs that you can't exactly assign directly but that you feel you need, sort of like the salaries of most middle managers, for example.

CO also deals with your company's costs and your budget for future costs. Middle managers, with upper management breathing down their necks about controlling costs, have to look pretty closely at some of the CO reports.

Managers using CO can make decisions that have some far-reaching effects, too. For example, in a manufacturing company, a manager can decide the rules and methods to have SAP apply to figure the cost of the manufacturing process from raw materials to finished goods. Those numbers ultimately determine the price of the product that the company sells. (Price the product too high, and the company could take a big hit in the marketplace, thereby costing that manager her job. Or more likely, some fall guy who had nothing to do with the costing will lose his job.)

Here's a list of primary things you do with CO:

✔ Activity-based accounting

✔ Cost center accounting

✔ Enterprise controlling

✔ Job order accounting

✔ Project accounting

✔ Product costing and analysis

✔ Profitability analysis

✔ Profit center accounting

Asset Management

AM, you may think, is the opposite of PM, but, of course, it's not. It's Asset Management. Now, if you've heard it once, you've heard it a million times — "A company's biggest asset is its employees." That may be true, but AM doesn't evaluate employees. It deals with fixed assets — machines, vehicles, buildings, office equipment . . . stuff, stuff, stuff. It sees how much they're worth, depreciates them over time, disposes of them, and replaces them. AM also has to get into maintaining and repairing fixed assets.

Project Systems

People use Project Systems (PS) to track projects. For example, a painting company may track each of its clients as a project. Basketball teams think of particularly bad players as "projects" and pay them enough to track each one of them with PS. Each project has revenues and expenses, and PS helps people manage that stuff (trying, often fruitlessly, to have revenues exceed expenses).

Throwing Stuff Around: Logistics

Logistics has a number of cute modules (refer to the list in Table 4-1) that managers use to evaluate actual data and to create theoretical data to use in planning. Logistics, in ordinary life, means things like strategies and techniques for moving stuff around. The same is true in SAP, but the stuff you move around are things like your company's sales force.

Logistics can concentrate a great deal of power in the hands of a few key managers, but if they use that power to advantage, logistics can really help the company.

Plant Maintenance

Plant Maintenance (PM) may not sound like a really glamorous module. The poor slob who walks around the plant cleaning up iron filings and scrubbing the floors doesn't pull down much of a salary. But the SAP Plant Maintenance person sits in a nice, carpeted office, drives a Lexus, works at a computer, and pulls down a hefty salary. That person plans and manages the company's facilities. For example, that boss may design a plan for periodic maintenance of the machinery.

Here are the things you do with PM:

- Manage information systems on PM activities
- Manage (but not actually perform) maintenance
- Manage maintenance bills
- Track your maintenance costs and resources
- Process unplanned tasks
- Manage periodic maintenance
- Manage service

Quality Management

Quality Management (QM) is for, you know, keeping people from getting totally shoddy in their work. You use QM to plan and carry out a quality assurance plan (which can never be totally successful, but it may be good). In a manufacturing organization, for example, the QM big shot plans and manages the process for keeping up quality throughout the manufacturing cycle.

Here's what you can do with QM:

- Work out your quality inspections
- Do a good job of quality planning
- Check out the information from your quality management

Production Planning

PP (Production Planning) is for managing your company's manufacturing activities. Say that you have a furniture company that makes really soft, couch-potato-style sofas. With PP, you manage all the raw materials, labor — everything it takes to get that couch from raw materials into a reliable resting place for an eager occupant waiting in front of a TV set somewhere.

Here are the PP elements:

- ✔ Activity-based costing
- ✔ Bill of materials
- ✔ KANBAN
- ✔ Master production scheduling
- ✔ Materials requirements planning
- ✔ Production planning
- ✔ Production orders
- ✔ Product costing
- ✔ Repetitive manufacturing
- ✔ Routings
- ✔ Sales and operations planning
- ✔ Shop floor control
- ✔ Work centers

Materials Management

Materials Management (MM) is for getting and managing your inventory (which you usually don't want too much of, because if you have it on hand, you haven't sold it). The furniture company, for example, uses MM to track how many couches it has stacked up in its warehouse. When a sales request comes in, the company can use MM to send a query to see whether the particular sofa inventory is committed to another order (which is called inventory management).

Main MM elements include the following:

- ✔ External services management
- ✔ Inventory management
- ✔ Information systems
- ✔ Invoice verification
- ✔ Materials procurement
- ✔ Materials valuation
- ✔ Reorder point processing
- ✔ Vendor evaluation

Sales and Distribution

Sales and Distribution (SD) has a more fun job than manufacturing, if you ask us, because it's more involved with people. It deals with sales, delivery, and billing. (Well, the billing can get pretty sticky sometimes — when people skip town and don't pay, or stuff like that.) SD is supposed to help the sales process go smoothly by doing things like telling a salesperson whether or not the stuff she wants to sell really does exist. If the customer wants to ask some hard question — such as "When can I expect to get my couches?" — SD gives you a shot at providing an answer.

Here are the key elements of SD:

- ✔ Billing
- ✔ Delivery processing
- ✔ Information systems
- ✔ Inquiry
- ✔ Pre-sales support
- ✔ Quotation processing
- ✔ Sales order processing

Getting a Handle on People: Human Resources

If you really want to work with people, you get into HR (Human Resources). Until a decade or so ago, HR was "personnel," and it didn't have a very good reputation. HR has gained a lot of respectability lately, though.

You use the SAP HR module to manage personnel. Stuff that you can do in the SAP HR module includes personnel administration, payroll, and personnel planning and development.

For example, a company can use SAP to track the dreaded time and expense monster. (How much are you spending on time and expenses, and how much should you be?) These capabilities are within HR:

- Benefits
- Organization management
- Personnel administration and planning
- Payroll
- Time, travel, and expense management
- Training management
- Recruitment
- Workforce planning

Getting People to Work Together: Common Systems

Sometimes you want to integrate different SAP modules. After all, the modules draw upon common databases and produce reports that cross the boundaries of the various modules. The Common Systems module is key to getting the modules to work together.

Workflow

With the Workflow module (WF), you control what you do when you integrate the different SAP modules. Using the business rules and events, WF moves information from one place to another in SAP. For example, you use WF when you send a purchase order (PO) through for approval. A PO request can originate from any business unit within the enterprise, and WF takes that request and routes it to the approving parties and, ultimately, creates a PO. (If you're lucky. Maybe the PO gets denied. That's been known to happen, too.)

Industry Solutions

Industry Solutions (IS) allows SAP to incorporate the special requirements and peculiarities of a particular type of business. The following list shows the different IS-specific modules:

- ✔ Automotive
- ✔ Consumer packaged goods
- ✔ High technology and electronics
- ✔ Healthcare
- ✔ Process industries
- ✔ Oil and gas
- ✔ Utilities and telecommunications

The Bottom Line

The functional modules, then, are the real applications that live inside SAP. Luckily, you don't have to run most of them yourself in your role as R/3 Administrator. You do have to keep them running, though, and support them in the ways that you find out about in Part III and the subsequent parts of this book.

This chapter is just to help you join in on the fun a little. Business people, on the whole, love arcane initials. They're short, for one thing. Get familiar with them, and they help make things easy. It's certainly easier to say "MRP" than "materials requirements planning." The initials also tend to create a kind of exclusive club of the people who actually know what the initials stand for. (But face it, outsiders are only slightly better off trying to figure out what "materials requirements planning" is than trying to fathom the shorter, simpler "MRP.")

SAP definitely has a bewildering alphabet soup of applications that intimidates, impresses, and in many cases, nicely serves business users in major corporations. If you're going to get really serious about one of the applications — or about all of them — you need to know more than you can find out in this chapter. This chapter just gives you a feel for the functional modules and the world that SAP end users inhabit.

Chapter 5

Proper Tiers Save Tears

· ·

· ·

*W*hen SAP talks about a *landscape,* it's not referring to anything that has anything to do with land. Before computers appropriated the term, a landscape used to be a panoramic view of an English countryside or something like that. In the 90s and beyond, though, a landscape is a panoramic view of the computers in your SAP system.

The whole landscape issue may not matter to you much. Chances are, your SAP system is already up and running, and you're supposed to administer it. Whatever tiers it has in its architecture are the ones it will have in the future, and you probably have other things on your mind. Nevertheless, maybe you have to help plan your installation, or maybe you're involved in discussions about improving the system.

This chapter introduces the innards of your SAP system — its clients, its servers, and their relationship to SAP. First, you find out about the three-tier architecture of Database Server, Application Server, and Presentation Server that helps your SAP system run at its fastest and best. Then, to give you a real-life feel for the architecture, you see how all three tiers participate in a simple action (a logon). Finally, we tell you about system landscapes for development systems.

Teaming Up: Client/Server in SAP

The basic concept in the SAP client/server architecture is teamwork. Share the work around. Distribute it, in other words. SAP allows some servers to do some tasks while other servers do other tasks at the same time. It's a division of labor. It's like at a construction site — some people operate bulldozers, others operate steam shovels, and others drink coffee (because somebody has to do that, too).

SAP divides labor among three servers — the database server, the application server, and the presentation server. The following sections explain briefly, in mostly simple terms, what these servers do. (Hey, this is a ...*For Dummies* book. It's our job to make things simple, even incredibly complicated things like the client/server setup in SAP.)

Bowing to the ruler: The database server

We find it difficult to say that one server is more important than any other. After all, take away any one of them, and the system wouldn't do its job very well.

Nevertheless, SAP does have its priorities, and the most important server in the system is the database system. Data is precious. You run R/3 so that you can get at data and produce reports. If you didn't have R/3, you'd find some other way to get at the data. On the other hand, if you didn't have R/3, you would probably never worry about getting, say, an application server.

The database processes tens of thousands of requests for data. Users spend the day creating updates, deletions, and queries; all these changes get processed at the database level. Enterprises usually put their largest and fastest resources with the database server.

Depending on the size and strategy of the SAP implementation, the actual database may physically reside internally within the server or separately in a cabinet of disks. The database and application servers may all be physically separate machines within the SAP system.

Standing in: The application server

The R/3 designers thought that they could lighten the burden of processing updates, deletions, and queries on the database servers by having an application server help with that processing. Like the database servers, the application servers are large and powerful machines, but application servers generally operate as stand-ins for the database servers.

The application server operates *asynchronously* from the database server, which just means that it doesn't have to be doing its processing at the same time as the database server. It stores a large portion of data in its *cache* — a special area in memory or on disk — and processes it there.

Take a closer look at the SAP technical architecture. A SAP system consists of a database and one or more SAP instances. We define a SAP *instance* as one dispatcher process, child processes, and memory. The dispatcher process manages the requests to the SAP instance. Keep it clear that the definition of *SAP instance* is different from the definition of an instance referring to a single database.

The dispatcher evenly distributes its requests to eight SAP processes to perform its various tasks. These SAP work processes are child processes from the dispatcher process. The following lists the SAP work processes and their functions:

- ✔ **Dialog work process:** Controls foreground actions — for example, any action such as entering a sales order, creating a user, or running an online report.

- ✔ **Background work process:** This work process runs the background jobs. If you schedule a cleanup job at 2300 hours, the background work process executes the task.

- ✔ **Spool work process:** This process executes all printing jobs in the SAP instance. Only one spool work process is allowed per SAP instance.

- ✔ **Gateway work process:** This process controls system-to-system communication requests. An example of a gateway work process is communication between two different SAP systems.

- ✔ **Update work process:** This process controls the update function in the database. The update work process starts working after a transaction is finished and needs to be saved in the database.

- ✔ **Update 2 work process:** Update 2 work process does the same task as the update work process. The only difference between the two is that the update 2 work process handles non-time-critical updates.

- ✔ **Message work process:** This process controls the communication between SAP instances in a SAP system. An example of a message work process is the communication between multiple application servers in a single SAP system. Only one message work process — called the *central instance* — exists per SAP system.

- ✔ **Enqueue work process:** This work process controls the locking and unlocking of objects in SAP, preventing multiple requests from attempting to change an object at once. This function is similar to the database row locking function.

Working the crowd: The presentation server

Database servers and application servers are, more or less, hard-core nerds. (We're using a little metaphor here.) They do phenomenal work, but they're so busy doing it that they can't spend much time combing their hair, shopping for the latest designer clothes, working on public speaking skills, and generally preparing themselves to meet the public.

In SAP, the application and database servers stay behind the scenes. Meeting the end users is the job of the presentation server, which is where the SAPGUI resides.

In many cases, the presentation server is the desktop PC that your end users have in their workspace. People often refer to what the presentation server does as *front-end processing.* Running SAPGUI on a physically separate machine frees up resources on the database and application servers so that they can do the hard-core work of the system.

Instead of using desktop PCs as the presentation server, companies can decide to devote a separate server as the presentation server. Which way to go is pretty much a company decision.

Putting things together: The SAP system

An SAP system is the combination of all three of the components that we describe in the preceding sections: database server, application server, and presentation server. All these combined servers work in unison to form a single SAP system.

So far in this chapter, we have spoken of each server as if it were physically separate from the others. Actually, that arrangement doesn't have to be true. Depending on the business as well as the technical need, you may combine some servers into the same physical host. It may be a little mind-bending at first to think of servers that aren't servers (well, not separate physical computers), but perhaps it's no more of a stretch than thinking of computers as being a landscape. When you combine servers into a single host, you then have *logical systems* and units instead of physical ones. That difference can confuse some end users and may even confuse you at first. The concepts are still the same, though — you still have database, application, and presentation servers. The only difference is where these servers reside — in separate computers or within one.

Three-Tier Architecture at Work

You have a classic three-tier client/server architecture when you put the three separate pieces together: database server, application server, and presentation server.

Consider what happens when a user processes one transaction. Suppose, for the example, that you have the user's desktop (presentation server), one application server, and one database server. You can follow the transaction from beginning to end as it involves the three servers. In this example, the user simply logs on to the SAP application server.

The user logs into the system at, of course, that server whose job is to meet the public — kind of a smarmy personality without a whole lot of brain power, namely, the presentation server (the desktop).

The user clicks an icon that executes the SAPGUI program on his desktop. As soon as SAPGUI starts, the presentation server is up and working.

In a single Pentium processor PC with 48MB RAM and a Windows NT desktop environment, SAPGUI takes up about 15 to 20MB of disk space (depending on what is installed), utilizes about 3MB of memory, and uses about 90 percent of CPU time when starting the GUI and changing GUI screens. That work of starting and changing screens, ever so little, is nevertheless work that's offloaded from the main SAP server. Keep in mind that the presentation server offloads that little bit of work for each user. Multiply the effect by the number of concurrent users, and the benefit to the application and database servers grows exponentially.

After the SAPGUI establishes connection with the server, actual logon takes place. (Even during the process of starting the GUI, the presentation server sends and receives information packets from the database and application servers. But you can see the interaction of the servers most readily by following the actual logon.)

After the user enters the user ID and password in the appropriate fields, he presses Enter. The game begins. The system routes a logon request to the application server and places it in the dispatcher queue. (Now both the presentation and application servers have participated.)

For the request to go into action, it has to have a dialog work process. If any such work processes are available, the dispatcher routes that logon request to the dialog work process.

Avoid two-tier architecture

Stay away from the two-tier client/server architecture. In a two-tier setup, less teamwork (distribution of work) occurs, and resources have to fight against each other more frequently. Although a one-tier approach is technically feasible, it's realistically impractical. The minimum acceptable configuration is a two-tier approach.

Many enterprises (large and small) deploy a two-tier SAP system. In many cases, the two-tier system is used in development and test environments. The benefits of this model are

✔ Reduced cost of the equipment (say, two servers instead of three)

✔ Speed to deliver because you set up faster

✔ Cheaper maintenance because you have fewer computers to maintain

On the flip side, the two-tier setup means

✔ Degraded performance when the processors conflict with each other

✔ Less speedy delivery of information

✔ Maybe more administration of the system to resolve conflicts

It's definitely better just to bite the bullet and go with a three-tier setup.

If no work processes are free, the request waits in line until a work process frees up. Which server does the processing during this waiting and passing of requests? The application server. When the request gets into a work process, that process performs the logon.

So far, two servers have participated. But the database server gets involved even in this simple series of steps. While the work process attempts to validate the logon, it searches for information on the user ID and password that the user has entered. If the application server doesn't have that information stored in cache, it goes to the database to get it.

The database server does a little work of its own. The database server must now go into its tables and query that information on the user ID and password. The database work processes retrieve the information and ultimately validate the user's logon request. That validation ends the request and allows the user to log on to the SAP system.

Many different things are happening at all different levels to get this user onto the system. Usually, this process takes less than a couple of seconds after the application server gets the logon request. But that's beside the point. The fact is that even this simple action — logging on — involves all three servers in the SAP three-tier architecture.

By contrast, if you process the request at one layer instead of three, the wait is longer and the process less efficient. Even this simple example shows the advantages of a three-tier client/server system.

Checking Out Three-System Landscapes: Development

During development (which is likely to go on continuously, even at established sites), companies can choose a single-system landscape, a two-system landscape, and a three-system landscape.

In this case, the systems aren't the familiar database server, application server, and presentation server from the previous sections in this chapter. These systems are your *development system* and your so-called *production system* — the one people use every day to do real work. (Sometimes it's debatable how real that work is, but that's another matter.)

When considering the questions of development and testing (you know, developing your own applications with ABAP and other stuff like that), SAP talks of these four types of systems:

✔ **DEV:** A system for customizing and developing your applications

✔ **TEST:** A unit for (you guessed it) testing your applications

✔ **QTST:** Another unit for testing, this one for quality assurance

✔ **PROD:** The actual working system; the production system where your users do all their grand Enterprise Resource Planning (and the occasional humdrum job, too)

What is best? The most expensive, of course — a three-system architecture. Here's a quick look at three possibilities:

✔ **Single-system landscape:** In a single-system landscape, all the systems reside in the same R/3 system but do different things — development, testing, quality assurance, and production. The problem with this system is that after you finish development and start production, you can't go back and do more development. You have to stop production so that you can do development and testing. Ask your users how they like the idea of having downtime for a couple of weeks so that you can do development.

✔ **Two-system landscape:** In a two-system landscape, you put production on one system and the other three (DEV, TEST, and QTST) on another. Still a bad idea. Doing both development and quality-assurance testing on the same system means that there's no turning back after you transport a tested program to the production system.

✔ **Three-system landscape:** This one is a good idea. You put development and testing on one computer, quality assurance testing and application testing on a second, and production on a third. You don't have to mingle your two kinds of testing on one computer. Above all, you neither have to halt production while you carry out your testing nor face the barrier of having to use your upgraded applications without being able to go back for more testing.

Chapter 6

Can You Get There from Here?

Sometimes being a great administrator doesn't mean that you know everything; it just means that you know where to *look* for everything. This chapter helps you strengthen that ability to look smart when, if the truth be known, maybe you're just a little above average. You can turn to help or to any of the other capabilities in this chapter, like menus, toolbars, and transaction codes.

One of the hazards of being an R/3 Administrator is that you have almost certainly had to jump into the middle of things. If you're like the rest of us, you probably started solving advanced problems and providing advanced solutions before reasonably getting the lay of the land yourself.

For a few moments in this chapter, enjoy the luxury of getting familiar with the clever, ingenious, and downright simple tools right at your fingertips whenever you start up SAP.

Getting Around with Menus, Toolbars, and the Fast Path

Getting there, for any activity, is half the battle, but you don't get much credit for it. It's like saying, "Hey, I showed up for the Boston Marathon." Likewise, you don't get much credit for knowing where to input data or how to put a function into action, log off (which, yes, is a function), click to print the present window, or key in a shortcut. You get credit for meeting somebody's business expectations (or, in the case of the marathon, finishing the race without dying in the process).

Nevertheless, being in the right place at the right time is an important skill. Here you find out some of those right places in R/3.

Taking charge of the R/3 window

You can save yourself plenty of time and trouble by knowing the parts of the R/3 window. Try working in a sample window:

1. **Start R/3.**

2. **Log in as an administrator.**

3. **Select a module.**

   For the example, click Accounting in the Menu bar.

4. **Navigate to a window.**

   For this example, we click Financial accounting, then General ledger, then Document entry, and then G/L account posting.

   A typical R/3 window comes up, as shown in Figure 6-1.

Table 6-1 summarizes the key use of each of the parts of the SAP window.

Table 6-1	Parts of the SAP Window
Window Part	*Use*
Title bar	Displays the name of the application or task. Click and drag here to move the window.
Menu bar	Displays the menus you can use in the present application or task. Menus change with the application.
Menu	Lists the functions you can actually perform in your present location.
Standard toolbar	Contains buttons for the most common SAP tasks, such as saving or exiting.
Application toolbar	Contains buttons for functions and choices in the current application.
Field name	To the left of the field box is the field name.

Window Part	Use
Input field	Inside the box itself, you input data in an input field.
Display field	Inside the box, you display data in a display field.
Screen	All the objects and data in an R/3 window.

Manipulating the menus

In the SAP R/3 window, you see a menu bar across the top. You use the menus, of course, to implement functions.

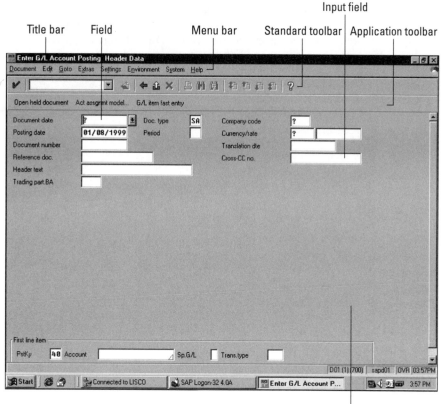

Figure 6-1: Check out the parts of a typical R/3 window.

The menus that appear in the menu bar neatly change depending on the application you're using and the task you're doing. Watch the change in action as you follow these steps:

1. **Start R/3 and log in as an administrator, if it isn't already running.**

2. **Choose Accounting⇨Financial Accounting⇨General Ledger to change to a different application.**

   As you can see in Figure 6-2, the menu choices change to reflect the new application.

3. **Choose Document⇨Display.**

   The menus again change to display menus for a document, as shown in Figure 6-3.

Certain menus are always available wherever you are in R/3: System, Help, and formatting. With System, for example, you do stuff like create a session, work with a user profile, or log off. Help, discussed later in the chapter, is the system administrator's second brain. Formatting allows you to change text colors, change how the Tab key behaves, and otherwise drive your users nuts by changing the way the screen looks. (Not really.)

Figure 6-2:
When you change to a new SAP application, the menus in the menu bar change to suit the task.

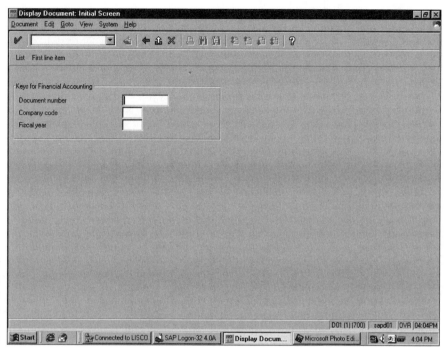

Figure 6-3:
The menus
change
dynamically.

Other menus are usually there, such as a menu for the object you're currently working in (such as Document Entry in the General Ledger module or Material in the Material Master module), Edit, and Goto. Some menus appear only some of the time, including Extras, Environment, View, Settings, and Utilities.

Checking out the System menu

A prime menu for an administrator is the System menu. You can try it out by following these steps:

1. **Start R/3 and log in as an administrator, if it isn't already running.**

2. **Choose System.**

   The System menu drops down, offering such choices as *Create Session*, *User Profile*, and *Log Off*.

3. **Choose User Profile⇨User Defaults.**

   The Maintain User: Defaults screen comes up, as shown in Figure 6-4.

4. **Click the Back arrow to return to the initial screen.**

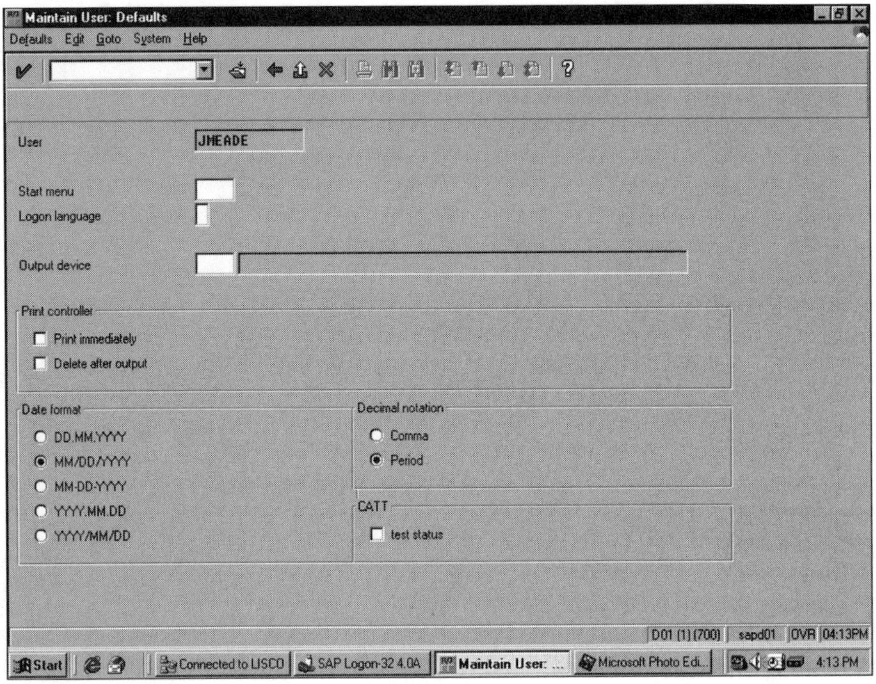

Figure 6-4:
Get to the
Maintain
User:
Defaults
screen from
the System
menu.

Using transaction codes

For administrators, transaction codes are often the choice over menus. A transaction code is a four-character code that you type into the command field to go to the initial screen of a task. The code saves you from two menu steps, one to go to the application, a second to start the task itself. For example, to go to the initial screen of Payroll, you type PC00.

Table 6-2 lists the transaction codes that we find ourselves using most often as consultants.

Table 6-2	Favorite Transaction Codes for Administrators
Code	*Use*
S000	Return to main menu screen
SU01	Users
SU02	Profiles
SU03	Authorization
SM36	Define job

Code	Use
SM37	Job overview
SPAD	Spool administration
SM04	System monitoring — User overview
SM50	Process overview
SM51	Servers
SM21	System log
ST22	Dump analysis
SCCL	Local client copy

Using the command field is quicker than navigating through the menu paths. Use the following codes before the transaction codes to navigate effectively.

/n   Closes the existing transaction and goes to the new transaction in the existing window. You need to enter this if your current transaction is not S000.

/o   Keeps the existing transaction and opens the new transaction in another window.

If you used the preceding example and were in the Maintain User: Defaults screen, you need to enter, for example, /OPC00 to go to the payroll screen in another window.

Finding transaction codes

Transaction codes are almost impossible to remember, except for a few that you do over and over again. And how do you find out a transaction code in the first place? Here's what you do:

1. **From the initial screen, choose Dynamic Menu from the application toolbar.**

   The Dynamic Menu screen appears, with a list of application areas.

2. **Double-click one of the menu choices.**

   A sublist appears, in some cases displaying tasks. Here's the cool part: Some of the tasks displayed also have transaction codes displayed. For example, as Figure 6-5 shows, the transaction code for Payroll is PC00.

   For items on the Dynamic Menu with a plus sign next to them, you can keep clicking until a task displays with its transaction code to the right.

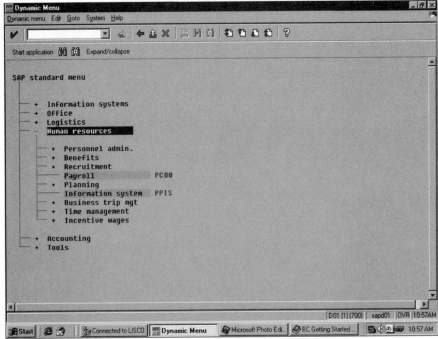

Figure 6-5:
You can use menus to find transaction codes.

A quick way to find the transaction code of where you are is by using the menu. Follow the menu path System⇨Status. A box with environmental information appears. In the field labeled Transaction code, you find the current transaction code.

Lost? You can always type **/nS000** to return to the main menu screen.

Turning to toolbars

Pictures are better than words. They just are, that's all. You can click once on a button instead of twice or more on a menu to get things done. Whenever possible, it's faster to use a toolbar.

The standard toolbar, right under the menu bar, has buttons for your most common tasks. Just click on a button to perform a task such as Save, Return to the previous screen, or Enter.

The application toolbar, underneath the standard toolbar, has buttons that allow you to choose functions quickly for the application you're using.

Taking a few minutes to learn the toolbars (both standard and application) is worthwhile. Clicking once instead of twice saves you a good bit of time over the months. Also, toolbars display the most important functions and the best way to do them. If you're not using the toolbar, you may be missing useful functions or taking too long to do the ones that you do perform.

Just as menus change depending on the task you're doing, buttons in the toolbars change, too.

Fiddling with function keys

In many ways, there is no substitute for good old function keys if you use a particular application extensively. In R/3, you can use the function keys on your keyboard. The function keys available change with the task you're doing, so you probably won't know every function key for every task. But you can get a handle on the functions for applications you love.

To find out the function keys available at any time, follow these steps:

1. **Put the pointer anywhere you like below the toolbars.**

2. **Click the right mouse button.**

    A menu appears, showing the active function keys. Figure 6-6 shows active function keys in the Inventory Management initial screen.

    You can click to choose an option. For the example, just click Exit.

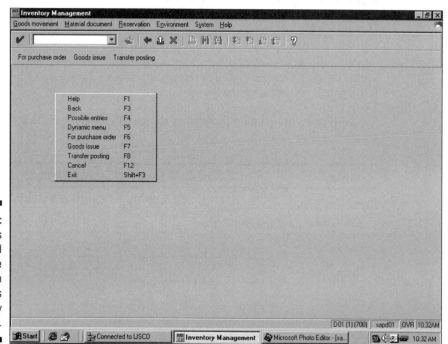

Figure 6-6: Use this menu to find out the function keys currently active.

But the real point of displaying the function key menu is to give you a chance to find out what function keys are active in certain places. Then just press the one you want.

Some of our favorite function keys for system administrators are shown in Table 6-3.

Table 6-3	Noteworthy Function Keys
Function Key	*Use*
F1	Gets you help on a field or an error message
F3	Go back
F4	See possible entries
F6	Create
F12	Cancel
Shift+F3	Exit session
Shift+F9	Go to first page

Speeding users with SAP naming conventions

SAP has a standard for naming everything in the system. It reserves certain naming ranges for SAP objects and others for the customer. You should follow the SAP recommended naming convention. If you do not, you may run into problems during upgrades.

Table 6-4 presents commonly used customer naming conventions and lengths.

Table 6-4	Standard Naming Conventions	
SAP Object	*Length*	*Customer Naming Convention*
Authorization/Authorization Profile	12	No "_" in second position
Codepage	4	9000—9999
Dialog Module	30	Y* Z* RP_9* RH_INFOTYP_9*
Enhancement Project	8	*
Function Library: Function Module	30	Y_* Z_*

SAP Object	Length	Customer Naming Convention
Function Library: User Exit Function Module	4	XZ*
Function Library: User Exit Function Module (Customer specific)	4	*
IDOC: Segment type	7	Z1*
IDOC: Enhancement type	8	*
Info Type Number	4	9000 – 9999
Matchcode: Matchcode ID	1	0 – 9
Menu	4	Y* Z* +*
Message: Number	23	900 – 999

Almost all customer objects start with a "Y" or "Z". If you have a large organization, SAP recommends starting with "Z" for branch offices and "Y" for head offices.

Getting to the Source: Online Documentation

System Administrators aren't supposed to need help. You give help. Other people may turn to you; you have to rely on yourself and whatever written documents you can scare up. Folks have to have their sources of information, though. Don't tell anybody, but medical doctors look things up in journals and check with their colleagues. Fortunately, you can find quite a bit of help within SAP R/3.

Finding help on applications

The business of SAP is doing business, and that means working in applications such as General Ledger and Accounts Receivable.

When you're doing your daily work, you don't usually want to know just how to get around in R/3 or how to put in shortcuts. You want to know how to do things like produce a report you want in General Ledger.

To get help on the application you're using in R/3, you use the menu bar. Suppose, for example, that you are in General Ledger and want help. Choose Help⟳Extended Help. The extended help for the General Ledger module appears, as shown in Figure 6-7.

With the application help, you can read up on the business application you're using.

Not every application has extended help, which can be a little disappointing. If the application doesn't have extended help, though, R/3 displays the R/3 library screen for you, where you can search for documents that can help you.

Getting help on a field

The gist of working in any application, of course, is putting information into the fields. Sometimes, though, a field can look about as inviting as, say, a Password prompt to a person who doesn't know the password. What do you put in when you don't know what to put in?

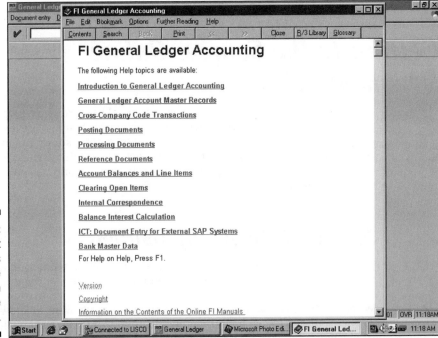

Figure 6-7:
You can get
help like this
on the
application
you're
using.

Finding out about the field

Fortunately, you can use the R/3 question mark button on the standard tool-bar to find out information on a field. Try it out.

1. **With the application running, click in the field you want help on.**

   For the example, we are running General Ledger, Chart of Accounts. We click in the Account Number field.

2. **Click the question mark button in the standard toolbar.**

   Help for the field appears, as shown in Figure 6-8.

The question mark from the toolbar is also helpful with system messages, which display in the status bar at the bottom of the window. Just put the cursor on the message and click the question mark (or press F1).

Finding what to put in the field

Oftentimes, you don't need to know technical, business stuff about how to use a field. You're the administrator. You're just trying to get the thing to work, not be an accountant. Actually, R/3 is quite thoughtful about helping you find what to put into a field.

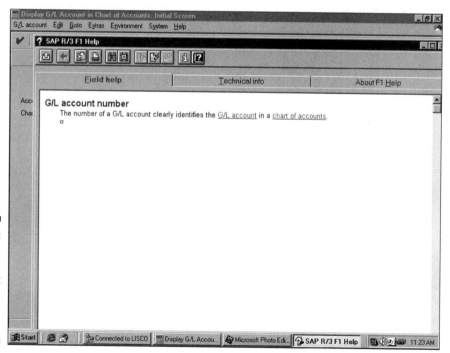

Figure 6-8:
Click the question mark to get help like this on the field you're in.

Here's what to do:

1. **Put the cursor in the field where you want help.**

   For the example, we put the cursor in the Chart of Accounts field.

   The possible entries arrow nicely appears at the right of the field.

2. **To see possible choices to put into the field, click on the possible entries arrow.**

   Proper entries mercifully appear, as shown in Figure 6-9.

Nobody should go through life using SAP without knowing about the possible entries arrow (though that arrow to the right is pretty hard to miss. And what else would it be for?).

To actually put the value you want into the field, put the cursor on the value that you want and double-click. (You can press F2 instead, if you want.) Bam. SAP puts the value into the field, and you go from looking stupid because you don't know what goes in there to looking good — at least for the moment.

Many values can be valid for a field, so SAP lets you narrow your search. If you know the first character or two of the value you want, type in those characters followed by the wildcard character (*). Then click on the possible entries arrow. You see only the appropriate values that start with the characters you entered.

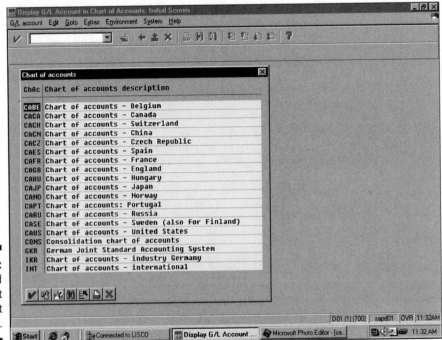

Figure 6-9:
You can find out what to put in a field.

Checking the status of the system

Users (including you at times, no doubt) can get their systems into all kinds of crazy states. To be able to help them, you first have to find out what state the system is in to begin with. (It's like knowing where you are in the mall before you can get much value out of using the map.) To get information about the status of R/3, choose System⇨Status from the menu bar. A dialog box appears, showing tons of helpful information that may get you oriented. Figure 6-10 shows a sample dialog box.

You can also get information about your graphical user interface, such as, "How much memory is available on my workstation?" To get there, click the color button on the menu bar, and then click About.

Getting help on reports

Doing business is all about generating reports. Once in a while, people need help backing up their systems or navigating or something, but they're likely to need help on reports anytime, because reports are what people churn out all day long.

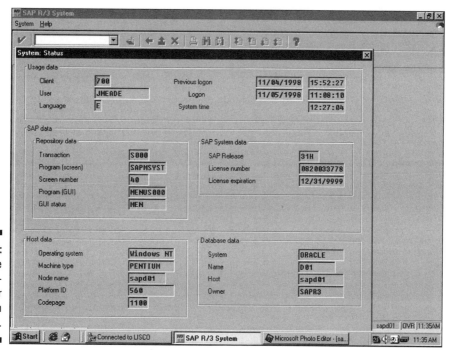

Figure 6-10:
Look here for information on your system status.

You can get help on a report from within the report the same way you get help on applications. Try it:

1. Put the cursor into the screen of a report you want help on.

For the example, we use the Treasury Report.

2. Choose Help⇨Extended help.

R/3 help comes up with information on that particular report, as shown in Figure 6-11.

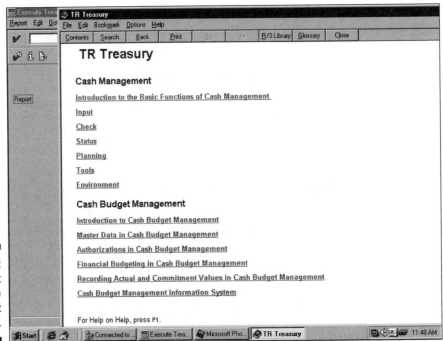

Figure 6-11: You can get help on the report you're in.

Getting Set Up in SAPGUI

With all that SAPGUI can do for you, naturally you want to be sure you have it all set up in the first place. Chances are you already have it for yourself. As administrator, though, you're probably going to be installing SAPGUI for lots of lucky folks.

Considering SAPGUI environments

You can install SAPGUI into most of the most popular environments. People use all kinds of systems, and they still want to get at SAP on your client/server network.

You can install SAP on these client systems:

- Windows 98/95
- Windows NT
- Apple Macintosh
- OS/2

Installing locally or on a server

If you decide to install on the desktop PC, you have all the necessary SAPGUI programs running on that PC.

If you decide to install on a server, most of the programs go on the server. On the PC, you end up with mostly references to the server.

Using the server gives you the advantages you usually get from installing on a server. Several PCs can run from the same copy of the programs (therefore saving the space you'd use to install the stuff on each PC). Installing on the PC means that you don't need network access to run SAPGUI.

Be sure that the version of SAPGUI that you're installing is not older than the version of SAP that you're using. If your SAPGUI is older than your SAP version, it won't work. The other way around is fine, though. A newer version of SAPGUI works with any previous version of SAP.

Starting the installation on Windows

If you have a previous version of SAPGUI, you already have a directory for it. Delete the previous version by deleting everything (files and subdirectories) in the directory `<SAPDIR>`.

Setup runs pretty much automatically. You just make a few choices from the Wizard that leads you through.

You can install from either a front-end server or a CD. For the example, we install SAPGUI 4.0 from a CD.

Here's what to do:

1. **On the CD, find and run the program SAPSETUP.EXE in the directory** `\GUI\WINDOWS\WIN32`.

   Figure 6-12 shows the SAP Frontend Setup screen.

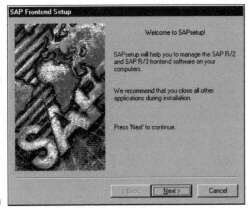

Figure 6-12:
You see this screen when you click SAPSETUP .EXE.

2. **Click Next to continue.**

3. **Choose whether to install on a client or a server.**

   For the example, click Next to accept the recommended client installation.

4. **Choose either Standard or Individual installation, then click Next.**

   If you choose Individual installation, you can choose all kinds of things yourself, such as whether or not to use a CAD Interface. Standard installation uses SAPGUI 32-bit.

5. **Choose either Server Dependent Installation or Local Installation, as shown in Figure 6-13.**

   The Wizard offers to create and register a directory for shared files on your computer. The default is `C:\PROGRAM FILES\COMMON FILES\SAP\SYSTEM`. Click Next to accept the default.

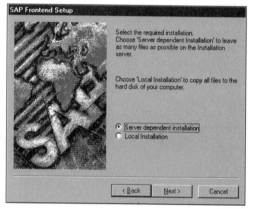

Figure 6-13:
You can choose to leave most files on the installation server.

Now you can provide information about your application server and copy files. Here's what to do:

1. **When the Wizard asks for information for a SAPGUI icon, type the information. Be sure that R/3 System is checked, and click Next.**

   If you plan to use SAPlogon, you can leave the fields empty.

2. **Type in the path to the CD with the SAP WinHelp files (or accept the path that appears on the Wizard), then click Next.**

3. **Choose a program group for your SAPGUI icons.**

   For this example, we clicked Finish to accept the default. The install program installs SAPGUI on the computer.

Part III
Doing Everyday Stuff

The 5th Wave By Rich Tennant

"I asked for software that would biodegrade after it was thrown out, not while it was running."

In this part . . .

R/3 administration is all about administering, and in this part you begin to do just that. You see how to perform some of your most frequently requested tasks as administrator — namely, setting up users with proper security, getting printers to work and using the print spooler, and running and scheduling background jobs so that the system runs most efficiently.

Chapter 7

(SA)People Skills

*T*he phrase "Check this one out," is one you often hear on the street. When used by a blue-clad member of the security force at a company, the phrase means, "See whether the person has a valid badge and any other required papers." Similarly, when you run a company, you have to make sure that the people who come in are the ones you want and not, for example, the misguided thieves who have come from the competition to steal secrets.

With SAP making the worldwide resources of the company available, "checking out people" is clearly much more important for the SAP administrator than for the person in blue at the door. It may sound a little bit unfriendly, but the top "people skill" for the R/3 administrator is making sure that the right people do get access to all the SAP information they need and that the wrong people don't. In this chapter, you find out everything you need to know to be effective at checking out the security of your people.

Seeing the Big Picture in User Security

You manage the R/3 user community with a user master record tied to a particular profile. Figure 7-1 shows the big picture in user administration.

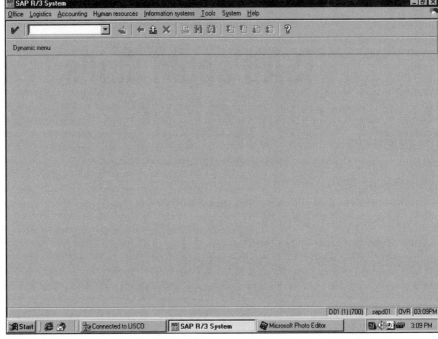

Figure 7-1:
Users,
profiles, and
authoriza-
tion
together
make the
authoriza-
tion model.

Anyone must pass over a series of hurdles before accessing the system. As system administrator, you control those hurdles — the items that the master record draws upon, shown in Figure 7-1. Every user master record draws on both composite profiles and profiles for its makeup. Feeding into a profile are both authorizations and authorization objects.

Looking over authorization objects

At the lowest level in the series of hurdles are authorization objects. *Authorization objects* are initial checkpoints within the ABAP programs. The ABAP statement AUTHORITY-CHECK triggers a check that compares the authorization that the user has with the values associated with the authorization object. For example, if the user enters transaction code SU01 and selects Create, the check determines whether the values are valid. If the values are valid, the user may continue with the transaction; otherwise, the user gets an error message.

SAP ABAP programs are programmed with many authorization checks. You may enhance the existing programs by inserting additional authorization checks. Also, if your organization requires even more authorization objects, you can create your own objects.

Understanding profiles

Your life as a security administrator could easily become overwhelming if you always had to deal with authorizations individually. Profiles simplify the administration tasks. A *profile* is a grouping of different authorizations, categorized by specific job roles, such as *sales entry clerk*. SAP comes standard with many profiles for the different roles within an enterprise. Customers often take the standard SAP profiles and modify them to fit their particular business needs.

Considering composite profiles

Composite profiles are similar to profiles in that both define job roles. The difference is in the organization of the authorizations. A *composite profile* is a "joining together" of profiles. For example, a sales order manager may have one profile for standard sales order entry and another profile for limited administration functions.

Reviewing user master records

A profile becomes functionally complete when you assign it to a user. Otherwise, the profile just doesn't amount to anything, like a Christmas tree that gets left on the sales lot and thrown away. The *user master records* contain a series of system users. Depending on the jobs the users perform within the enterprise, they have different profiles and composite profiles. Profiles associated with user master records are the fundamentals to the SAP security model.

Creating a User

Naturally, you can't just close everybody out of the system and claim that you have done your job effectively. Like it or not, you have to give some people some access. Creating users is the first step in allowing access to the system.

First, make sure that you have the rights you need to set up users. Then you need to find two sets of information to proceed:

- ✔ Who needs access?
- ✔ What rights do they need?

Giving yourself super rights

To be able to set up other users, you need the authorization to

✔ Create and maintain users

✔ Give authorization to the profiles you want to assign

✔ Give authorization to a group you want to assign

In other words, you need to be a *superuser*. If you have the composite profiles SAP_ALL and SAP_NEW, you have complete security access to the system and are a superuser.

Here's how to check your username and see what profiles you have:

1. **Choose Tools➪Administration➪Maintain Users or enter transaction code** SU01 **in the command field.**

If this SAP installation is new, log on to the 000 client as SAP* with password 06071992, the standard R/3 password for user SAP* for all new installations.

The Maintain Users: Initial Screen appears, as shown in Figure 7-2.

2. **Enter your username in the User field.**

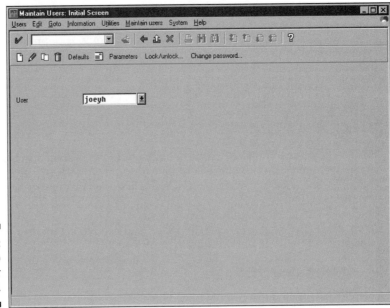

Figure 7-2:
Start here to
check your
authorizations.

3. **Click the Change icon (the one with the pencil on it) to check the profiles assigned to you.**

   The profiles assigned to you appear, as shown in Figure 7-3.

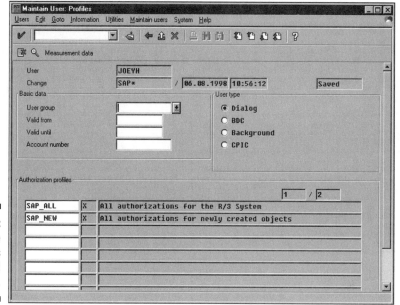

Figure 7-3:
You can see
the profiles
assigned
to you.

The composite profile SAP_ALL opens the system wide open. Be careful to whom you give this type of access.

Creating a user

Your users aren't impressed by your super rights until you use those capabilities to benefit them. That is, you have to set them up as users who can access SAP.

To define a user, you complete a series of fields. Follow these steps:

1. **Choose Tools⇨Administration⇨Maintain Users or enter** SU01 **in the command field.**

   The Maintain Users: Initial Screen appears.

2. **Enter the username you want to create — JOEYH for this example, as shown in Figure 7-2.**

   The username is not case-sensitive.

Naming your user

Coming up with names can be tough. You ought to be able to buy books for creating usernames the way you can for naming babies. In SAP, you define a user by a combination of characters. Many IS departments already have naming conventions for system users, which is perfectly okay and probably a good idea. Here are some common naming conventions:

✔ First name + First letter of the last name

✔ Last name + First letter of the first name

Any naming convention works as long as it abides by these rules:

✔ The maximum length is 12 characters.

✔ The name is case-insensitive.

3. **Click the Create icon (the one with a picture of a piece of paper with a corner folded down) or press F6.**

   This step takes you to the Create User Master Record screen, shown in Figure 7-4.

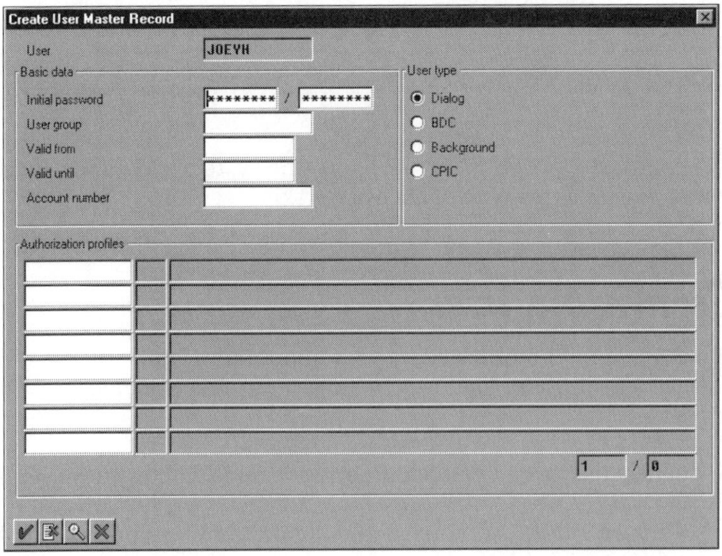

Figure 7-4:
Create a user master record here.

4. **Enter the initial password for the user in the Create User Master Record screen.**

   By default, the password must be between three and eight characters long and may not start with a question mark. All characters and numbers are valid. Also, the password you enter is not case-sensitive.

The password doesn't appear on the screen. Instead, you see asterisks.

The next time JOEYH attempts to log on to the system, he is prompted to use a new password.

5. **Leave the User Group field blank in the Create User Master Record screen.**

   User groups allow distributed maintenance of users. A superuser of a user group can, with proper authorization, maintain users of that group. This field is not mandatory; leave it blank if no user groups are defined.

6. **Enter** SAP_ALL **and** SAP_NEW **in the Authorization Profile.**

7. **When you finish making entries in the Authorization Profile, press F5 or click the green check mark to advance to the Maintain Address Data screen, shown in Figure 7-5.**

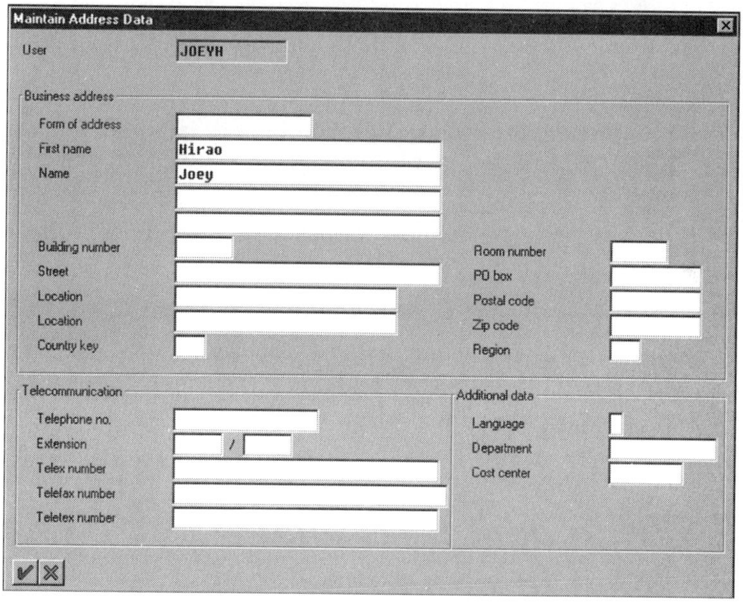

Figure 7-5:
You don't
have to
complete
the Maintain
Address
Data
screen.

Entries in this screen are not mandatory, but enter address information here if you want to.

8. **Press Enter or click the green check mark to advance to the Maintain Fixed Values screen.**

Here is a detailed description of the other fields in the Create User Master Record screen:

- ✓ The **Valid From** and **Valid Until** fields specify the valid dates of the new user created.

- ✓ **User Type: Dialog** is for interactive users. Dialog users use dialog work processes.

- ✓ **User Type: BDC** is for a batch input session special user.

- ✓ **User Type: Background** is for system background user. Background users use background work processes.

- ✓ **User Type: CPIC** is for a CPI-C special user.

- ✓ The **Account Number** field specifies the account number or name that the user is associated with. The number or name is user-definable. An example of an account number is a company code or business unit. SAP recommends entering a value to allow Accounting to logically group users.

9. **Enter any defaults in the Maintain User Defaults screen, as shown in Figure 7-6, and then press Enter or click the green check mark to continue.**

Check the date and number format to see the number format applicable to your country.

10. **In the Maintain User: Parameters screen, enter any default values you want.**

Entries in this screen are optional. You can select values from the list provided in the drop-down menu.

11. **Press Enter or click the green check mark to finish.**

Entering addresses and personal information

Your R/3 security system doesn't much care about a person's address or other personal information, although the company is likely to need it. Therefore, you also enter some supplemental information when setting up your user — information that's useful if you want to invite someone to an office party but not needed for your security system to check out that person.

Putting in address information

Here's how to put in the additional address data for a user you've created:

1. **In the user maintenance screen, transaction code SU01, enter a user-name and click the Address icon or press Shift+F6.**

   The Maintain User: Address screen appears. The information in this section refers to mail-type data (you know, postal addresses). None of the fields in this section are required.

2. **Enter supplemental information about the user.**

3. **Click the Save icon to record any changes.**

Setting some user defaults

You can set defaults for Output Device, Date Format, and a few other things you may want to regulate for the user.

1. **From the user maintenance screen, transaction code SU01, enter a username and click the Defaults button or press Shift+F5.**

   The Maintain User: Defaults screen appears, as shown in Figure 7-6. Here is where you populate user default values. SAP doesn't require you to set any defaults. The defaults are for user convenience.

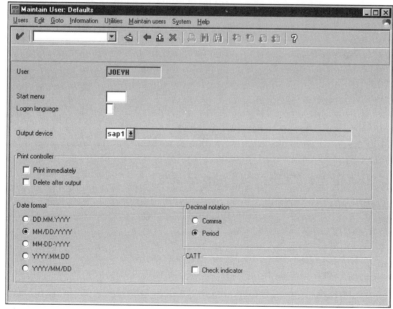

Figure 7-6: You can set a few defaults to help your user.

2. **Enter any of the values explained in Table 7-1.**

3. **Click the Save icon to record any changes.**

Table 7-1	User Defaults
Setting	**What It Does**
Start Menu	Allows users to have their own personalized Startup menu or have their Startup menu be something other than the default S000 Startup menu.
Start Language	Allows the user to set the language to one other than the system default language. SAP is capable of displaying many different languages. However, you have to import these languages into the system before you can use them.
Default Device	Sets the default printer to an SAP defined printer.
Print Controller	Allows the user to have specific printing values. You can elect to print immediately or to delete your spool request after printing. Click the check boxes to activate these values.
Date Format	Lets you set different formats for dates. For example, in the U.S., the format is usually in this order: month, date, year. In Europe, the order is typically date, month, year. Other options are also available. Select the format that best meets your needs.
Decimal Point Format	Allows you to choose either a comma or a period as the decimal character.
CATT	Allows for specific parameters for the CATT tool (Computer Aided Test Tool). For example, if the Test Status flag is set, a test status is set when CATTs are started. This is a special feature for the CATT tool.

Saving users' time with parameters

You can put in some PIDs (identification numbers) that save your users some time. PIDs automatically put information in certain fields as those users work merrily along. Here's what to do:

1. **From the user maintenance screen, transaction code SU01, enter a username and click the Parameters button or press Shift+F7.**

   The Maintain User: Parameters screen, shown in Figure 7-7, appears. In this screen you can set default parameters. SAP does not require you to set any defaults; the settings are more for user convenience.

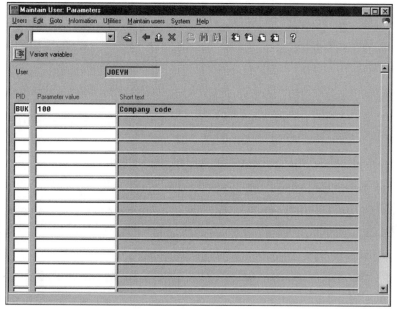

Figure 7-7:
Set user
parameters
here.

2. Put in any PIDs.

For example, suppose you have an order entry clerk who deals only with Company Code 100. You would enter PID (BUK), for Company Code, with a value of 100. This way, every time the clerk encounters a data entry field for Company Code, SAP automatically enters the value of 100.

Security is one area in the world of the Basis administrator that closely parallels concerns of your cohorts on the functional side. Basis needs to look at the business requirements for security and configure those requirements into SAP. Sounds sort of like what the FI/CO (Financial Accounting/Controlling) team does with the accounting requirements of the enterprise. In this security endeavor, Basis and the functional team members need to unite to define the enterprise's security requirements. Face it — when all is said and done, security is customarily a Basis duty.

Administering Users

Getting users set up in the first place is important, of course. The work really begins, though, after you implement security strategy and start supporting real users. You get all sorts of requests from users, from the ever-popular "I can't *fill-in-the-blank*" to the equally memorable "I forgot my password." The following sections can help you in your day-to-day security administration challenges.

Displaying the user master records

You can display master records to check a user's password or any of his or her other key information. To do so, follow these steps:

1. **Choose Tools⇨Administration⇨Maintain Users⇨Users, or enter the transaction code** SU01 **in the command field.**

   You go to the user maintenance screen, from which you start many of your security functions.

2. **Click the drop-down button of the User field.**

   This smaller window (called the List Selection Screen, shown in Figure 7-8) allows you to choose users based on criteria you enter. You can enter wildcards to search on particular strings. For example, entering **A*** in the User field retrieves a list of all usernames starting with A. You can use the same technique for the other fields.

Figure 7-8:
Choose
users based
on criteria
you enter.

List Selection Screen	⊠
User	
Profile	Display
User group	○ Profiles
	◉ Other data
Auth. object	
▦ Choose object ✕	

3. **Press Enter to continue.**

   A list of users appears. The first view is a summary list of the users selected from your search criteria.

4. **To select a user, double-click on the username.**

   You go to the initial user maintenance screen in transaction code SU01. From the initial screen you can do detailed maintenance on the user.

   Another way of looking at these records is to go directly to the underlying tables:

1. **In the command field, enter the transaction code** SE16 **or choose Tools⇨ABAP/4 Workbench⇨Overview⇨Data Browser.**

   See Figure 7-9.

   Avoid altering any records within a table directly. Always attempt to use the SAP R/3 layer and its front-end utility for any changes. SAP R/3 has an enormous data map of all the tables and their relationships. Changing one record in one table without fully knowing the entire structure may introduce data inconsistency.

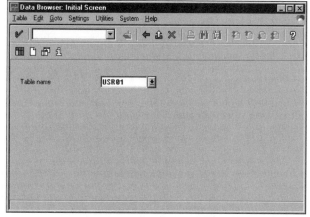

Figure 7-9:
Data
Browser:
Initial
Screen

2. **Enter the name of the table and press Enter to continue.**

In this example, enter table **USR01**.

The Data Browser selection screen appears, as shown in Figure 7-10. It allows you to limit your search on the records in the table selected. Various field are available to limit your search; exactly which fields are available depends on the table itself.

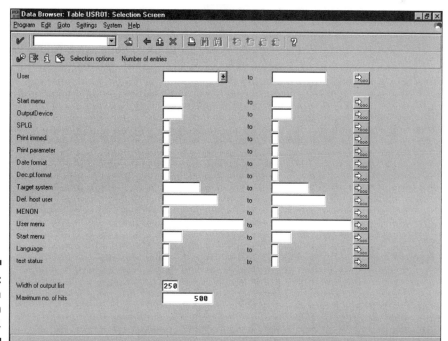

Figure 7-10:
Select data
to search
for.

3. **To see all the records in the table, leave the field values blank and click the Execute icon or press F8.**

Unlocking users and changing passwords

Displaying information is certainly useful, but your users won't be impressed if you can look at their information but not do anything with it. For example, a common security request from a user is to look up a forgotten password. Not a problem. You can not only look up passwords, but you can also change them.

In addition, you can deny users permission to use the system — or *lock them out.* Or the system itself may lock them out — for example, if they try to use an invalid password too many times. After users are locked out, they look to you to unlock them, as explained in the next section.

Unlocking users

Nobody likes being locked out. Here's how to unlock the poor soul who's being denied access.

1. **Choose Tools⇨Administration⇨Maintain Users⇨Users or enter the transaction code SU01 in the command field.**

2. **Select the locked username from the drop-down list. Display the entire user master record.**

   In this example, use JOEYH.

3. **Enter JOEYH or search for all users. If you search for all users, you can see all the accounts that are locked. Do so by clicking the drop-down and pressing Enter.**

   Figure 7-11 shows the locked users.

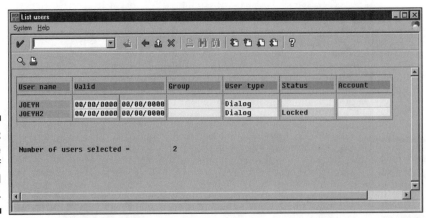

Figure 7-11: You can see a list of locked users.

4. **After selecting the user to unlock, click the Lock/Unlock button to unlock the user, as shown in Figure 7-12.**

Figure 7-12:
Click to
unlock a
user.

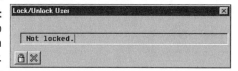

Make sure that the users SAP* and DDIC are never locked. SAP uses these users to perform certain internal functions. Use report RUSR006 to see the locked users within an R/3 system. This report may also indicate attempted security breaches.

Even if a user is unlocked, the person can't get into the system without knowing her password. The next section explains how to change a password.

Changing a password

Follow these steps to give users their cherished passwords for getting into the system:

1. **Follow the menu path Tools⇨Administration⇨Maintain Users⇨Users or enter the transaction code SU01 in the command field.**

2. **In the Maintain Users screen, enter the username and click the Change Password button.**

3. **Enter the password twice.**

The password does not appear in the field. All characters are valid, and passwords are not case-sensitive. SAP prompts the users to change their password on their next logon session.

Setting security parameters

You may want to control settings such as how many times a user can try to log in with an invalid password or the minimum length for a password. For example, when setting up support for a project that will run for six months, you may want to make passwords invalid after that time. (Although, when you think about it, how many six-month projects actually finish in six months?)

You control security variables with *instance parameters.* Go to the Edit Profiles screen to view some of these settings.

1. **Choose Tools➪Administration➪Computing Center➪Management System➪Configuration➪Profile Maintenance or enter** RZ10 **in the command field.**

   Figure 7-13 shows the Edit Profiles screen.

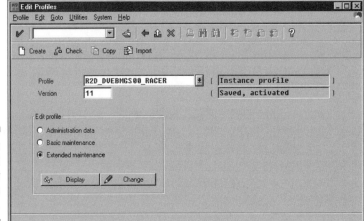

Figure 7-13:
Control
security
variables
here.

2. **Choose Instance Profile from the drop-down menu (at the right of the Profile field in Figure 7-13).**

3. **Select the Extended Maintenance option and click the Change button to maintain the parameters.**

   Table 7-2 shows key security parameters.

Table 7-2	Security Parameters
Parameter	**Description**
login/ext_security	System access with external security
login/fails_to_session_end	Number of invalid login attempts until session end
login/fails_to_user_lock	Number of invalid login attempts until user lock
login/min_password_lng	Minimum password length
login/no_automatic_user_sapstar	Control of the automatic login user SAP*

Parameter	Description
login/password_expiration_time	Date password must be changed
snc/permit_insecure_gui	Permit insecure GUI logins to SNC-enabled server

To add the parameter login/password_expiration_time, follow these steps:

4. Click the Create icon and then enter the parameter's name, login/password_expiration_time.

5. In the Parameter Val: field, enter 90, **as shown in Figure 7-14.**

This value forces all users to change their password in 90 days.

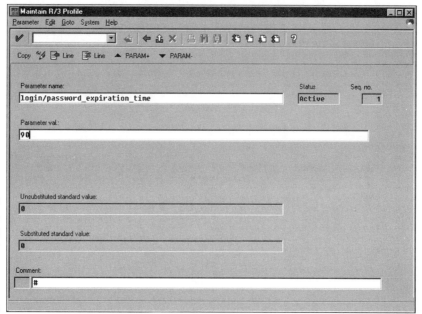

Figure 7-14:
You can set a parameter for when the password will expire.

6. After you enter the parameter and values, click the Copy button or press Shift+F4 to insert the new parameter into the instance profile.

7. Click the Left Arrow button to take you back to the Maintain R/3 Profile screen.

8. Click the Left Arrow button again to go back to the Edit Profiles screen.

9. **Click the Save icon to save your changes.**

10. **When asked "Do you want to activate the profile?" click Yes.**

SAP informs you of any warnings. Usually, these messages contain general information. To make the new instance parameter active, you have to stop and restart the SAP instance.

Administering Profiles

Profiles, as we explain earlier in this chapter, are job roles such as sales entry clerk. These prepackaged authorizations simplify your job by saving you from having to enter all the details for each profile every time. You simply assign one of these profiles to a user in the appropriate job role.

Up to this point, you have been using standard R/3 profiles. These 50 or so "canned" profiles provide a solid base to work from. To see the available profiles, follow these steps:

1. **Choose Tools⇨Administration⇨Maintain Users⇨Profiles or enter the transaction code** SU02 **in the command field.**

2. **Click the Generate button or click F5.**

   See Figure 7-15 for the results.

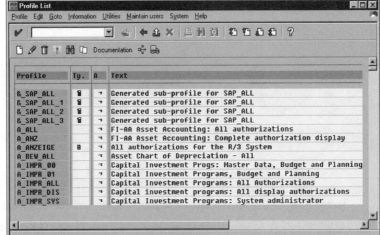

Figure 7-15:
You can see a list of available profiles.

This list displays profiles by module. The descriptive text helps you feel out these profiles. But in all reality, you need to go to the individual authorization level to really see what the profiles do.

Each functional module has a naming convention associated with it. The following list shows the first letter and its representation of the SAP profiles and composite profiles.

Letter	Representation
S	Basis Component
A	Asset Management
C	Production Planning
V	Sales and Distribution
P	Human Resources
M	Materials Management
L	Warehouse Management
K	Controlling
F	Finance
G	General Ledger

SAP recommends that your custom created profiles not have a "_" in the second position. For example, US:FI_MGR is a valid profile name.

3. Double-click on a profile to get detailed information on that profile.

Figure 7-16 shows the result of double-clicking on the A_ALL profile.

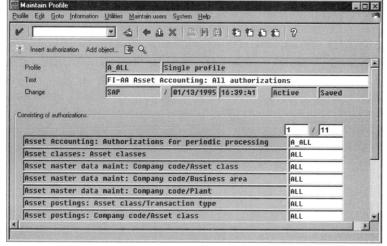

Figure 7-16:
Check out detailed information on a profile.

4. Double-click on the individual authorization to get detailed information on the authorizations that make up that profile.

Maintaining authorizations

If you have specific needs, you can change the values of the standard authorizations and make your own authorization object.

Always make a copy of the SAP standard authorization before changing it. A copy allows you to keep the standard authorization objects and create a new customer authorization object.

Before you begin, know exactly what change you want to make. Changing authorizations is a manual process, and it's pretty precise.

Checking out current authorizations

You have full control of the field values of the authorization checks on the authorization objects, which gives the security administrator added flexibility.

Follow these steps:

1. **Choose Tools⇨Administration⇨Maintain Users⇨Authorization or enter the transaction code SU03 in the command field.**

   The Maintain Authorization screen comes up. From here, select the object class you want to maintain.

2. **Double-click on the object class to get detailed information it.**

   Figure 7-17 shows the results when you double-click on the Basis: Administration object class.

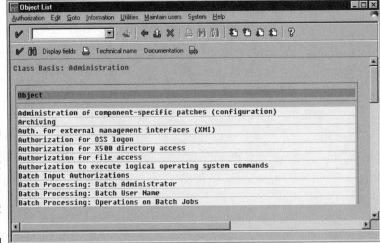

Figure 7-17:
You can get detailed information on an object class.

3. Double-click on the authorization object to see its authorizations.

Figure 7-18 shows the results when you double-click on the Authorization for OSS Logon authorization object.

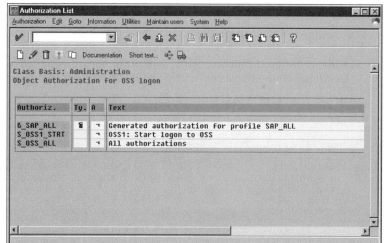

Figure 7-18:
The author-
ization list.

4. To see the field values of the authorization, double-click on the authorization.

Figure 7-19 shows the results when you double-click on the S_OSS1_STRT authorization.

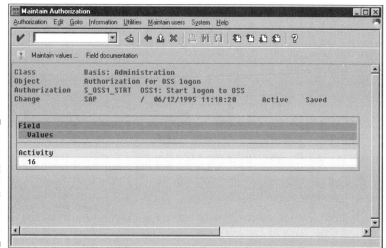

Figure 7-19:
You can
check out
the field
values of
an author-
ization.

Copying an authorization

Suppose you want an authorization that is different from the SAP authorizations. You can use one of the SAP standard authorizations as the pattern for your own, customized authorization.

You should never change SAP standard authorizations. It's always best to make a copy and start from there.

1. **Choose Tools⇨Administration⇨Maintain Users⇨Authorization or enter the transaction code SU03 in the command field.**

2. **Select the object class from the list.**

   In this example, select Basis: Authorization.

3. **Select the authorization object.**

   In this example, select S_OSS1_STRT. Figure 7-20 shows the selected authorization object.

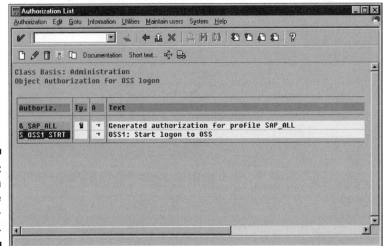

Figure 7-20:
Select an object in the authorization list.

4. **Click the Copy icon and then enter the name of the new authorization in the Copy Authorization screen.**

   The selected authorization is copied.

   For naming customers, you can use anything that doesn't have a "_" in the second position.

5. **Double-click on the newly copied authorization from the Authorization List screen.**

   From the Maintain Authorization screen, you can enter specific field values.

6. **Double-click on the field values and enter new values.**

   To see the meaning of the field values, press F4.

7. **After entering the new values, click the Save icon.**

   Figure 7-21 shows new field values.

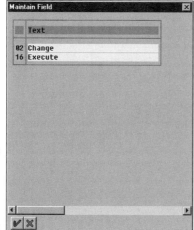

Figure 7-21:
Maintain
field values
here.

After you enter new authorization field values, you have to activate the authorization.

8. **Click the Activate icon or press F7.**

   SAP shows you the before and after values of the authorization, as shown in Figure 7-22.

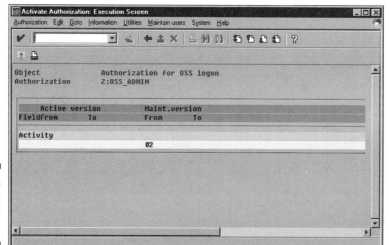

Figure 7-22:
Activate an
authoriza-
tion here.

9. **If the field values are correct, click on the Activate icon or F7 again.**

   The last step is to change the authorization description.

10. **Go to the authorization list, select your new authorization by clicking on it, and then click the Short Text button to change the text.**

11. **Enter descriptive text, as shown in Figure 7-23, and press Enter.**

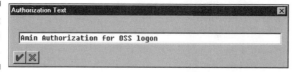

The authorization doesn't take effect until it is activated. Also, users with this new authorization don't feel the effect until they log out and log back into the system.

Maintaining profiles

You apply the same technique to maintaining profiles as you do to maintaining authorizations: Copy, change, save, and activate. To create a new profile from one of the standard SAP profiles, follow these steps:

1. **Choose Tools⇨Administration⇨Maintain Users⇨Profiles or enter the transaction code SU02 in the command field.**

2. **To see the available profiles, click the Generate button or click F5.**

   See Figure 7-24 for the results.

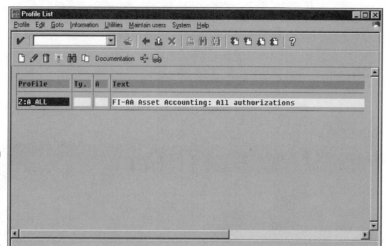

You can also enter a search string, such as **s***, and then press Enter.
This search string displays all profiles that start with, uh, *s*.

3. **Select the profile you want to copy by clicking once on the profile.**

   For the example, select the profile Z_ALL.

4. **Click the Copy button and enter the name for the copy.**

   Figure 7-25 shows the Copy Profile dialog box where you enter the new
   name. For customer naming, you can use anything that doesn't have a
   "_" in the second position. For this example, use the name Z:A_ALL.

Figure 7-25:
Enter a new
name here
for your
profile.

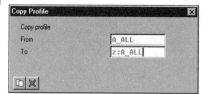

5. **Select the new profile, Z:A_ALL, from the Profile List screen to maintain its contents.**

6. **Enter a new description into the Text field.**

   The next step is to add or delete authorizations from Z:A_ALL.

7. **Delete an authorization by selecting a line and then pressing the
   right mouse button and choosing Delete Line or Shift+F2. Add a new
   authorization by clicking the Insert Authorization button or pressing
   F8 and then selecting the authorization and pressing Enter.**

8. **Press the Save icon to save the changes.**

   Next, you activate the maintained profile.

9. **Click the Activate icon or press F7.**

   SAP shows you the before and after values of the profile.

10. **If the values are correct, click on the Activate icon or press F7 again.**

Setting Up the Profile Generator

Profile Generator is a relatively new tool to the R/3 security module. It's a
front-end utility to configure and maintain security profiles. If you want to use
the Profile Generator, you need to configure a few settings. The Implementation
Guide (IMG) is helpful in configuring settings. Start by following these steps:

1. **Access the IMG by entering SPRO in the command field or by choosing Tools⇨Business Engineering⇨Customizing⇨Basic Function⇨ Enterprise IMG⇨Display.**

   Figure 7-26 shows the IMG screen.

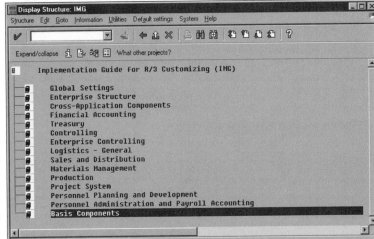

2. **Expand the Basis folder in the IMG tree.**

   The different sections in the IMG are organized in a folder format with subfolders.

3. **Choose Basis Components⇨System Administration⇨Users and Authorization⇨Maintain Authorizations and Profiles using Profile Generator, as shown in Figure 7-27.**

4. **Configure the profile generator by following the IMG instructions for activating the profile generator.**

   Use the instructions from the sections "Activating the profile generator," "Working on SAP check indicators and field values," "Generating the Enterprise menu," and "Generating activity group/profile and assigning users" to configure the profile generator. Perform all the steps in sequential order.

The steps in the following sections can help you configure the profile generator.

Activating the profile generator

Activate the profile generator by clicking the Activate Profile Generator check mark. The Select Transaction dialog box comes up, as shown in Figure 7-28.

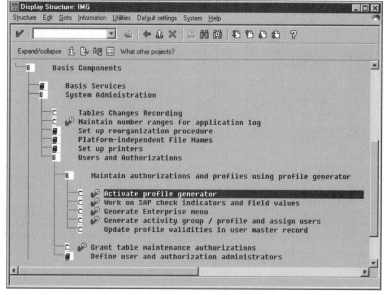

Figure 7-27:
Start here to
activate the
profile
generator.

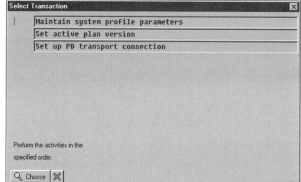

Figure 7-28:
Select
transaction.

Perform all the configuration by double-clicking on each step in the screen in
order. The first item is Maintain System Profile Parameters.

Maintaining system profile parameters

Double-clicking the Maintain System Profile Parameters folder takes you to
Edit Profiles. These profiles are system parameters, not parameters just for
authorizing users. Follow these steps to configure the Maintain System Profile
Parameters setting:

1. **Click the drop-down arrow and select the instance profile.**

2. **Click Extended Maintenance and then click the Change button, as shown in Figure 7-29.**

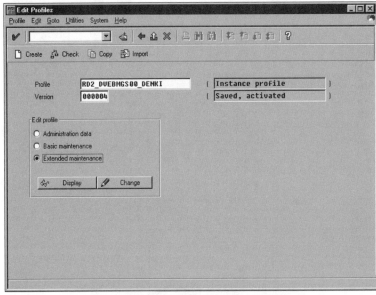

The Maintain R/3 Profile screen, shown in Figure 7-30, comes up.

3. **Click the Create icon (the one with a picture of a piece of paper with a corner folded down) or press F5 to create the new parameter.**

4. **Enter the parameter name:** `auth/no_check_in_some_cases` **with a value of** Y.

Figure 7-31 shows the Maintain R/3 Profile screen with a parameter typed in.

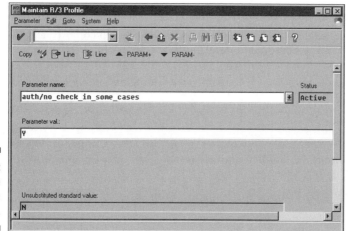

Figure 7-31:
Type in the
name of a
parameter.

Pay close attention to the syntax of the parameters. These settings are all case-sensitive, as well.

5. **Click the Copy button and then click the Back arrow.**

You go back to the first Maintain R/3 Profile screen.

6. **Click the Copy button again and then click the Back arrow again.**

You go back to the Edit Profiles screen.

7. **Click the Save icon to save and activate your changes.**

A series of information messages appears. Look at them carefully to make sure you haven't made an error. If everything is all right, confirm and activate.

The changes become active only after you stop and restart SAP. Click the Back arrow to continue with the configuration.

8. **Click the Back arrow to get back to the IMG Select Transaction screen.**

Setting the active plan version

Back at the Select Transaction screen, you can continue with the next item, Set Active Plan Version. This configuration allows the profile generator to integrate other SAP modules. Follow these steps:

1. **Double-click the second item, Set Active Plan Version.**

2. **Enter** 01 **for the active plan version.**

   To see other available options, press F4 on the configurable field.

3. **Click the Save icon and click the Back arrow to get back to the IMG Select Transaction screen.**

Setting up PD transport connection

Working again from the Select Transaction screen (refer to Figure 7-28), you configure the Personal Planning and Development (PD) Transport system. Transport, in SAP, is copying between systems. The default selection is Automatic Transport Connection. To change the default, follow these steps:

1. **Double-click the last item, Set Up PD Transport Connection, to configure it.**

   The Set Up PD Transport Connection screen appears. The field should be blank to allow automatic transport connection, as shown. The possible entries are

   (Blank) = Automatic transport connection is activated.

   X = No automatic transport connection.

   T = Transport using object lock (repair flag).

2. **Click the Save icon and click the Back arrow to get back to the IMG Select Transaction screen.**

Working on SAP check indicators and field values

On the Select Transaction screen, the next folder in the list is Working on SAP Check Indicators and Field Values. Click on the Check icon to continue.

Select all the steps in the screen to complete this configuration, as described in the following sections.

Creating a development class

A *development class* groups similar types of objects by one key value. Customers who want to do their own development need to create their own development classes. Think about the types of development classes needed for the implementation and create them. You can always return later and create more as needed.

The names of these development classes must start with a Y or Z. To create a development class, follow these steps:

1. **Double-click Development Class.**

   The IMG takes you to table TDEVC, shown in Figure 7-32. This table defines development classes. All development should be grouped by a development class to keep similar objects in the same class.

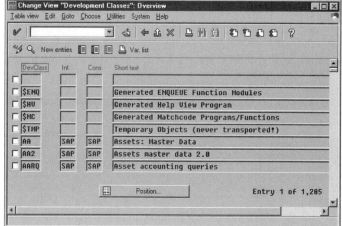

Figure 7-32: Use this table to define development ment classes.

2. **Click the New Entries button.**

   You can now enter new development classes.

3. **Enter the name of the new development class and enter a description.**

   See Figure 7-33 for an example.

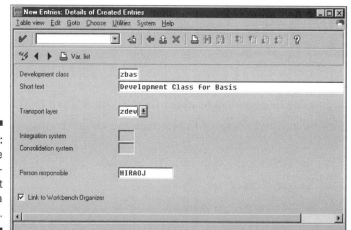

Figure 7-33: Put in the new development class and a description.

4. **Click the Save icon and then click the Back arrow to get back to the IMG Select Transaction screen.**

Copying SAP test status and field values

When you click the Copy SAP Test Status and Field Values folder in the Select Transaction screen, you go to transaction SU25. With this transaction you transfer the standard SAP authorization objects to all SAP transaction codes. Every time you perform transactions in SAP, SAP executes authorization checks. This transaction imports the defaults for the SAP authorization check indicators into the tables USOBX_C and USOBT_C.

Select the default and click the Execute button or press F8. Click the Save icon when done. Figure 7-34 shows a report for the copying of SAP defaults.

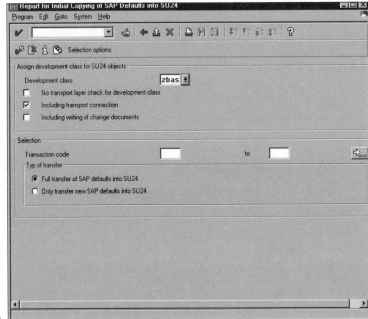

Figure 7-34: Here's a sample screen for copying SAP defaults.

1. **Enter a development class in the Development Class field.**

2. **Click Including Transport Connection to enable the transport you select.**

3. **Leave the fields for transaction codes blank.**

4. **Click the Save icon.**

5. **Click the Back arrow to get back to the IMG Select Transaction screen.**

Changing the test status

When you select Change Test Status in the Select Transaction screen, you go to transaction SU24 — a transaction you use to deactivate or activate authorization checks for all the transaction codes. Follow these steps:

1. **Click the radio button Maintain Check Indicators For Transaction Codes. Leave all other fields blank to see the authorization checks for all transactions.**

2. **Click the Execute button or press F8.**

   SAP generates a list of all transaction codes. You don't need to change anything; just keep the standard authorization check.

3. **Click the Back arrow to get back to the IMG Select Transaction screen.**

Generating the Enterprise menu

When you use the Profile Generator, you use the SAP menu tree to develop activity groups. But the menu tree doesn't just "go live" on its own. You have to activate it.

To generate the menu tree, follow the numbered steps in the SAP menu screen, as shown in Figure 7-35.

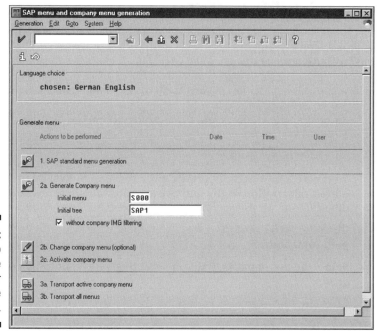

Figure 7-35: Start here to generate menus for the Profile Generator.

1. **Click the Execute icon in SAP Standard Menu Generation to generate the standard SAP menu.**

   SAP may take its sweet time to generate the menus, so don't be surprised.

2. **Select Generate a Company Menu.**

   From the standard menu structure, you can create a menu specific to the company. The company menu becomes a subset of the SAP standard menu.

3. **To keep the SAP-generated company menu, skip step 2.b.**

   Step 2.b. allows you to change the company menu generated. Again, making the menus isn't instantaneous.

   Now that you've generated the SAP standard and company menus, you need to activate the company menu.

4. **Click 2.c Activate Company Menu.**

5. **Execute step 3.a and 3.b.**

   These steps assign a change request to the company menu and all generated menus.

You're done! Now you can use the Profile Generator.

Generating activity groups/profiles and assigning users

The profiles created by Profile Generator are called activity groups. An *activity group* is practically the same as a profile, except that it was created with the Profile Generator.

Follow these steps for the quickest way to get to the Profile Generator.

1. **Enter the transaction code** PFCG **in the command field.**

   Alternatively, you can choose Tools⇨Administration⇨Maintain Users⇨Activity Groups.

2. **To create a new activity group, click the Create icon or press F5; enter a brief description of the activity group on the first line and a more detailed one on the second line, as shown in Figure 7-36.**

3. **Click the Menu button to see a graphical representation of the menu path selections.**

4. **Select the menu paths that you want to give access to this activity group.**

5. **Click the plus sign to open up the tree for further drilldown.**

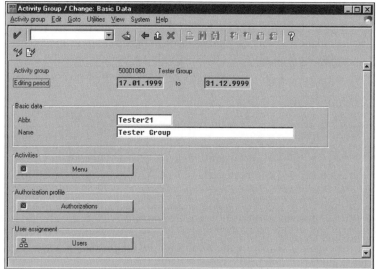

Figure 7-36:
Activity
group/create:
basic data.

6. **Select the menu paths you want to assign to your activity group.**

   A green traffic light indicates access, and a red traffic light indicates no access.

   Turning on the technical names is a good idea because then you can see where you're going and what transaction codes are associated with your selection. To turn the names on, click Ctrl+F1 or choose Edit⇨Technical Names⇨Technical Names On.

   If you want to see the transaction associated with the menu path, click the Execute icon on the transaction code. The Execute icon takes you to the associated transaction. When you finish viewing the transaction, click the Back arrow to return to the Profile Generator.

7. **After you finished selecting the menu paths, click the Save icon.**

   The next step is to define the authorization associated with your activity group.

8. **Click Ctrl+Shift F7 or click the Authorization Profile button.**

Authorization selection for activity group

After you complete your menu selection, you need to maintain the authorization fields. The next steps enable you to define the authorization parameters of the activity group.

1. **Open the authorization folders to maintain the authorization field values.**

   The authorizations that are maintained are marked Maintained and the ones that are not maintained are marked Standard.

2. **Maintain all the authorization field values.**

   The field values represent the authorizations needed to complete the transactions for the activity group. Depending on the access you want to allow, enter values for the fields that appear.

3. **When you finish updating these values, click the Save icon.**

4. **Enter a name for this profile.**

5. **Click the Generate icon or press Shift+F5.**

   This step generates the activity group to make it available for use. If any unmaintained authorizations exist, the system alerts you. If everything is complete, you are ready to test your activity group. If the generation is successful, you get a message telling you so.

If you want to associate other authorizations with this activity group, press F9 or choose Edit⇨Insert Authorization⇨Insert Manually from the Change Activity Group: Authorization screen. Always test your Activity group before releasing it to the world.

User assignment for activity group

Now that you know how to create an activity group, you need to assign it to a test user. Start from the Activity Group/Change: Basic Data screen.

1. **Enter transaction code PFCG in the command field, or choose Tools⇨Administration⇨Maintain Users⇨Activity groups.**

2. **Select an activity group and click the Change icon or F7.**

   This step brings you back to the Activity Group/Change: Basic Data screen.

3. **Assign new users to this activity group by clicking the Users button and entering the username.**

   This step creates the relationship between the activity group and the user master record, user21. A message appears in the lower-left corner, indicating the relationship.

4. **Tie the activity group to the user master record by clicking the User Master Data button in the User Master Update Data screen.**

   This updates the user master record with the activity group assignment.

   The final step is to test the activity group.

5. **Log in with the test user and thoroughly test the activity group.**

   Testing before releasing the group to the user community is very important.

Tracing Authorizations

As you test and develop authorizations (whether manually or with the Profile Generator), you'll come across some specific questions, such as "I need to do this but I can't" or "What are the authorizations I need to do this?" The following sections help you face up to those questions with some answer other than, "Uh, well, gosh, how should I know?"

Using SU53 to see what you are denied

It is good practice to include an authorization to allow access to transaction code SU53. SU53 shows you whether all authorization checks have been successful or not. If they are not successful, the code returns the needed authorizations.

First off, create an authorization that allows you to use SU53:

1. **Type in transaction code** SU03 **to go into Authorization Maintenance and then select Non-Application-Specific Authorization Objects.**

2. **Select the object Authorization Check for Transaction Start.**

3. **Create an authorization for authorization S_TCODE with field value SU53.**

   Refer back to the "Maintaining authorizations" section earlier in the chapter to see how to complete this step.

4. **Assign the authorization to a profile that is assigned to a user.**

   Now you are authorized to use the Check Authorization function.

Suppose that you want to perform a task but you don't have the proper authorization. Immediately after SAP denies you, enter **/nSU53** in the command field. You then see the check results.

By looking at the Object Class, Object, and Field Value, you can create the proper authorization needed to allow access into this transaction. From this message you can create a solution. (See the "Maintaining authorizations" section for more details.)

1. **Go into Authorization Maintenance by using transaction code SU03.**

2. **Select Non-Application-Specific Authorization Objects and then select the object Authorization Check for Transaction Start.**

3. **Create a new authorization with value SU01.**

   Voilà! Now attach this authorization to your test user's profile, and you solved the access problem to SU01.

Authorizations to do specific tasks are usually controlled by many different authorization objects. Therefore, you need to go through the entire task to see whether other checks are involved. In the preceding example, the solution was only for entering into transaction SU01, not performing any other function beyond that. You need to do further testing of all needed functions.

Tracing authorizations

Tracing authorizations is helpful when you need to create an authorization profile to perform certain tasks. The job is tedious but gives you a complete "blueprint" to work from.

Starting a trace

Follow these steps to trace an authorization:

1. **Log in with a user with SAP_ALL and SAP_NEW profiles.**

   Using these profiles prevents any failed authorization checks during the trace.

2. **Enter ST01 via the command field to see the trace screen.**

   From this initial screen, you can see the last time a trace occurred as well as whether one is active. See Figure 7-37 for the trace screen.

   You can do only one trace at a time. Make sure that traces are turned off when they're not needed, because unneeded traces create an unnecessary load on the system and make performance suffer. Status of "0" in the Active Trace Types shows that the tracing is off.

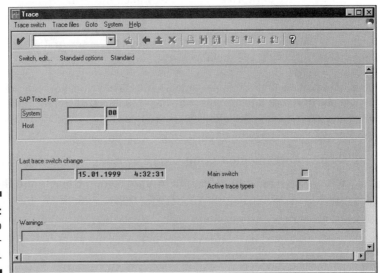

Figure 7-37:
Start here to trace authorizations.

3. **To start tracing, click the Switch Edit button.**

4. **In the Trace Types section, click on Authorization and click off any other selection.**

5. **To limit the trace, click the right arrow on General Filters in the General Management section.**

   Figure 7-38 shows the dialog box where you limit the trace.

6. **Type in the username and click Back.**

   The General Filter box displays "Active."

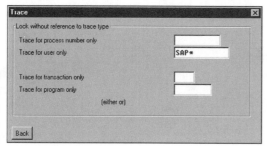

7. **Click the box underneath Write Options in the General Management section.**

8. **Click on "Trace:write to disk," and then click Back when done.**

   Afterwards, Write Options displays *To disk.*

9. **In the Filter Recs in the Database, enter** MY_Checks.

10. **To save this entry from going to the menu and making its selection, choose Trace Switch⇨Editor Save In⇨In Database (New).**

    Figure 7-39 shows your settings before you start, when you're ready to trace.

11. **Open another session by choosing System⇨Create Session.**

    The new session is where you perform the transactions to be traced. The first screen records the trace.

12. **When you're ready, click the S in your first screen.**

13. **When you're done, click the Stop button to stop tracing and No Trace to turn off tracing on the toolbar.**

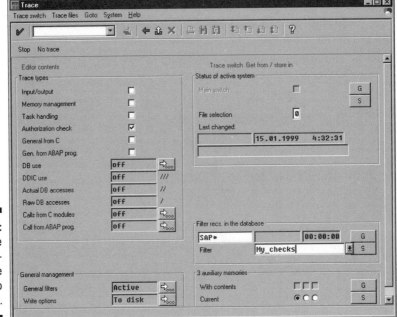

Figure 7-39:
Here are
sample set-
tings before
starting to
trace.

Looking at your trace

After you complete the trace, you can review it to check the authorizations in the profile.

First, be sure you stopped the tracing and turned it off completely.

1. **From the trace screen ST01, choose Trace File⇨Standard Options or enter F6.**

   You go to the Options for Trace Analysis screen.

2. **Click off all checks except Trace for Authorization Checks; enter the date and time to limit your results to your one trace; click the Accept button when finished.**

3. **Choose Trace Files⇨Analyze Standard, or press F7, and then click on the NewList to see a refreshed list of trace files.**

4. **Double-click on your file to see the results of the trace.**

   Here you see only the authorization traces, as shown in Figure 7-40. Listed in the files are the authorization object and the appropriate field value of the transactions performed.

From this information, you can create a profile to match this task or function. Tracing authorizations is a very powerful tool. Although it is time-consuming, it is very specific and exact.

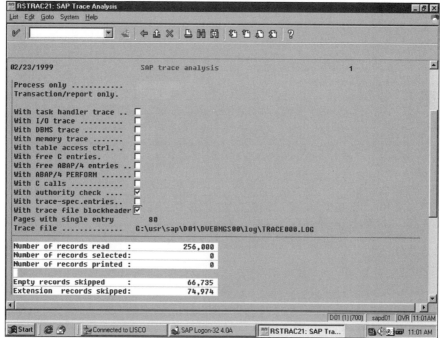

List Edit Goto System Help

```
02/23/1999                    SAP trace analysis                    1

Process only ...........
Transaction/report only.

With task handler trace ..  ☐
With I/O trace ..........   ☐
With DBMS trace .........   ☐
With memory trace .......   ☐
With table access ctrl. .   ☐
With free C entries.        ☐
With free ABAP/4 entries .. ☐
With ABAP/4 PERFORM .......  ☐
With C calls ...........    ☐
With authority check ....   ☑
With trace-spec.entries..   ☐
With trace file blockheader ☑
Pages with single entry        80
Trace file .............    G:\usr\sap\D01\DVEBMGS00\log\TRACE000.LOG

Number of records read    :        256,000
Number of records selected:              0
Number of records printed :              0

Empty records skipped     :         66,735
Extension  records skipped:         74,974
```

D01 (1) (700) sapd01 OVR 11:01AM

Start | Connected to LISCO | SAP Logon-32 4.0A | RSTRAC21: SAP Tra... | 11:01 AM

Figure 7-40:
Here you
see the
results of
your trace.

Test your newfound knowledge

How do you unlock a locked user?

A. *Lock* is a euphemism for brain-locked. There's nothing you can do.

B. Start with transaction code SU01. Select the locked user from the drop-down list. Select the user to unlock and then click the Lock/Unlock button.

C. Just laugh at the person and taunt him or her, saying, "You got yourself locked. You get yourself unlocked."

D. None of the above.

What is the purpose of the profile generator?

A. You can efficiently generate electricity with it.

B. You use it to save yourself some time and trouble when you configure and maintain security profiles.

C. You can substitute it for a conventional camera. It's especially helpful in crime work.

D. It serves no purpose at all.

Chapter 8

You Ain't Got a Thing If You Ain't Got Printing

*T*o your users, printing is just a given, isn't it? Like making a phone call, or breathing, or sitting down on a chair. Even sending a fax from SAP is pretty ho-hum to them. Talk about your thankless jobs. Printer administrator would be high on the list. Nobody is going to think you did anything hot by allowing them to exercise their natural-born right to print their work.

But you have done something considerable in getting printing to work efficiently in your networked SAP system with all its servers and local workstations.

In this chapter, you first find out how to set up printers (and faxes, too) so that they'll work from SAP. Then you see how to delve into your private domain, the spooler, and do things like check on the status of jobs being printed.

Getting Printers to Work in SAP

Setting up printers to work with SAP isn't entirely automatic because, for one thing, it's not obvious what you connect the printers to. If you're running an individual PC, you connect the printer to the PC. If you're running a network, you connect to a server on the network.

If you're running SAP, though, well, what do you connect to?

SAP R/3 has a simple enough solution, which is, basically, to leave printing to the operating system. In all respects, it is probably the best strategy. What R/3 provides — ingeniously, even if it looks lazy — is a seamless interface to the operating system through R/3's *spool system*.

That little spool system is the key to the printing. R/3's spool work process formats the data and sends it to the operating system, which manages the output.

To print successfully from R/3, you first have to be able to print from the underlying operating system. In the next section, we talk about getting your local printer set up properly, the basis of printing from SAP.

Connecting a local printer

Whenever you're setting up your system to print, you have to follow the steps to get that local printer working in its local environment. Here's how to set up a printer in Windows 95/98 or Windows NT.

1. **From the Desktop, choose Start⇨Settings⇨Printers.**

2. **Double-click Add Printer.**

3. **In the dialog box, shown in Figure 8-1, select either a network or local printer.**

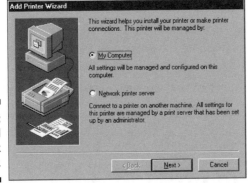

Figure 8-1:
Select local
or network
printer.

4. **Tell Windows to use this printer as your default.**

   To select this printer as your default, click the Yes radio button in the Add Printer Wizard screen (shown in Figure 8-2).

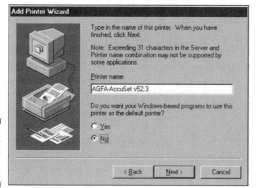

Figure 8-2:
Click the Yes
radio button.

5. **Follow the Add Printer wizard to test your printer and set a default printer.**

If you have other printers defined, go into the printer's screen via Start⇨ Settings⇨Printers and highlight a printer you want to set as your default. Right-click on that printer; from the pop-up menu, select Set as Default, as shown in Figure 8-3.

Figure 8-3:
Here, set
your printer
as the
default.

When you have your local printer working properly, you can invite that printer into the world of SAP, as explained in the next section.

Configuring the local printer to run with SAP

The key step, from the SAP perspective, is getting that local printer to respond when SAP tells it to print. Here's how to do that:

1. **Log on to the SAP system as a user with system administration privileges.**

2. **Go to the Printer Administration menu. Follow the menu path Tools⇨Administration⇨Spool⇨Spool Administration.**

If you prefer, use the command field and enter transaction code **SPAD**. Either way, you arrive at Spool Administration: Initial Screen, as shown in Figure 8-4.

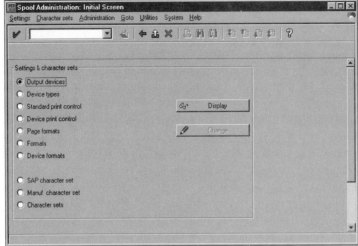

Figure 8-4:
Start spool
administra-
tion here.

3. Click the Change button (the one with a pencil on it).

The list of output devices appears, as shown in Figure 8-5.

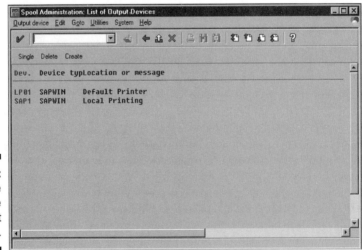

Figure 8-5:
Choose one
of these
output
devices.

4. Click the Create button in the application toolbar.

The configuration screen of printers appears, as shown in Figure 8-6.

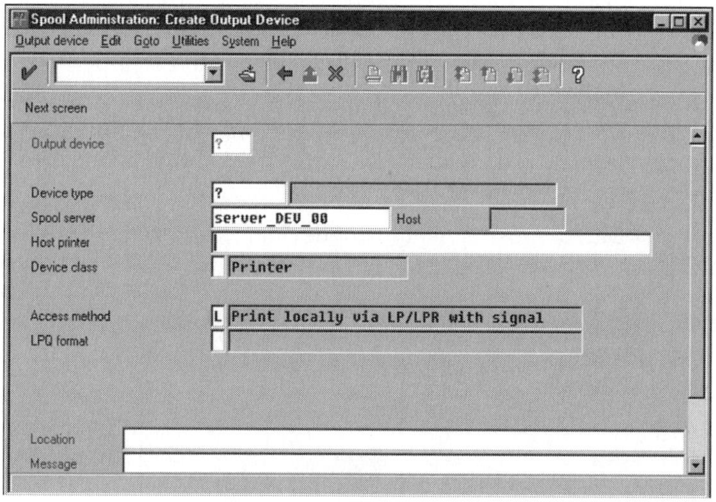

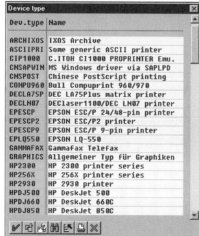

Figure 8-6:
The Spool
Administration window
configures
print
devices.

5. Fill the output device fields.

Enter these values for the output device, as shown in Figure 8-6:

- *Output device* is a four-character code that identifies the printer.

- *Device type* is a selection from a list of common printers, as shown in Figure 8-7.

Figure 8-7:
Select from
a list of
common
printers.

- *Spool server* is the application server where the spool work process is configured. The naming convention is (Host_SID_SystemNumber).

- *Host* is the physical host where the print formatting server resides.

- *Destination Host is* the physical host where the actual output is managed.

- *Host Printer* is the actual printer name at the operating system level. If you are using NT, enter the full UNC name, like `\\ServerNamer\PrinterName`.

- *Device Class* is the type of device, as shown in Figure 8-8.

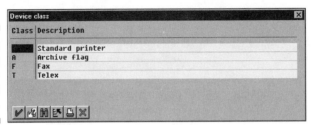

Figure 8-8: Check the list of available device types.

- *Access Method* specifies the printing type, as shown in Figure 8-9.

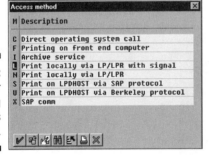

Figure 8-9: Choose your printing access method.

For default PC printing, use printing type F (front end printing).

- *SAP Title Page* prints cover sheets for all spool requests for this printer, if selected.

- *Lock printer in R/3 system,* if selected, prohibits printing from SAP systems if selected.

With your configuration set up as shown in Figure 8-10, you've accomplished the mission. SAP pushes all output to the PC's default printer.

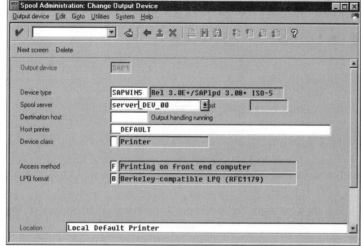

Figure 8-10:
Here's the completed printer configuration screen.

Controlling the local print server: SAPLPD

One way to print from SAP is to have the small transfer program, SAPLPD, running on your desktop.

You can check whether SAPLPD is installed on your system. If `saplpd.exe` exists in your SAPGUI directory, as noted above, SAPLPD has been installed on your desktop.

Put a shortcut for SAPLPD in your Windows Startup group, so SAPLPD automatically runs when Windows starts.

A quick way to see whether SAPLPD is working is to run `saplpd.exe`. In the screen Spool Administration: List of Output Devices in SAP, go to the menu and select Qutput Device⇨Print This List. If a list is printed at your default printer, you are ready to print at this station.

Setting up specific printer types is like the steps previously discussed for connecting a Windows printer. Two scenarios are particularly common:

✔ Configuring the printer as a local printer in SAP

✔ Setting up a fax

Configuring a printer as an SAP local printer

As administrator, you have to decide whether to print *locally* or *remotely*. In R/3 speak

> ✔ *Printing locally* uses the host's operating systems facilities. Output requests go directly from the R/3 spool server to the Windows spool system.
>
> ✔ *Printing remotely* usually passes the print data to an external host not running an SAP spool work process but instead using SAPLPD.

Whenever possible, it's best to use a local connection. Thanks to the speed and efficiency contributed by the R/3 spool application server, a local connection is the fastest connection. Most reliable, too.

You need first to define a printer at the operating system level where the SAP application server resides. Refer to your particular operating system's printing guide to accomplish this task.

If you are implementing SAP on NT 4.0 server, define printing by using Microsoft's TCP/IP for Printing service. There may be problems when attempting to unite protocols other than TCP/IP with R/3. Remember, R/3 only utilizes the TCP/IP protocol. A preferred technique is to configure the data as type RAW when setting up printers via Printing for TCP/IP. This allows unformatted data (RAW data) to go to the printer.

Follow these steps to configure the printer as local.

1. **Log onto SAP with an administrator's user ID.**

2. **At the initial screen, type** SPAD **to go to the Spool Administration screen.**

3. **Click the Change button and then the Create button to define a new printer.**

Figure 8-11 shows the architecture of our example.

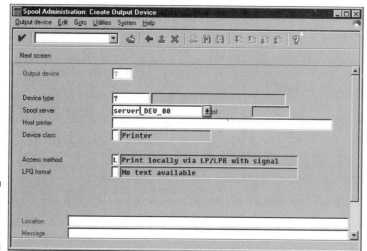

Figure 8-12 shows a configured local printer. If your setup doesn't have an R/3 application server running on the PC, you have to set up a remote connection (using SAPLPD) to the printer.

Setting up a fax

Sometimes, users won't settle for just printing a piece of paper at a central printer down the hall. They want to engage in a special, highly advanced form of printing — faxing.

Like other device options, you must be able to fax from your PC before configuring the PC fax for R/3. You have to install PC fax software and configure the fax on the PC.

If the PC fax software works, you can configure the fax to work with R/3. Here's what to do:

1. **Confirm that the** `sapfx.exe` **and** `sapfx.dll` **files are present on your PC.**

   These files should reside in the same directory as `saplpd.exe`.

2. **On the SAP menu, choose** **Tools**⇨**Adminstration**⇨**Spool**⇨**Spool Administration.**

   If you prefer, enter the command field transaction code **SPAD**.

3. **Click Change.**

   The list of output devices appears.

4. **Click Create.**

   The configuration screen of devices appears.

5. **Enter the configuration fields as shown in Figure 8-13.**

   For Host printer, use the name of the fax as defined in the PC.

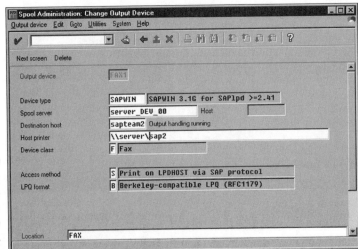

Figure 8-13:
Complete
this screen
to define
a fax.

Sometimes the fax software doesn't work if you start SAPLD or SAPGUI before starting the fax software. Start the applications in the following order:

✔ Fax software

✔ SAPLPD

✔ SAPGUI

Spinning and Spanking Your Spooler: Managing Print Requests

The spool area is the heart of SAP printing. For you, the SAP R/3 administrator, the spool system is your private little bailiwick. Others may know about the local printer and the local operating system and about using SAP. The spool system, though, is a big mystery to them.

A *spool* is pretty much what its name suggests. It's a place where you store stuff, the way you store thread on a spool of thread. In the world of computers, a spooler is software. It uses the computer's memory or hard disk to store requests. As administrator, you can go into the spooler software and perform all kinds of neat operations:

✔ Managing print jobs and other requests (which are formal operations)

✔ Spinning and spanking (which aren't formal operations)

Managing spool requests

After you have printers set up to work with SAP, you can manage the spooler to control all the print requests that come in from the various users. You can

✔ Print a spool request

✔ Check a spool request (and change the destination printer or the number of copies)

✔ Look at the data being printed

✔ Track jobs being printed

To get to the spool area, choose Tools⇨Administration⇨Spool⇨Output Control. The Spool: Request Screen appears. You can also access the spool area by entering **SP01** in the command field. This screen allows you to narrow your research of print request, as shown in Figure 8-14.

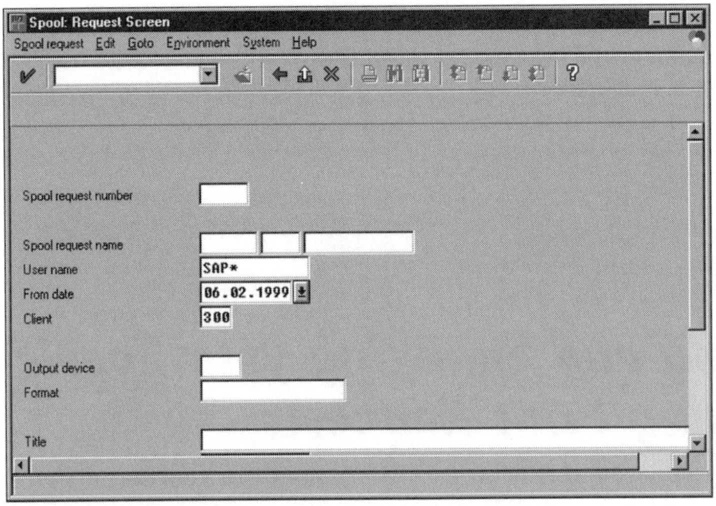

Figure 8-14:
Use this
screen to
control print
requests.

From here, you can administer some common printing requirements.

1. **Click the check button on the left side of the request form.**

2. **Select the print administration function.**

   • To display the spool request, press F6 or choose Spool
     Request⇨Display.

   • To print the spool request, press Shift+F1 or choose Spool⇨Print.

   • To delete the spool request, press Shift+F2 or choose
     Spool⇨Delete.

   • To display the attribute, double-click the spool request itself.

To get more attributes, press the Attributes II button or choose Goto⇨
Attributes II. The default priority is 3. You can change that from 1 (highest)
to 9 (lowest). If you make a change, click the yellow folder on the menu
bar to save the change.

Customizing spooling

These are some customizing settings that a Basis administrator will
encounter. Not all application SAP instances need to have a spool work
process running. In contrast, only one spool work process can be defined in
an SAP instance.

Whenever you modify an instance parameter, ensure that there are appropriate resources available to handle the change imposed on the system.

To configure an SAP instance to run a spool work process, you must edit the instance profile. Follow these steps to accomplish this task.

1. **Select** **T**ools⇨**A**dministration⇨**C**omputing Center⇨**M**anagement **System⇨C**onfiguration⇨**P**rofile Maintenance.

   The Edit Profiles screen appears. You can also get to this screen by entering the command **RZ10**. Figure 8-15 shows the screen.

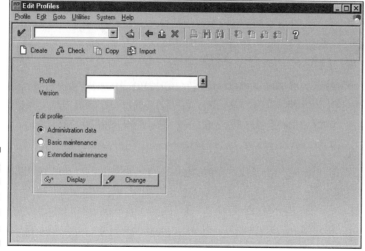

Figure 8-15: Start here to modify an instance parameter.

2. **Select the specific instance profile, using the selection arrow on the Profile field, and then double-click on the instance profile that you want.**

3. **In the Edit Profile section of the Edit Profiles screen, click the Basic Maintenance button and then click the Change icon.**

4. **On the right-hand side, enter 1 in the field for spool, as shown in Figure 8-16.**

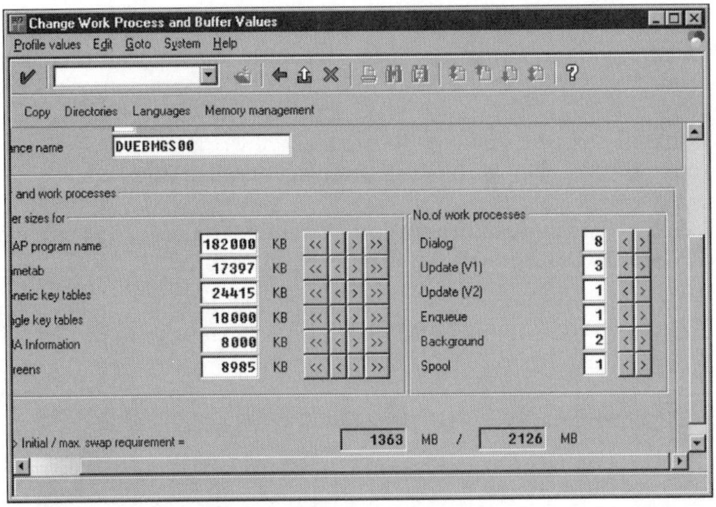

Figure 8-16:
Set your
final values
in this
screen.

5. **Click Copy and then click the button with the yellow folder to save your change.**

6. **Review and accept each of the confirmation questions.**

You're done! Now you can use this instance as a SAP spool server.

Remember, this change is only effective after you stop and restart SAP.

Chapter 9

Working Behind the Scenes

*I*n theater, the people on stage may get most of the credit, but the people behind the scenes do at least as much work as the famous actors in the foreground. What good is a play without a decent director, for example? (Not much. And we've seen some of those structureless plays that seem to have no director.) Lighting is pretty essential. Costumes make a big difference. Stagehands come in handy for moving props around.

SAP has all kinds of opportunities for work behind the scenes. Here is this humongous computing force in SAP; but thousands of people pounding keys on it in the foreground create a need for help in the background.

Background jobs help make efficient use of your SAP system's resources. For a Basis administrator, for example, background jobs mean doing cleanup jobs during hours of lower activity. On the business side of things, background jobs mean running batch jobs to process routine transactions. For example, an organization may choose to run a nightly batch job to print purchase orders (POs) so that employees don't have to wait for the printing during the day.

The computer, for its part, does basically the same thing for a background job as for a foreground job — it processes and gives a result. The only difference between background and foreground jobs is that the background jobs use work processes that are very forgiving, allowing time-critical processes to gobble up the system's resources (like those egoistic actors on stage, who insist on having the limelight).

In this chapter you see how to create, schedule, and reschedule background jobs.

Setting Up Background Jobs

As Basis administrator, you need to run some daily housekeeping jobs. These jobs are mostly ABAP programs that run in the background. In this section, we take, as an example, the job that cleans up old spool requests, RSPO0041.

Your SAP instance needs to have at least one background work process configured. Go to transaction code SM50, Process Overview, from the command field. You should have at least one background work process, BTC, configured.

Also, before you can configure and schedule background jobs, you need authorization. The obvious benefit to requiring authorization is that you don't have your whole user community scheduling jobs and generally creating conflicts, incoherence, and chaos. You want only designated individuals to have this authorization. To set up administrator authorization, go to transaction code SU01 via the command field. If you are the Basis administrator with profile SAP_ALL, you have access to background job configuration and maintenance. Background authorizations are controlled by the following authorization objects:

S_BTCH_ADM: Batch Processing: Batch Administrator

S_BTCH_JOB: Batch Processing: Operations on Batch Jobs

S_BTCH_NAM: Batch Processing: Batch User Name

S_ADMI_FCD: System Authorizations

Take a look at some standard SAP authorizations for these objects from transaction code SU03.

Some jobs are initiated from a user. If you schedule jobs with a normal account like JOEYH, the job disappears if JOEYH disappears as a user. We usually run all cleanup jobs as user DDIC (SAP data dictionary user), which doesn't disappear from the system.

Creating a background job

To be able to run a background job, you first have to create it. When SAP can identify the job, it can go to the next step — namely, running it. Create a background job like this:

1. **Choose Tools➪Administration➪Jobs➪Define Jobs or enter transaction code** SM36 **in the command field.**

   The Define Background Job screen appears, as shown in Figure 9-1.

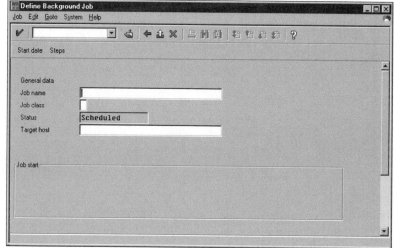

Figure 9-1:
Start here to
create a
background
job.

2. **In the Job Name field, enter a description of the job.**

   In this case, enter the program's name, RSPO0041.

   You don't have to enter the name, of course. But to keep it simple, enter the ABAP program's name here. That way, you can readily identify the process that runs when this job runs.

3. **In the Job Class field, enter a letter code for the priority to be given to the job.**

   Use letter codes A, B, and C, with A being the highest priority and C being the lowest. If you enter A or B, you should have at least two background work processes configured for that SAP instance. Enter C for all jobs unless they are super-critical, in order to minimize the misallocation of resources. For the example, enter **C**.

4. **In the Target Host field, enter the application server that processes this background request. If it is not specified, the background job will be processed on any available server.**

   Figure 9-2 shows a completed sample Define Background Jobs screen.

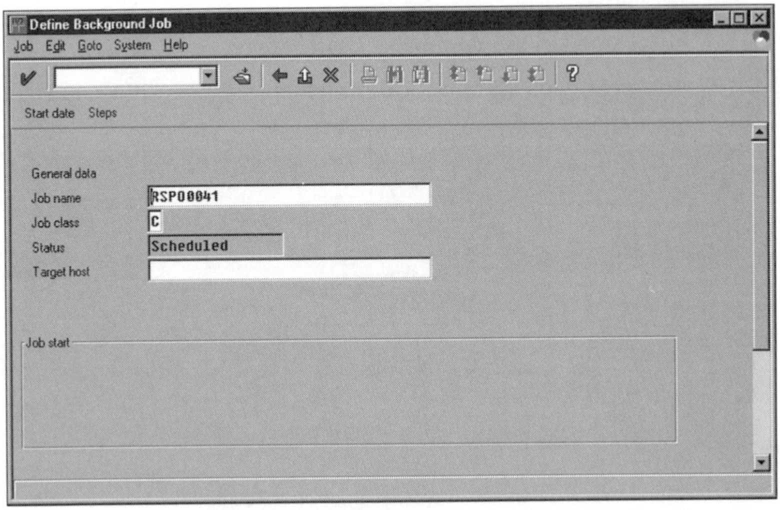

Figure 9-2:
A completed
Define
Background
Jobs
screen.

After creating a job, you need to configure the specific program to run. The following steps take you through assigning a job to run in the background.

The next step is to define the program to run in the job.

5. **Click the Steps button at the top of the Define Background Jobs screen to reach the Create Step 1 screen, shown in Figure 9-3.**

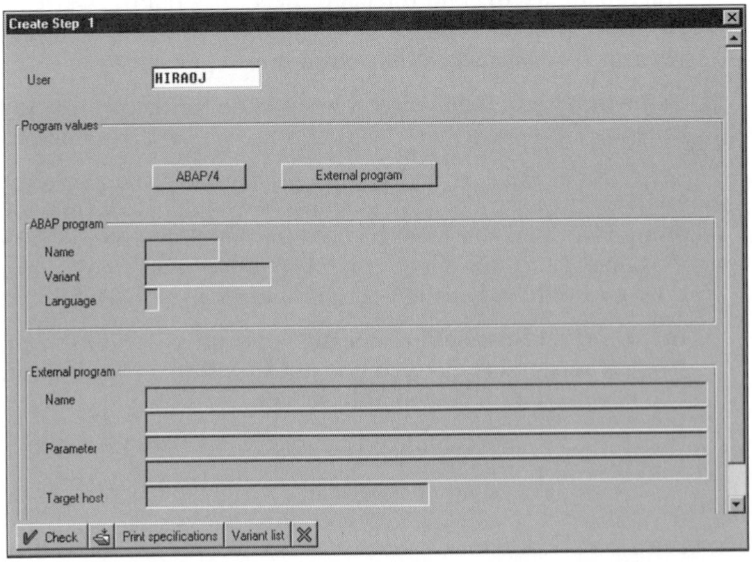

Figure 9-3:
When you
click the
Steps
button, you
reach the
Create Step
1 screen.

You can schedule outside programs as well as an ABAP program to run. In the example, you schedule an ABAP program to run.

6. **Click the ABAP/4 button and enter the program name to run.**

   This action ungrays the Name, Variant, and Language fields, making them available for input. Fill in the Name field with ABAP program name RSPO0041.

7. **Bring up a list of variants for this program by clicking the Variant List button at the bottom of the screen. Select the variant by double-clicking the one you want.**

   The Variant Directory for the program appears. In this case, you have three variants to choose from, shown in Figure 9-4.

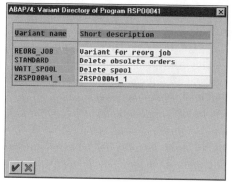

Figure 9-4:
Click the
Variant List
button to
see a list of
variants.

8. **Finish by clicking the Save icon at the bottom.**

   The job has been created to run program RSPO0041 with variant ZRSPO0041_1.

Creating a variant

A *variant* is a way that SAP tells its ABAP programs to run. For example, in program RSPO0041, the variant ZRSPO0041_1 tells the ABAP program to delete items which are older than one day. Depending on the ABAP program scheduled, SAP requires that you specify a variant for the program. If the program requires a variant but none is set up, you need to create one.

Follow these steps to create a variant for an ABAP program:

1. **Enter transaction code SE38 or choose Tools⇨ABAP/4 Workbench and then click the ABAP/4 Editor button.**

   The ABAP/4 Editor: Initial Screen appears, as shown in Figure 9-5.

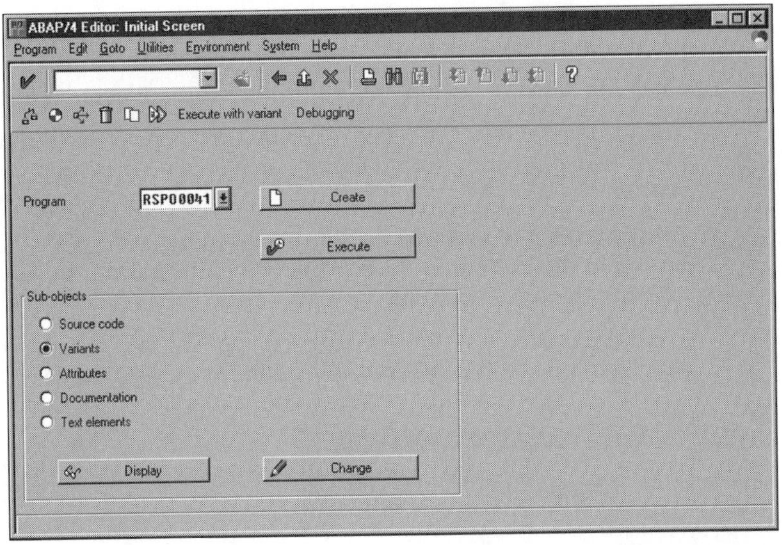

Figure 9-5:
Start here to
create a
variant.

2. **Enter the program name and click the radio button Variants on the lower left side. Click the Change icon (a pencil) to continue to the Variant screen.**

3. **Click the Create button from the Variant initial screen, shown in Figure 9-6.**

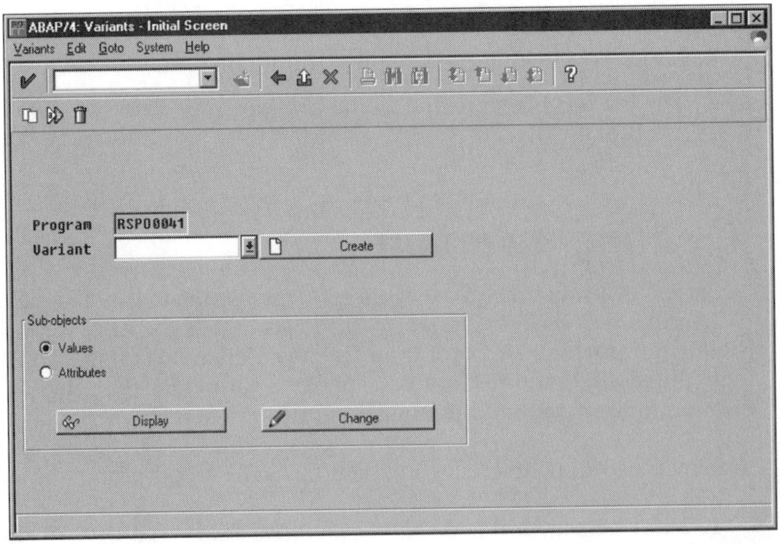

Figure 9-6:
Here's the
Variant ini-
tial screen.

4. Enter a name beginning with Z or Y.

Figure 9-7 shows the field where you enter the name.

Figure 9-7:
Name the
variant
(starting
with Z or Y).

5. Fill in variant-specific options for the program in the remaining screens.

In this case, see Figure 9-8 for the first Maintain Variant screen. An asterisk in the Client field means that this job runs for all clients within the system. The default is the current client.

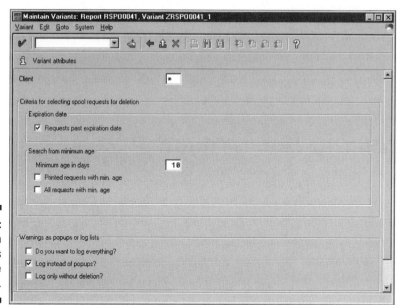

Figure 9-8:
Fill in
options
for the
program.

6. Click the Continue button to get to the next Maintain Variant screen. Enter a short text in the Description field.

Figure 9-9 shows the field.

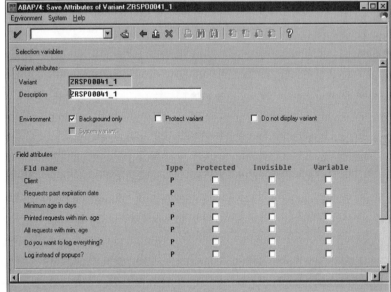

Figure 9-9:
Put text
in the
Description
field.

7. **Click the Save icon at the end.**

Scheduling Background Jobs

Scheduling, of course, is a large part of the whole point when you're doing background processing. Often, you want to schedule the job to run at a time when it doesn't conflict with a bunch of other jobs (like at night, for example). You can schedule the job to run once or periodically.

In the following sections, you see how to schedule a job, how to check it out after you schedule it, and how to change it when the inevitable urge comes along to do just that.

Scheduling a job

Now that you have created a job, you need to schedule the job to run. Suppose, for example, that you want to schedule a job to run at 6:00 a.m. every day. Here's how to do it:

1. **Enter** SM36 **in the command field and enter the job name. Click the Start Date button to summon the scheduler shown in Figure 9-10.**

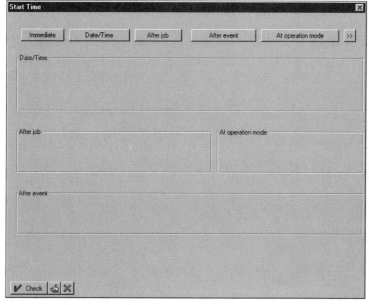

Figure 9-10: You can schedule when a background job starts.

2. **Click the Date/Time button and enter the date on which you want the job to run and then enter the time at which you want the job to run in the Time field.**

   In this example, fill in the next day's date and a time of 6:00 a.m. This schedules the job to run tomorrow at 6:00 a.m.

   Next, you need to configure frequency.

3. **Click the Periodic Job check box at the lower-left and then click the Period Values button.**

   The Period Values dialog box appears.

4. **Select Daily and then click the Save button to exit the Period Values dialog box.**

   See Figure 9-11 for an illustration of the Period Values dialog box.

Figure 9-11: Here's how to select time and frequency.

5. **Click the Save icon at the bottom of the Start Time screen to save.**

   After clicking the Save icon, you return to the Define Background Job screen.

6. **Now your job is scheduled to run daily at 6:00 a.m. If this is correct, click the Save icon at the top of the Define Background Job screen to save.**

   A message appears in the lower-left corner of the screen, "Job RSPO0041 has been created," as shown in Figure 9-12.

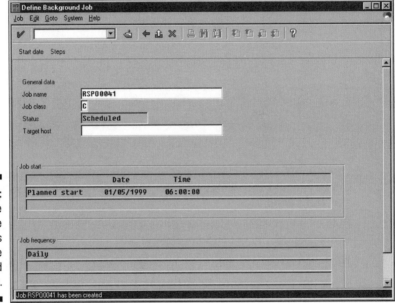

Figure 9-12:
A welcome message confirms that you've created the job.

Maybe you think that creating and scheduling your background job ought to take care of matters pretty well. But people expect you, the administrator, to be perfect. You better have ways to double-check yourself. The next section shows how to review your scheduled background job.

Reviewing scheduled jobs

Who knows who may have made a mistake? Maybe you or your other Basis teammates. In any case, you had best make sure the job is scheduled the way you want. Here's what to do:

1. **Follow the menu path Tools⇨Administration⇨Jobs⇨Job Overview or enter** SM37 **in the command field.**

   This takes you to the Select Background Jobs main screen, shown in Figure 9-13.

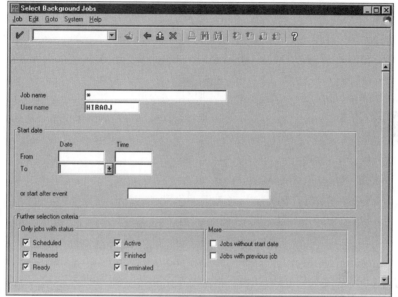

Figure 9-13: Start here to select background jobs.

2. **Fill in the search criteria to select the job you just scheduled.**

   In this example, we've entered RSPO0041.

3. **After entering your search criteria, press Enter.**

   The Job Overview screen appears, as shown in Figure 9-14. The column headings — Scheduled, Released, Ready, Active, Finished, and Cancelled — reflect the possible status of the job. An X in a column shows the status of that job.

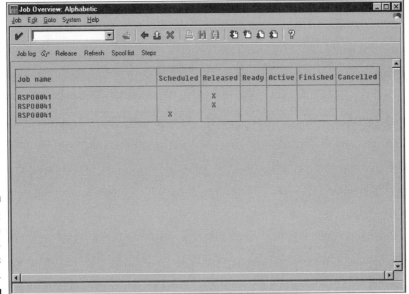

Monitor the job over several days to ensure that it is set up properly. After a job runs, you can get information about it by following this step: In the Job Overview screen, double-click on a completed job to see the results.

- ✓ The output shows you when the job started and ended. In the unfortu-nate event that an error occurred, the output also shows you a brief error message.

- ✓ You can see messages about your background job only if the job is in the Finished or Cancelled phase.

   The job for the example in Figure 9-15 was in the Finished state when we double-clicked it. This example shows that the job started and finished without any problems.

Changing scheduled jobs

After you put in these convenient background jobs, you may want to change them in some way, such as by changing the start date or the frequency for the jobs. (Face it, those are the two options you're most likely to want to change, and only if you find that you don't need the jobs so often or something.)

To set the schedule, go to the Job Overview screen by either

✔ Following the menu path Tools⇨Administration⇨Jobs⇨Job Overview

✔ Entering transaction code SM37 in the command field

This screen allows you to query on Job Name, User Name, and dates. In the following steps, you're going to check out what kind of jobs user DDIC has scheduled.

The list produced is *client-independent.* Regardless of where a job was scheduled, the job shows up on your search.

A wild card * is valid for the Job Name and User Name. If you leave blanks for the Date fields, R/3 disregards that search criteria. You use the Or Start After Event field when you have scheduled a job to run after a certain configurable event. Select the check boxes for Jobs without Start Date and Jobs with Previous Jobs if you want to see those jobs as well.

To look at all jobs for a user, follow these steps:

1. **Enter * in the Job Name field.**

2. **Enter the User Name.**

   For this example, we use HIRAOJ. Figure 9-16 shows the Select Background Jobs screen filled in with the search criteria.

3. **Press Enter to see the query results.**

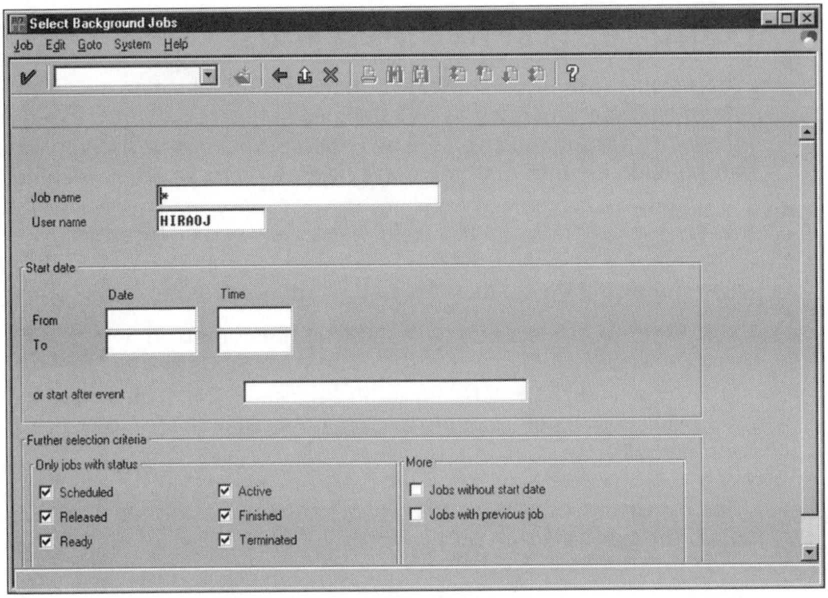

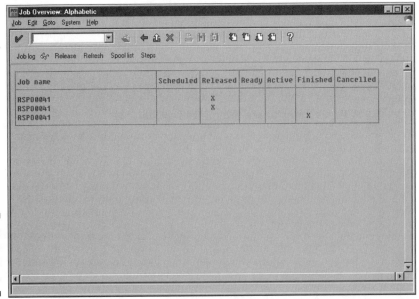

Figure 9-16:
You can review your scheduled jobs.

The example search returns three line items, as shown in Figure 9-17. SAP only returns job logs that haven't been deleted.

Figure 9-17:
Here's the requested list of jobs.

To modify the settings on a background job, follow these steps:

1. **Select the first line item to modify by placing your cursor on it.**

2. **Choose Job⇨Change.**

   This step takes you to the Edit Job screen. In this example, you're going to change the start time.

3. **Click the Start Date button and alter the time from 6:00 to 6:15.**

4. **Click the Save button (the one with the folder on it) to record your change.**

   Figure 9-18 shows the screen with the change.

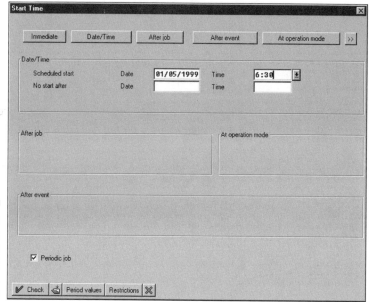

Figure 9-18:
You can
see your
changed
start time.

After you click the Save icon, you return to the Edit Job screen.

5. **Click the Save button again to reschedule the changes made to the job.**

Cleaning house with background jobs

In most offices, the cleaning crew comes in after normal hours. Who wants to hear vacuum cleaners and step over cords at very important meetings? People hate that. Clean up at night, though, and people really appreciate it.

As a Basis administrator, likewise, you can run your SAP "vacuum cleaners" at night. You can schedule jobs that clean up SAP nicely, and people really appreciate it. (Actually, people don't notice it that much. The same is true for nighttime vacuuming. Neglect to do either one, though, and people notice, and they aren't very nice to you about it.)

Table 9-1 is a list of the recommended jobs and their descriptions. To run one of them, you follow the procedures in "Setting Up Background Jobs" in this chapter.

Table 9-1	Recommended Background Jobs		
Program (Job Name)	*Description*	*Frequency*	*Details*
RSBDCREO (SAP_ REORG_BATCHINPUT)	Deletes dated batch input sessions	Daily	Must create variant; client-dependent
RSBPCOLL (SAP_ COLLECTOR_FOR_ PERFMONITOR)	Creates statistics for background jobs	Daily	Client-independent
RSBTCDEL (SAP_ REORG_JOBS)	Deletes dated back-ground jobs	Daily	Must create variant; may be client-dependent
RSM13002 (SAP_ REORG_ UPDATERECORDS)	Deletes dated update records	Daily	Client-independent
RSPO0041 (SAP_ REORG_SPOOL)	Deletes dated spool requests	Daily	Must create variant; may be client-dependent
RSSNAPDL (SAP_ REORG_ABAPDUMPS)	Deletes dated ABAP dumps	Daily	Must create variant; client-independent
RSCOLL00 (SAP_ COLLECTOR_FOR_ JOBSTATISTIC)	Creates perfor-mance statistics	Hourly	Client-independent
RSBPSTDE (SAP_ REORG_ JOBSTATISTIC)	Deletes dated statistics for jobs	Monthly	Must create variant; client-independent

Checking the status of these jobs as well as scheduling them is always a good idea. Whenever you create a client or re-create a client, be aware of the nec-essary cleanup jobs.

Background jobs may not involve much glory for you. If you do them right, people don't even know they're going on at all. In fact, background jobs say a great deal about the life of the average SAP R/3 administrator. Do your job right, and you don't get any credit at all. People don't even know you're doing it. They get all caught up in doing their own business and forget about you entirely. SAP R/3 administration, if you think about it, is pretty much a background job itself. But you do have the quiet satisfaction of knowing that you are helping people, even if they don't even think about it.

Part IV

Somebody's Gotta Do It: R/3 Tuning and Maintenance

The 5th Wave   By Rich Tennant

"OH YEAH, AND TRY NOT TO ENTER THE WRONG PASSWORD."

In this part . . .

*L*et's face it — you get into some pretty heady stuff as administrator. (We try to lead you through it step by step, though.) You see how to schedule your R/3 system's operation modes so that R/3 runs most efficiently. You see how to copy clients within a system or between systems. You see how to actually monitor the performance of the operating system, networks, databases, and SAP itself. And you get the inside scoop on starting and stopping R/3 and on managing memory. Phew. Good part.

Chapter 10

What an Operator!

In This Chapter

▶ Creating an operation mode of your own

▶ Assigning work processes to give your operation mode its own personality

▶ Scheduling when your operation mode gets to run

The fact is, your R/3 system can run in a number of different ways — any number of different ways, in fact. Only one of them probably interests you, though. You'd like your system to run "efficiently."

But efficiency calls for different things at different times. If you're driving a Jeep, it's efficient to be in low gear when you're hauling a big load, in four-wheel drive when doing a little all-terrain driving, and in basic two-wheel drive when cruising the highways at 80 mph. You change gears to suit your circumstances.

As R/3 administrator, you can "change the gears" of R/3 so that it runs most efficiently for the conditions — mud, snow, open highway, or whatever. Well, for an R/3 system, the conditions are more likely to be "heavy interactive use," "lots of batch processing," and things like that.

In this chapter, you find out how operation modes can radically throw your system out of whack with these babies . . . or fine-tune it so it runs really great.

Defining an Operation Mode

What do you configure when you configure an R/3 system? Well, you work with *operation modes*. If you were new to R/3 and just had to guess what an operation mode was, you might say something like, "Uh, I don't know, 'on' and 'off?'" Or you might try "fast" and "slow" or "zippy" and "bogged down."

If you guessed at something like "zippy" and "bogged down," you'd be pretty close to right. There are certain processes, completely mysterious to end users, that you can readily control as system administrator. These processes, which in fact are called *work processes,* you can configure so that your system works properly for, say, daytime with heavy interactive use, or night time with lots of batch processing. Each configuration is an *operation mode.*

For each mode, you manage the number of particular work processes available. During normal business hours, like 9 a.m. to 5 p.m., a company has many interactive dialog users. During this time you would probably want to maximize the number of work processes for dialog users. During the night, most of the users are at home. At night, many batch jobs may run, so you would want to maximize background work processes and minimize dialog work processes. In short, the operation modes control the number of work processes available to the system throughout the day.

The number of work processes is directly proportional to the amount of memory and CPU horsepower of the hardware. In general, each work process gobbles about 12MB of memory. Remember, in an SAP system many variables are fighting for the precious memory. Just to name a few heavy hitters in the memory battle, you have

- ✔ The database
- ✔ The operating system
- ✔ SAP and all its pieces

Be cautious when increasing the number of work processes:

- ✔ Compare the number of 12MB work processes with the memory available.
- ✔ Make changes gradually and carefully.

Operation modes do not increase the number of total work processes. They simply make one work process act as another type during the operation mode. In the next section, you configure day and night operations.

Follow these steps to define your operation mode:

1. **Go to the operation mode configuration screen by choosing Tools➪ Administration➪Computing Center➪Management Systems➪ Configuration➪Op Modes/Servers.**

   This takes you to the CCMS: Maintain Operation Modes and Instances screen. You can also enter RZ04 in the command field to get to this configuration screen.

2. **Click the Create icon.**

   Boxes appear for you to define your day and night operation. You can also press F5 to access this control.

In this example, we enter **Day** in the operation mode field and enter a brief description in the next field, such as **Normal Daylight Operations.**

3. **Select Operation Mode as Normal.**

   In the lower half of the screen, be sure the radio button is clicked for "Productive Operation Mode (Normal Operation)." The normal type allows the switches to occur automatically. The test mode allows the changes to occur manually.

4. **To save the new operation mode, press F11 (or choose Operation mode on the menu and then choose Save).**

   You return to the initial screen in the Maintain Operation Modes and instances screen.

Follow the same steps to create another operation mode for off-hours operation. (Call it "Night.")

Assigning an Instance to the Mode

"Instance?" "Instance?" Who sits up nights thinking of terms like "object" and "instance" to keep SAP administrators going bonkers?

If an instance were called, say, a "processor," or a "computer," or a "server," you'd know what was under discussion. Call it R/3 itself and you'd be fine, because one installed R/3 system is an "instance." But nooo. We need another name altogether — a name that almost sounds like something familiar in English.

An instance is a computer or server or R/3, really, but there's a distinction because a server can have a number of different faces (or, to use the assigned word, "instances"). An instance is the resources like memory and work processes that go with one application server or database server. You can vary those instances as system administrator. So the term "instance" may be necessary, but the distinction between an "instance" and, say, a "server" can seem pretty nitpicking.

Creating an instance

To give a personality to the operation mode you created in the previous section, you assign an instance profile to it. The instance profile contains work processes appropriate for administering dialog processing (common during the day) or background processing (which tends to be rife at night).

Here's how to assign an instance to your operation mode:

1. **Click the button Instances/Op Modes.**

2. **Select Settings⟿Based on Act Status⟿New Instances⟿Create.**

   The screen displays "Productive instances and their wp distribution."

After you've created your instance, you do the nitty-gritty work of putting work processes into it, as explained in the next section.

Putting work processes into the instance

In the next step, you set the number of work process types available for each operation mode.

1. **Double-click the operation mode you want to configure.**

   You're ready to configure the number of work processes. In this example, we're configuring the Day operation mode we created.

   Any modifications to the Day operation mode are made by clicking the plus or minus sign to increase or decrease the number of work processes.

2. **Click the background work process box and set the number.**

   The dialog work process count decreases as you increase the number of background work processes. During the operation mode configuration, only the number of background and dialog work processes can be modified.

   Your changes only affect the instance you've selected. A system with multiple instances (application servers) can run different work process distributions in one operation mode.

3. **Click Save.**

SAP has some rules and recommendations in regards to the number of specific work processes you can put in an instance.

   ✔ Only one spool work process per instance.

   ✔ At least two dialog and two background work processes per instance.

During the night, we want to maximize background job processing, so follow these steps:

1. **Reduce the number of dialog work processes to 2.**

2. **Increase the background work processes to 8 and reserve one of the 8 for class "A" background jobs.**

This means that one background work process is always waiting for a class "A" job. After you've configured Day and Night, click Save to keep the changes. You can now set a timetable for when the modes will run automatically.

Setting an Op Mode Timetable

Your various operations modes wouldn't be that useful if you had to start them running manually, but that's not necessary. You schedule when they'll run.

Scheduling your op modes

To schedule your op modes, you use the Timetable Maintenance screen. Follow these steps:

1. **Go to the operation mode configuration screen by choosing Tools⇨ Administration⇨Computing Center⇨Management Systems⇨ Configuration⇨Op Modes/Servers.**

   This takes you to the Timetable Maintenance screen. You can also enter SM63 in the command field to get to this configuration screen.

2. **Click the Normal Operation radio button and select Change.**

   You can set a new timetable. Initially, nothing is set.

3. **To select a time frame, double-click the beginning of the time period and then double-click the end time period.**

   The selected period changes to black from blue.

4. **Click the Assign button and then select the operation mode.**

   Repeat this process for each operation mode you use.

For our example, the work system switches from Day to Night without any user intervention. Nothing other than the passing of time is necessary to induce these changes.

There is no need to start and restart SAP for this configuration to take effect.

Scheduling an exception

At times, you may need to make an exception to the configured schedule. R/3 has the option "Exception operation," which allows you to change the schedule without deleting your existing configuration.

Here's an example. On December 31, 1999, you have a long work day. The accounting department will have two shifts of workers:

- 6 a.m. to 3 p.m.
- 3 p.m. to 9 p.m.

To adjust for the long day, you, the Basis administrator, have to delay the switching of the operation mode from Day to Night. Follow these steps:

1. **Go to the Maintain Operation Mode Timetable screen.**

2. **Click the Exception Operation button.**

   The Exception Operation Timetable screen appears. Its layout is the same as the normal scheduling screen. The only difference is that you can specify the operation mode exception by date.

3. **Click the By Date button.**

4. **Set the time for each operation mode and then click Save.**

   The top of the screen displays the date of the exception. As the Basis administrator, you have scheduled in advance for this change. Now you can get on with New Year's Eve!

Chapter 11

Cloning a Client

- -

In This Chapter

▶ Creating an empty prototype client

▶ Copying an elaborate original onto the prototype

▶ Getting rid of a client if it's bad, useless, or just past its time

▶ Copying the "other" way — transporting between systems

- -

Copying has all kinds of great uses. If you've worked long and hard to get a client to just the state you want, it's nice to be able to copy it when you plan to experiment with it. That way, you can keep the original in pristine form.

At times, you need to copy R/3 clients. Copying anything as big and ambitious as an R/3 client definitely involves hazards. In this chapter, you find out how to perform a copy and how to avoid some of the hazards of doing so. You also see how to clean house by deleting a client and how to do a *transport* — a copy between two systems.

Copying a Client

Why would you want to copy a client in the first place? Situations come up where you do want to. If you're going to do some testing on a client, for example, you're likely to mess it up. Why not mess up a copy instead of the original? Want to try out a creative new idea? Try it on a copy, not the original.

Here, first we clarify what a client is and what you copy when you copy a client. In real life, a *client* is a customer — sort of a pretty important customer for professional services. In the world of computers, a client is a computer on a network (and it functions as a customer for a server).

In SAP, a client is a computer — kind of. In SAP, a client is not necessarily a separate piece of computer hardware. It's a *logical system,* where you have master records and tables set up.

- *Master records* are key information. For your users, it's usernames, authorizations, and other really important stuff. For vendors, the master records are addresses, phone numbers, banking information . . . also really useful stuff. Master records are permanent — categories like *address* that you aren't going to change.

- *Tables* are collections of actual data. If somebody changes an address (which people have a pesky habit of doing when bored, broke, restless, or evicted), you change the data in the table but keep the master record the same.

After you get a client the way you want it, you don't have to start from scratch every time you need a separate client based on the same information. Copy the original and then customize the copy. This way

- You don't need to test on your production system.

- You can customize a client for a special group of users (maybe for just the folks in the finance department), and then personalize a copy for each user.

If you have to train a bunch of novices — who make lots of mistakes and do weird things — copy a client for training. You don't want those inexperienced clunkers playing with your everyday system. Let them trash the copy.

Creating a prototype client to copy onto

In SAP, when you copy, you copy master records and tables. Before you can copy them, though, you have to have a new client — called a *prototype client* — to copy them from. In this section you see how to set up that new client.

The *client copy tool,* as its name suggests, allows you to copy a client you already have and call it by a different name. For example, say that you want to copy the SAP reference client 000 and name the new copy *client 300.* From a technical perspective, the client copy makes a duplicate copy of the database records where the client field equals 000.

The client copy tool is powerful as copy utilities go. It lets you determine the types of data to copy over. In the examples in this chapter, you see how to define those fields (sometimes referred to as a *copy profile).*

Defining a new client

In this example, use client 000 as a pattern to create your own client. First, you need to define the new client in table T000. Follow these steps:

1. **Log into the system and choose <u>T</u>ools⇨<u>A</u>dministration⇨ <u>A</u>dministration⇨Client Ad<u>m</u>in⇨Clie<u>n</u>t Maintenance or enter transaction code** SCC4 **in the command field.**

   SAP lists your current clients. Figure 11-1 shows clients for one sample system (your system is probably different). In this screen, you define a new client.

2. **Click the Change icon or press Ctrl+F1.**

   A warning appears, informing you that you are changing a client-independent table (an array of information that could be used by multiple clients). Each change you make will affect all the other clients in your system. That's okay.

3. **Click the green check icon on the warning dialog box, and continue.**

   A new button called New Entries appears on the toolbar.

4. **Click the New Entries button.**

   You're now ready to put data into a new table. It's covered in the following section.

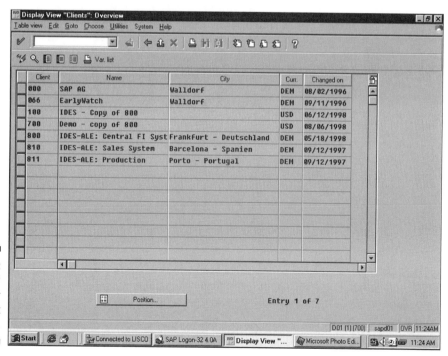

Figure 11-1:
Here SAP lists your current clients.

Putting in metadata

Metadata, as you see from the data you enter in the next set of steps, is data that describes other data — the kind of data definitions that you put into a data dictionary. You insert metadata in the New Entries screen, which is shown in Figure 11-2.

Don't go around creating clients willy-nilly. Each client is big — practically a separate computer. Your company doesn't want piles of clients lying around. Create clients according to the client deployment strategy at your organization. Hey, sticking to your plan is always wise — and besides, it's good for your job security.

1. **Enter a client number and a description at the top of the New Entries screen.**

   For this example, create client 300, an empty client. Call it the *prototype client*.

2. **Enter the city where your system is located.**

   This information is for reference only.

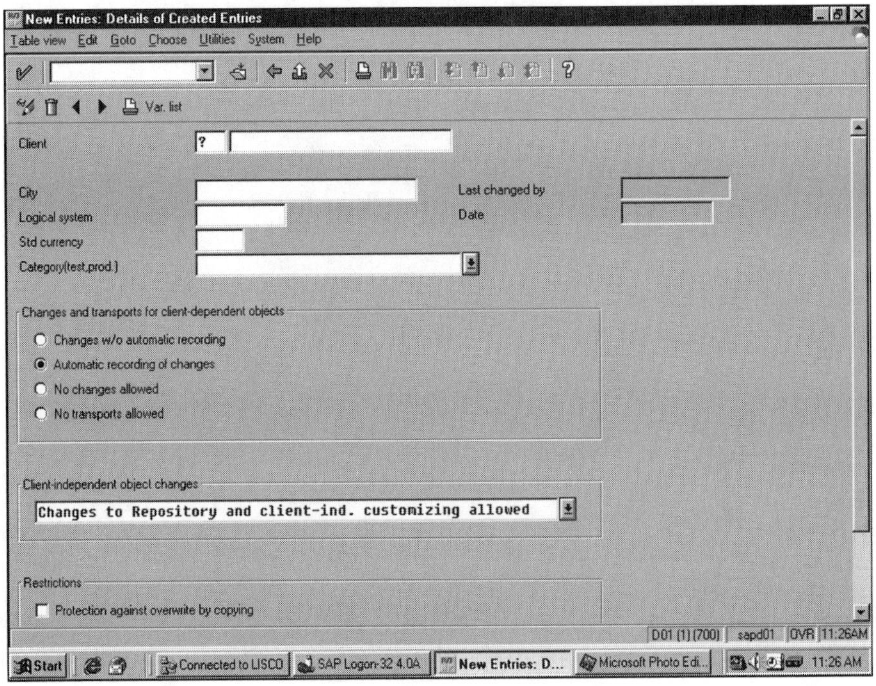

Figure 11-2: Put information for new entries here.

3. **If your organization uses logical systems, enter the name of the appropriate logical system.**

   Logical systems identify available SAP systems that aren't necessarily physically separate but act like it. Logical systems come into play when using ALE (application link enablement) between distributed logical systems. In this example, you are not using logical systems, so leave this spot blank.

4. **Enter the standard currency utilized in this client in the Std Currency space.**

   If you click in the field, a possible entries arrow appears at the right of the field. You can click it to see a drop-down list box of choices. In this example, you use U.S. currency, so enter **USD**.

5. **Put in the category of the client, which in this case is Test.**

   The options available for the Category(test,prod.) blank, which are accessible through a drop-down list box, are

   - Productive
   - Test
   - Customizing
   - Demo
   - Training/Education
   - SAP reference

6. **Select the appropriate option in the Changes and Transports for Client-Dependent Objects space.**

   For the example, select No Transports Allowed, which disables you from moving any customizing changes.

   In general, your organization's client deployment strategy determines how you handle changes and transports. Your options are

   - *No Changes Allowed.* This turns off the ability to make any customizing changes. No Changes Allowed is the option you need to set for this example.

   - *Changes w/o Automatic Recording.* You aren't automatically prompted to include any customizing changes in a change request.

   - *Automatic Recording of Changes.* All customizing changes are prompted with an option to include the change in a change request.

   Don't allow any client-independent maintenance in this client.

7. **Select No Changes to Repository and Client-Independent Customizing allowed.**

   The other options available are

   - Changes to Repository and Client-Independent Customizing Allowed

   - No Changes to Client-Independent Customizing Objects

   - No Changes to Repository Objects

   Do not click any of the restrictions available for Restriction. Without the restrictions set, you can copy over this client as well as use the CATT tool (a testing tool) for data input.

   Your screen looks something like Figure 11-3.

8. **Click the Save icon.**

   You're done!

Copying a client onto the prototype

After you have your new client, you can use it as the *target* and copy from the original client onto it. Use client 000 as your base to create clients.

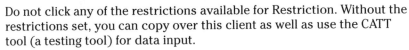

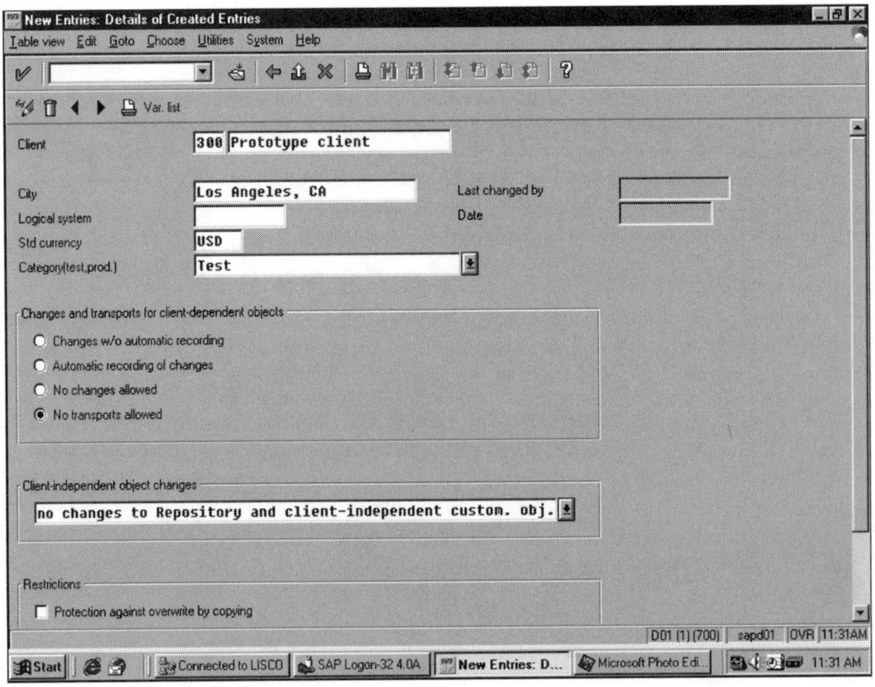

Figure 11-3:
Your completed screen looks like this.

Local or remote client copy?

Client copying falls into two classes: local copies and remote copies. A *local client copy* is a copy performed within one system. A *remote client copy* is a copy between systems.

If you need to make a client copy between systems, it may be better to perform a client export and import, because a remote client copy produces significant network traffic. See "Exporting and Importing a Client" in this chapter.

SAP provides handy, prepackaged clients, available after the initial installation. SAP R/3 comes standard with three clients: 000, 001, and 066. 000 and 001 are the same. 066 is the Early Watch client, where SAP logs in to peek at your system. (Don't get paranoid. It only does that when you request the Early Watch service.) 000 and 001 represent SAP's version of a reference client. You can utilize the 000 model as a baseline to create your own client. 000 and 001 start differing after you implement items such as languages and other system customizations. Any global changes to client-dependent objects also affect 000 but not 001. Always use 000 as your base to create clients.

You initiate all client copies from the *target* client and not from the source client.

Never, under any circumstances, alter or delete 000 and 001. SAP strongly recommends against such wanton vandalism against your baseline system. Use a *copy* of 000 to start your tinkering.

Starting the copy

Log in to the client that you created in the preceding set of steps. All new clients have one special user and a password. Log in as SAP* with the password **PASS**.

Neither the source client nor the target client should have users. Users on the source client are undoubtedly changing the tables there. Likewise, users on the target client are putting in data that's not on the original client, meaning that the copy isn't exactly like the original. If either the source client or the target client has users, you're "shooting at a moving target," and that's not good.

Plan to sneak around and run the copy when not too many users are around, and keep even those few away from the source and target clients. In other words, run the client copy in the background and at night.

Backing up the database before copying

Before you begin, it's always a good idea to have a backup of the database *as it was* right before you start the copy. Invest a little time up front to avoid a disaster in the end.

If you have a fairly large database, your client copy may run into some rollback segment problems (Oracle). To avoid these problems, create a large rollback segment and put it online during the copy. Put the smaller rollback segments offline during the copy.

Before you begin, make sure you have adequate space in the database for the copy. The size of the database doesn't necessarily double, but some additional space is necessary to duplicate the records. The actual amount you need really depends on the size of your system and database.

The client copy is like one huge transaction. If you keep logging turned on, you can end up with a ton of logs. Keeping all those logs affects the speed as well as the success of the client copy. Put your database in nonlogging mode to avoid this problem.

Space needed depends on the database used. In an Informix and Oracle database, check for these:

- ✔ *bspaces* (Informix)
- ✔ *tablespaces* (Oracle)

Target 70 percent or less utilized in

- ✔ PSAPBTAB
- ✔ PSAPSTAB
- ✔ PSAPCLU
- ✔ PSAPOOL

Keep in mind that 70 percent is only an estimate.

1. **Choose Tools➪Administration➪Administration➪Client Admin➪Client Copy➪Local Client Copy or enter the transaction code** SCCL **in the command field.**

   The Client Copy - Copy a Client screen appears, as you see in Figure 11-4.

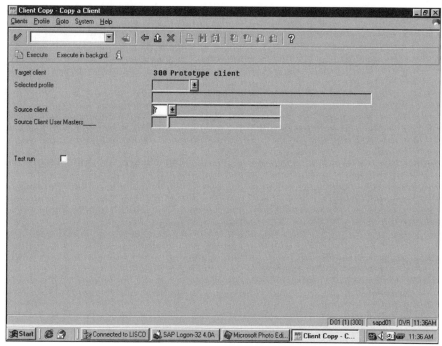

Figure 11-4:
Start your
client copy
here.

2. Click the down arrow on the drop-down list for Selected Profile and select the profile for the copy.

See Figure 11-5 for a list of sample options for Selected Profile. The client copy tool allows you to choose the type of data to copy.

You can't separate master data and transaction data. It's all or nothing.

3. Select SAP_ALL to capture all the data from the source client.

4. Select 000 as the Source Client and 000 as the source client for User Masters.

The Test Run checkbox in the lower left enables you to run through the copy in test mode, a sort of dry run. You run through the entire copy without committing any changes to the database. Doing a test run is good if you're shy or nervous, and it does allow you to see whether you're going to have any space issues in the database. If you're confident with your calculations about space, though, carry on without checking for the test. The time to do the test takes just as much time as the real thing.

5. Run the copy in background mode. To do that, click the Execute in Background button on the application toolbar.

You see the screen titled Schedule Client Copy in the Background, shown in Figure 11-6.

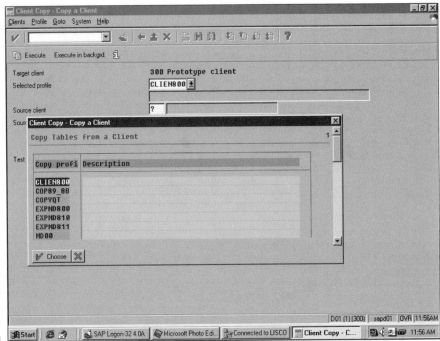

Figure 11-5:
Choose a copy profile here.

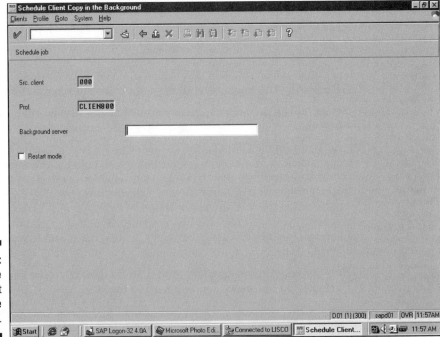

Figure 11-6:
Schedule your client copy in the background.

Scheduling the job

As administrator, you control when the copy takes place. Often, you want to run the job at night. For this example, though, run it immediately, as explained in the following steps:

1. **To schedule the job, click the Schedule Job button on the application toolbar and click the button with the green check.**

   Restart Mode should be unchecked. Figure 11-7 shows the dialog box that verifies your choices for the client copy.

2. **If all is correct, click Yes and continue on.**

3. **In the Start Time dialog box, shown in Figure 11-8, click the Immediate button and then click Save to start the job.**

   You can check on the status by entering **SCC3** in the command field. You can also check status by starting at the initial SAP screen and choosing Tools⇨Administration⇨Administration⇨Client Admin⇨Copy Logs.

4. **In the Client Copy Log Analysis screen, select the appropriate target client by double-clicking on the name of the client, and then double-click on Processing (in the Status text column).**

   The Client Copy Log Analysis screen is shown in Figure 11-9.

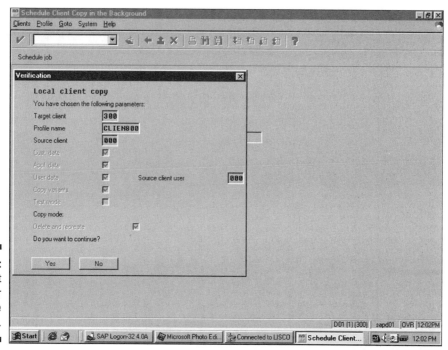

Figure 11-7:
Verify that your choices are correct.

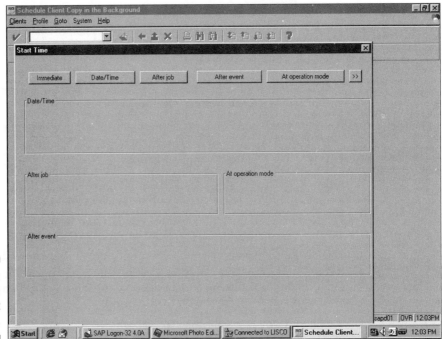

Figure 11-8:
Schedule
your start
time here.

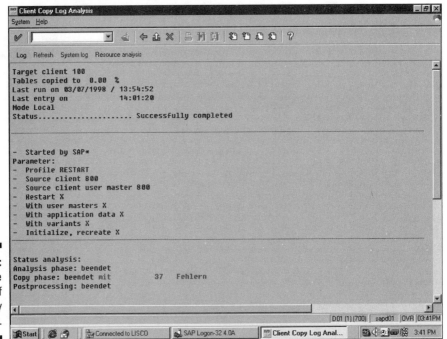

Figure 11-9:
Check the
status of
your copy
here.

5. **Double-click on the name of the client to choose the specific client copy run, and then double-click on Processing again.**

    This step brings up a screen that shows the status of client copies in the current client.

    To monitor the status, click on the Monitor button on the application toolbar in the Client Copy Log Analysis screen. A graphical representation displays the progress; the speed depends on your system. Plan for at least a few hours.

Checking the log file and creating source code

At the end, check the logs via the Log button to see whether your attempt to copy a client ended successfully. Checking the logs thoroughly after all copies is always advisable.

To see the log file, follow these steps:

1. **Click the Log button on the Client Copy Log Analysis screen.**

    Figure 11-10 shows the log analysis for a successful run.

2. **Enter Expansion Level 4 to see a detailed analysis of the copy; enter 1 for a summary. Press Enter.**

    Figure 11-11 shows a detailed analysis.

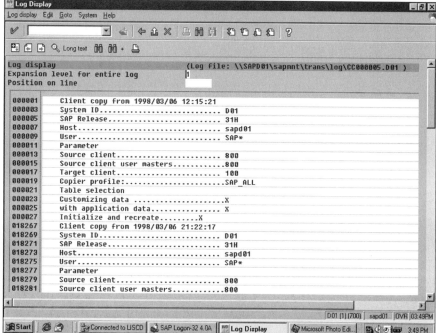

Figure 11-10:
Here's the
log analysis
for a
successful
run.

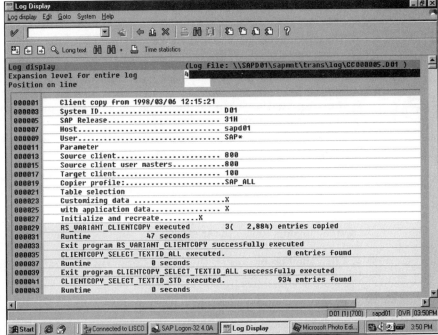

Figure 11-11:
You can see a detailed analysis of your run.

Once you've completed the run, you take the big step of generating actual SAP source code for what you've done.

1. **To generate ABAP source code, enter** SE38 **in the command field of the SAP R/3 System initial screen, or choose Tools⇨ABAP/4 Workbench⇨ABAP/4 Editor from the application toolbar.**

2. **Call report RGUGBR00 from the Program field of the ABAP Editor: Initial Screen (Figure 11-12), and click on the Execute button.**

   The Utilities for Validation/Substitution/Rules screen appears.

3. **Select all the flags except the usage flags and all substitution routines flags.**

   Figure 11-13 shows a sample completed screen.

4. **Execute the program by clicking the Execute icon or pressing F8.**

   The log file is shown back in Figure 11-11. SAP completes the copy by generating its own source code for the new client.

Congratulations! You've cloned that puppy.

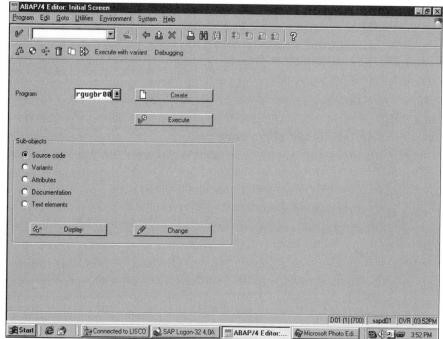

Figure 11-12:
Here, call
for the
log analysis
report.

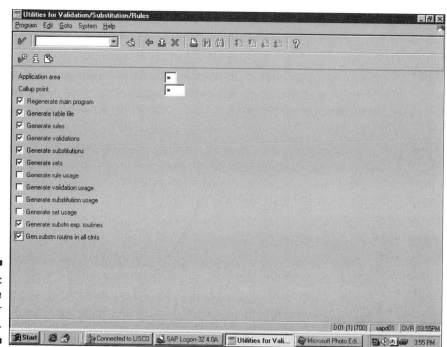

Figure 11-13:
Select the
items for
your report.

When copying doesn't go right

Why is it that stuff always seems to happen? Why can't you just run a client copy and end up with a new copy? Sometimes you can, but some of the time, nooooo. Stuff happens. Well, that's part of the fun of a client copy, and it gives you, the R/3 administrator, a chance to show that you don't quit when the going gets tough.

Restarting the client copy

At times, a client copy may fail. It's a bummer, but you need to keep your cool.

- ✔ Investigate the cause of the problem.

- ✔ Document a solution.

- ✔ Make the change.

- ✔ Restart the client copy.

SAP has a default option of starting the client copy in RESTART mode. The client copy process looks at the client copy log files and continues from the last commit. If the client copy is unable to restart, you may have to start the client copy from the very beginning. Do so by pressing the RESTART⇨NEW Start button. Carry on with the process as though it were a new client copy.

The following sections look at some common reasons why SAP may terminate your well-intended copy.

Resolving database issues

Copying a database can be a bit harrowing, and the database can cause a number of problems for you. In the following list, we don't resolve specific database problems, but we do indicate some of the more common faults that can come up and give you some advice as to what you can do about them.

Often, the way you resolve the problem depends on the specific database you're using. Check for the name of your database in this list. If you see the name, try that list item first.

- ✔ **You didn't turn off logging in the database.** The database may have run out of room to write logs. A fix to this problem is to truncate the existing logs by archiving them offline and then turn off logging on the subsequent client copy run.

  The specific way to archive offline and turn off logging depends on the database you're using.

- ✔ **The rollback segment ran out of space.** Create a larger rollback segment and put it online. Take the smaller rollback segments and put them offline. These tasks are also database-specific. (Rollback segments are primarily Oracle-specific.)

✔ **Client copies aren't correctly synchronized.** This is associated with
SQL Server 6.5.

To resolve this problem, try checking the parameter
`sdb/mssql/sync_tables_lists`. Often, you can solve the problem by
setting the parameter value to
`TBTCO,TSP01+TSP02,D010S+D010SINF+D010L+D010LINF`.

✔ **The number of locks may be insufficient in the database.** Increase the
number of locks and continue on with the client copy. Increasing the
number of locks may mean allocating more memory to the database as
well. (The way you allocate memory depends on the database you're
using.)

Resolving SAP R/3 issues

The databases just discussed aren't the only sources of snafus. SAP can
cause hang-ups quite nicely on its own.

For instance, perhaps the user SAP* did not have the adequate authorization
to perform the client copy. If this appears to be the case, at the termination of
the client copy, see whether SAP_ALL and SAP_NEW are in `SAP*'s` security
profile. If you are copying into an empty client, no security profiles are initially available for `SAP*`. In this case, enter the two profiles for `SAP*` in the
source client.

See Chapter 7 to see how to work with users and profiles.

Another possible SAP problem is that at the end of the client copy, the log
indicates that certain tables were not copied over. You may have to manually
copy the tables over with the transport utility, which is described at the end
of this chapter.

Deleting a Client

Sometimes nothing is more gratifying than just rubbing out a client
altogether . . . obliterating it, snuffing it out, annihilating it, sending it off to
oblivion. Sometimes you delete a client because you just don't need it any-
more; sometimes you delete a client before running a refresh to create a new
one just like it.

You can delete a client in one of two ways:

✔ From within the SAP application

✔ Through the command line at the operating system level

Some inconsistencies have been noted with the delete utility that is available from the application. For this reason, we cover the client delete process from the command line.

You do the client delete routine in two phases:

1. Delete the entry in table T000.

2. Delete all the data within a client.

Deleting the client from table T000

Deleting a client from table T000 is similar to creating a client (described earlier in this chapter). Here's how to delete the client:

1. **Log into the system and either choose <u>T</u>ools➪<u>A</u>dministration➪ <u>A</u>dministration➪Client ad<u>m</u>in➪Clie<u>n</u>t maintenance or enter SCC4 in the command field.**

   If you want, you can refer back to Figure 11-1 to see the initial client maintenance screen.

   Click the Change icon in the application toolbar, and click the Enter button to confirm that you've seen the warning message about client-independent tables.

2. **Highlight the client you want to delete.**

3. **Choose <u>E</u>dit➪<u>D</u>elete.**

4. **Click the Save icon to save the changes.**

   Figure 11-14 shows the screen after you delete the client. It no longer appears in the list.

You may think that deleting a client gets rid of its data. Not so fast, Sparky. In SAP, you deal with logical systems. The client data resides on a database; you have to delete *its* data, too.

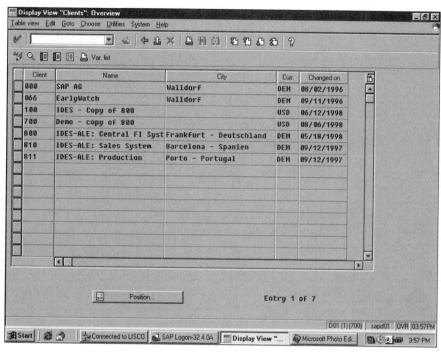

Figure 11-14:
The deleted
client is
gone from
the list.

Deleting the data from the client

To actually delete the data from the client, follow these steps:

1. **Log into the operating system as** `<sid>adm`.

2. **Create the following script to use the SAP R3trans program.**

   The script calls upon the SAP R3trans program, which does most of the
   work in the delete. The following script has been tested in both HP-UX
   and NT 4.0. Other operating systems probably need small adjustments
   to the script to make it work. Any modifications to this small script for
   your particular operating system are probably minor.

```
Delete Script for NT 4.0, save as delclient.cmd
REM Delete script for SAP Clients
REM Tested on NT 4.0 on 31H systems
r3trans control.ctl
```

(continued)

(continued)

```
Delete Control file for NT 4.0, save as control.ctl
REM This is the control file for the Client Delete script
REM Tested on NT 4.0 on 31H systems
clientremove
client=300
select *

Delete Script for HPUX, save as delclient
# Delete script for SAP Clients
# Tested on HPUX on 31H systems
r3trans control.ctl
Delete Control file for HPUX, save as control.ctl
# This is the control file for the Client Delete script
# Tested on HPUX on 31H systems
clientremove
client=300
select *
```

Before running these scripts, make sure you have followed the same precautions you would for running a client copy. (See the section called "Copying a client onto the prototype," earlier in this chapter.)

✔ In an NT environment, use the change directory command (cd) to select `drive:\usr\sap\trans\bin`. Run the script with this command: `>delclient.cmd`.

✔ In an HP-UX environment, use the change directory command to select `/usr/sap/trans/bin`. Run the script in the background as follows:

`>nohup delclient &`

Refer to "Copying a client onto the prototype," earlier in this chapter, for more information on checking log files.

Exporting and Importing a Client

When you need to create a client copy from a remote system, the client export and import utility is very handy. A fancy name for the means by which you export and import clients is the *client transport system*.

Transporting actually exports R/3 clients from the database to the transport directory. You can break the process down into three steps: export, import, and post-processing. The following sections give you a brief explanation of each of the steps.

Exporting a client

To copy a client to a remote computer, first you export the client from the source computer. (Later, you import it into the target computer.) To export the client, follow these steps:

1. **Choose Tools⇨Administration⇨Administration⇨Client admin⇨Client transport⇨Client export or enter** SCC8 **in the command field.**

   You go to the Client Export screen, shown in Figure 11-15.

2. **In the Selected Profile field, click the possible entries arrow at the right of the field and select from the available profiles.**

   The profiles are the same ones displayed for client copies. You may also create a customizing profile, explained later in this chapter in the section "Exporting just specific information."

   For this example, select SAP_ALL. This profile captures all data from the client.

   The other necessary field is the target system's SID (system identification number).

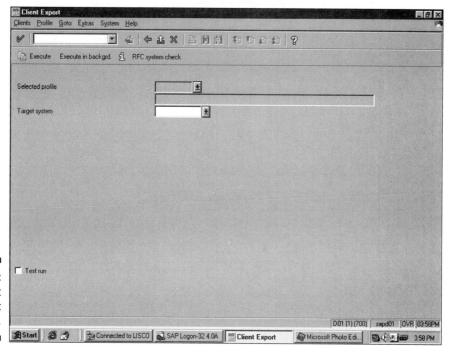

Figure 11-15:
Conduct
your client
export here.

You can click in the field, then use the possible entries arrow to find appropriate entries for the SID (system ID).

3. **After entering the appropriate options, click the Execute in Background button from the application toolbar in the Client Export screen.**

   Clicking this button allows you to schedule the job.

   From this point forward, the process is the same as for a client copy, explained earlier in the chapter in the section "Copying a client onto the prototype." Monitor the status with transaction code SCC3. When the job is completed, SAP creates these three change requests:

   ```
   a) <SID>KO<No.> (client-independent data)
   b) <SID>KT<No.> (client-dependent data)
   c) <SID>KX<No.> (client specific text)
   ```

Finishing the export takes some time, perhaps hours, so time the export to take place during periods of low activity.

Importing a client

After successfully exporting the client, you need to import the change requests into the target system. Follow these steps:

1. **Log into the target system as** `<sid>adm`.

   In the example, the source system is DEV and the target system is ACP.

2. **Log in as** `acpadm` **and process the transaction outlined next.**

   For this example, you log in as `acpadm` and process the transaction outlined next.

3. **Change directory with the** `cd` **command.**

   In an NT environment, to drive: `\usr\sap\trans\bin`. If you're using UNIX, use the `cd` command to go to `/usr/sap/trans/bin`. Either puts you in the common transport directory of system landscape. The format for the `tp` command is

   ```
   tp import <sid>ko<No.> <sid> client<clientno.>
   ```

4. **If the change request is not already in the buffer, add it by using the** `tp` **command.**

   ```
   tp addtobuffer <sid>ko<No.> <sid>
   ```

5. Import the change request. Use the following command.

```
tp import devko01242 acp client110 u8
tp import devkt01242 acp client110 u8
```

The unconditional code is 8, "disregard restrictions based on table classification."

Import both change requests. The third is used during the post-processing phase.

Be sure you understand the implications of importing client-independent customization. If you have existing clients running in your target system, client-independent imports may invalidate those clients.

Checking up afterwards

After you think you've done your successful import, you should check to be sure that your optimism is justified.

1. Log in to the target system.

2. From the command line, enter SCC7 **or go there by choosing Tools⇨ Administration⇨Administration⇨Client admin⇨Client transport⇨ Client import.**

3. Start the post-processing procedure from here.

You should review copy logs to be sure things occur as planned.

Exporting just specific information

You may, at some time, want to export specific information from the source. To do so, you may need to create a customizing profile. Here's how:

1. Choose Tools⇨Administration⇨Administration⇨Client admin⇨Client transport⇨Client export or enter SCC8 **and go in the command field.**

2. Choose Profile⇨Create Profile.

You go to the screen with the title Client Copy, Selection of Tables to Be Selected, shown in Figure 11-16. Whether you use the menus or the transaction code, this step is the same.

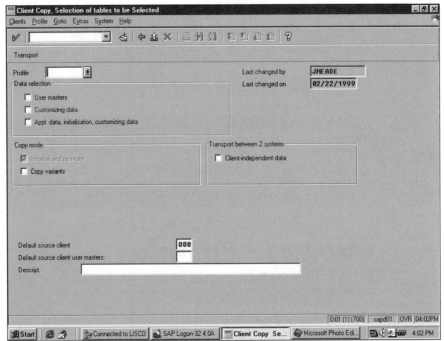

Figure 11-16:
Here, make
selections
for creating
a profile.

3. **Select from the list of options to create a profile.**

   In this example, you create a profile that captures the user masters (authorizations, as explained in Chapter 7) from DEV/100. That is, click the selection box for User Masters, and type in **100** in the Default Source Client field at the bottom of the screen.

   Figure 11-17 shows the completed Client Copy, Selection of Tables to Be Selected screen.

4. **Click the Save icon when you are finished.**

Reviewing other client export/import issues

You can see the portability of SAP R/3 with the client export and import utility. After you create an export, you can import it into any R/3 system as long as the release levels of the R/3 systems are equivalent.

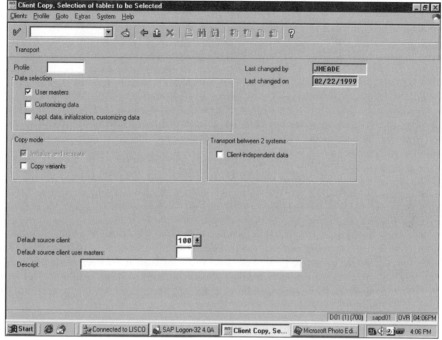

Figure 11-17:
Capture
user mas-
ters, and
designate a
source
client.

The export and import utilities do have technical limitations. The following list illustrates a few examples, by release, of things you can't export and import. (Numbers in parentheses are version numbers.)

- ✔ User master (can't import and export in 3.1G and 3.1H)
- ✔ Tax types and document data (can't import and export up to 3.0F)
- ✔ Addresses (can't import and export up to 3.0F)
- ✔ Client-independent objects transported separately (can't import and export from Version 3.0E)

You can transport Repository objects (objects you manage with the ABAP/4 Development Workbench, discussed in Chapter 14).

As a result of these limitations, you have to move these objects in separate change requests or reenter them manually.

Before moving in client-independent objects, you must think about the impact on the target system. Essentially, two scenarios are possible. Scenario one involves a target system with no clients. Scenario two deals with a system with active clients.

- ✔ In scenario one, you probably don't want to import client-independent customizing data. This action invalidates any existing clients in that system. The preferred technique is to import only client-dependent data. After the import, you may have to do some manual updates to configuration.

- ✔ In scenario two, you import client-independent data as well as client-dependent data. You create a profile for client-independent data and import that into the target system. Afterward, you elect a profile like SAP_ALL, create a client export, and import that into the target system.

Copying a client, then, isn't exactly like photocopying a picture or, say, copying a word-processing file. Clients are big and usually have plenty of data in them. Copying them takes a long time and is fraught with peril. At times, however, a client copy can save you from peril as well, such as when you want to have trainees working away at a client, so it is a process that you need to know.

Test your SAP knowledge

What is the likely cause when a client copy doesn't go right?

A. Sabotage. It's almost sabotage. People love to mess up the work of R/3 administrators.

B. Pure, unmitigated stubbornness by SAP. Sometimes it "just says no."

C. Excessive heat in the office. Turn down all the office thermostats to 50 degrees.

D. Try restarting the copy. If that doesn't work, check into issues with the database or R/3.

Does deleting a client get rid of its data?

A. Of course it does. If the client isn't there, how can it have any data, silly.

B. No. You have to delete its data from the database where it resides.

C. That just depends. If you do a good data delete, then you get rid of the data, too. Bad client deletes don't do it, though.

D. That is one of the great mysteries of the universe. Nobody really knows (though many may pretend to).

Chapter 12

Monitoring Performance
with CCMS

In This Chapter

▶ Establishing CCMS alert thresholds

▶ Monitoring performance in the operating system and other sticky places

▶ Gazing at the graphical alert monitor

*S*AP is such a monster of a system — with so many servers (called *instances*), databases, network activities, and unruly users — that somebody somewhere has to be able to look over what's happening everywhere and monitor it a little bit.

As administrator, you're like a worker looking at the dial on a big boiler. You can see whether it's going to overheat, and you can turn the boiler down before it explodes (which would create a real mess and make you quite uncomfortable).

With CCMS (Computing Center Management System), the "boiler" you monitor and configure is SAP — its operating system, network, databases, and SAP R/3 itself. From CCMS, you can see what's going on in the system and make adjustments. (You can also really screw things up, but you're not supposed to do that.)

In this chapter, you see how to set the little alarms (called *alert thresholds*) that you use to monitor the system. Then you get to work and actually monitor performance. Finally, you look over the cool graphical system for monitoring alerts.

Setting CCMS Alert Thresholds

Alerts, as the name more or less suggests, are little warnings that tell you that something may be out of whack. *Alert thresholds* are the points at which such warning signals come up. For example, if you didn't want a glass more than half full of water, you could set an alert threshold for the halfway point in the glass.

CCMS has alert thresholds for all the things that SAP monitors — operating system, database, network, and SAP itself. And with CCMS, you can monitor detailed statistics within each of those categories. As you play around in your role as administrator, you get familiar with many of those little monitors. Or maybe you develop certain favorites and forget about the others.

Before looking over some actual monitoring in SAP, you may want to look over alert thresholds in SAP so that you can understand a bit more about the monitoring that's going on. (On the other hand, you may not want to look those things over. That's fine. Just skip to the next section in this chapter — "Monitoring Performance.")

Starting CCMS and checking your authorization

Because you no doubt end up starting CCMS pretty often as administrator, you may as well see how to do it. Here's what you do: Go to CCMS via the menu path Tools⇨Administration⇨Computing Center⇨Management System or enter transaction code **SZRL** in the command field. To be able to do much damage, er, to put in appropriate settings, you have to have an administrator's authorization for CCMS, S_RZL_ADM. If you have the SAP_ALL profile, you're set. See Chapter 7 to find out about authorizations.

Setting default alert thresholds

To be able to monitor things, you have to set th ethresholds in the first place. You do so in the Maintain Alert Thresholds window, which you access by choosing Configuration⇨Alert Thresholds from the main CCMS window or by entering transaction code RZo6 in the command field.

Before you randomly assign alert thresholds, SAP recommends that you start with its default alert values. Then you can alter the default values depending on your particular needs. By starting with the defaults, at least you know you're getting off to a sensible start. Here's how to set the baseline values:

1. **From the main Maintain Alert Thresholds screen, highlight Database and click the Change button.**

2. **Click the Set to SAP Defaults button at the top and then click the Save icon. See Figure 12-1 for the database Alerts Thresholds screen.**

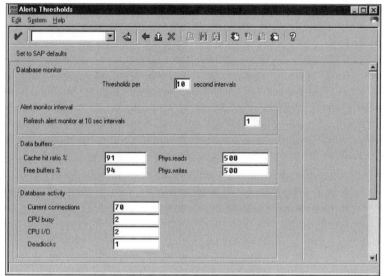

Figure 12-1:
Alerts
Thresholds
for the
database.

3. **Go back to the main screen and highlight the server in the Active Server selection. Click the Change icon to set the threshold values.**

   You go to the Alert Threshold Server screen. You see the configurable options for this screen. Click on each of the 5 buttons: Operating system, Syslog, Performance, Buffer, Other alerts. See Figure 12-2 for the Alerts Thresholds screen.

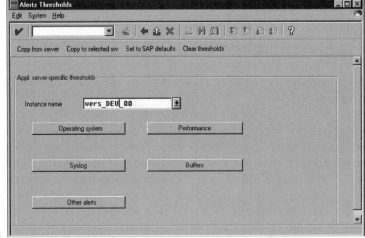

4. **To set all the values to the SAP defaults, click the Set to SAP Defaults button at the top and agree to the changes.**

Really, those defaults are a great idea. Somebody who built the system and knows good settings has put them in place.

Looking over the various thresholds

Good as the defaults may be, the way to have fun and impress people as administrator is to tinker with those defaults. The next few sections look in detail at the various alerts you can set and lay the foundation for you to go in and really have a ball by setting them yourself.

Checking out operating system alerts thresholds

You like to know that your operating system is working well, but what do you look at to see whether it is? Well, you look at things like the number of processes per minute in the CPU queue. This section reviews what you monitor when you check out your operating system.

From the main Maintain Alert Thresholds screen, transaction code RZ06, highlight the active server and click the Change icon. Then click the Operating System button. The Operating System Alerts Thresholds screen comes up, as shown in Figure 12-3.

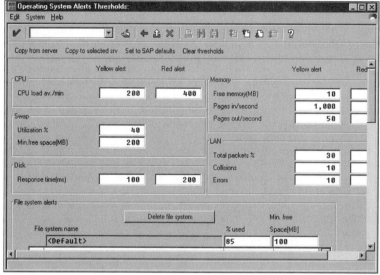

Figure 12-3:
Check oper-
ating system
alerts
thresholds
here.

Notice that the screen is divided into six areas: CPU, Swap, Disk, File System Alerts, Memory, and LAN. Each section gives the parameters that you config-ure to set alert levels for that area. SAP offers default values. You can adjust the numbers based on your preferences and your experience.

Here's a look at some of these configurable variables:

- ✔ **CPU** represents the number of processes in the CPU queue per minute in increments of 100. For example, the red alert value of 400 represents an average of four processes per minute in the CPU queue. The number of processes in the queue and system performance are directly propor-tional. As one goes up, the other goes down. Overworked CPUs may indicate problems within the system or simply the need for more horsepower.

  For a description of yellow and red alerts, see the section "Monitoring Alerts Graphically" later in this chapter. Basically, they operate like yellow and red traffic lights. Yellow is a caution, and red means trouble.

- ✔ **Swap** parameters fall into two areas: Utilization Percentage and Minimum Free Space. Swap refers to temporarily placing material from memory onto the hard drive.

  If the Utilization Percentage of swap is greater in actual use than the value set in this screen, SAP displays an alert. The Minimum Free Space is measured in megabytes. CCMS creates an alert if the space left falls below the space specified on this screen. Swap is a critical area for per-formance. It measures the amount of data that had to go to disk because adequate memory was not available to store it. If the world were perfect, everything would be performed in memory. Swapping is perfectly normal; don't get me wrong. But attempting to swap beyond the available space causes some performance problems.

✔ **Disk** parameter is defined by Response Time. The number in the box represents an average response time in milliseconds.

Some time is always involved when measuring disk performance. The disk drives within the server are all mechanical pieces constantly moving. A long response time may represent possible hardware issues, as well as the need for a better disk layout.

✔ **File System** monitor keeps track of space utilization. The percentage used triggers a yellow alert if the actual percentage is higher than the stated value. A red alert occurs if the percentage used is 10 percent greater than the stated value.

Utilization is primarily a space issue but may also indicate other problems. For example, file systems may fill up immediately if the operating system crashes or dumps.

✔ **Memory** alert parameters are divided into three areas: Free memory, Pages in/second, and Pages out/second. Memory is a crucial part of performance. SAP, the database, and the particular operating system gobble up more and more memory as the load on the system increases. The Free Memory parameter is measured in megabytes. It represents the actual free memory within the system. Pages in/out represent the number of pages in/out per second. You can enter appropriate values to trigger a yellow or red alert.

✔ **LAN** thresholds monitor basic statistical data. The Total Pvackets % measure utilization. The Collisions and Errors metrics are measured in number of occurrences. Enter the values of a yellow and red alert for these variables. The LAN component is a critical point of performance. A small network error may have a global impact.

Reviewing performance alerts thresholds

The performance alerts thresholds measure the work process response/wait times (in milliseconds). SAP has four work processes:

✔ Dialog

✔ Update

✔ Background

✔ Spool

From the main Maintain Alerts Thresholds screen, transaction code RZ06, highlight the active server and click the Change icon. From here, the Performance button. See Figure 12-4 for the Performance Alerts Thresholds screen.

The performance metrics shown in this screen represent only the time statistics after the request goes into a work process queue. These numbers do not represent response/wait time from the presentation server to the application servers. Average response time should be about one to two seconds for dialog work processes and less than one second for update work processes. Wait times should be less than one second. High wait times may indicate the need for more work processes.

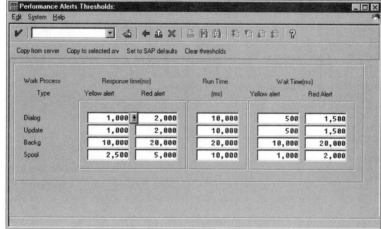

Figure 12-4: Set performance alerts thresholds here.

Another statistic to monitor is long-running dialog work processes. High run-times for dialog work processes (measured in milliseconds) means that a given work process is not available to service other requests. A runaway dialog work process may indicate many problems. Some common problems stem from inefficient configuration and development.

Looking over syslog alerts thresholds

The system log records SAP errors and events. You use it to find out stuff about programs or transactions that get terminated, errors in databases, and other troublesome things.

From the main Maintain Alerts Thresholds screen, transaction code RZ06, highlight the active server and click the Change icon. From here, click the Sysylog button. See Figure 12-5 for the syslog thresholds.

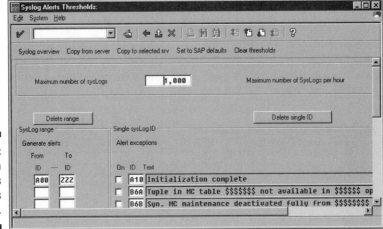

Figure 12-5:
Work with
syslog alerts
thresholds
here.

The Syslog Alerts Thresholds screen comes up for the server you're analyzing.

These thresholds configure the system alert logs. They act as filters for the messages shown in the system log. The parameters are divided into two areas: range of log file IDs and individual IDs.

Whenever a message comes up that falls within the range values, the system gives an alert. You can configure up to 20 different ranges. Any overlap in the ranges is logically joined as one. You can also configure up to 100 individual alerts. For example, if you have an alert range from A00 to ZZZ and click the button Alert On for message A10, message A10 is not alerted. Conversely, if you have a range from BB0 to ZZZ and have A10 clicked, message A10 is logged as an alert. You can also configure the number of total alerts and the number of alerts per hour. Whenever SAP reaches the threshold you've set here, an alert is triggered.

Scrutinizing buffer alerts thresholds

Buffers are areas set aside in memory for temporary storage. From the main Maintain Alerts Thresholds screen, transaction code RZ06, highlight the active server and click the Change icon. From there, click the Buffers button. See Figure 12-6 for the buffer thresholds.

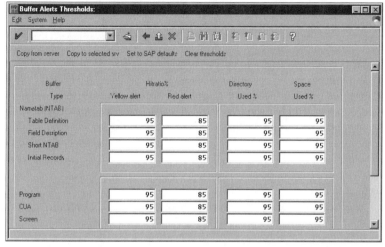

Figure 12-6:
Check your buffer alerts thresholds here.

This screen allows you to configure the alerts thresholds for the buffers in SAP R/3. The screen is divided into four columns: Buffer, Hitratio%, Directory Used % and Space Used %. The following list describes the different buffers being monitored:

The **Nametab** buffer stores SAP R/3 data dictionary information, which is information on information (metadata) of the ABAP dictionary. Nametab data is stored in four buffers:

- ✔ **Table definition:** The TTAB buffer stores the table definitions defined in the dictionary in table DDNTT.

- ✔ **Field Description:** The FTAB buffer stores the field definitions of tables in table DDNTF.

- ✔ **Short NTAB:** The NTAB buffer stores a brief summary of TTAB and FTAB buffers. The information comes from the contents of the DDNTT and DDNTF tables.

- ✔ **Initial Records:** The IREC buffer stores the initial record layout depending on the field type. Like the NTAB buffer, the IREC buffer gets its information from the DDNTT and DDNTF tables.

The **Program** buffer stores the ABAP programs. It is also known as the *program execution area* (PXA).

The **CUA** buffer is the menu buffer. It stores GUI objects, including buttons, icons, and menu items.

The **Screen** buffer stores DYNPRO loads, meaning that it stores the GUI screens.

The buffers described in the preceding paragraphs should be large enough to prevent excessive paging. These buffers are needed for all transactions. For example, whenever you call a transaction, it looks for programs to execute, tables to use, and images to display. Of course, these actions aren't the only events that happen. The less the system needs to read to disk to obtain this basic information, the more efficiently a transaction executes. In a perfect world, almost everything would be buffered so that the system could run at peak speed. Because you work in a not-so-perfect world, you want to minimize the effect of paging.

Table buffers come in two types:

- **Generic Key table buffer** stores a range of table entries.
- **Single Record table buffer** stores single table entries.

The greater the efficiency in table buffering, the less the system needs to read from disk. The name of the game is maximizing efficiency.

The first two columns in the buffer alerts thresholds screen show the Hitratio, which is calculated as 100 * (buffer read/total reads). Reaching 100 percent — which means that every time someone requests an object, it's already in the buffer — is the goal.

The last two columns in the buffer alerts thresholds screen show the Directory Used Percentage and Space Used Percentage. Every buffer has a directory pointing to the location of objects buffered. If no free directories are available, no more objects can be buffered. Monitoring this metric is just as important as monitoring the buffers' quality. The Space Used Percentage measures the amount of space left in the buffer. If the buffer doesn't have enough room to store objects in it, the objects are swapped to disk. Swapping reduces performance.

Glancing at other alerts thresholds

You can also monitor these other cool alerts thresholds:

- Roll/Paging Files
- Enqueue
- Dispatcher utilization

From the main Maintain Alerts Thresholds screen, transaction code RZ06, highlight the active server and click the Change icon. From here, click the Other Alerts button. See Figure 12-7 for the miscellaneous thresholds.

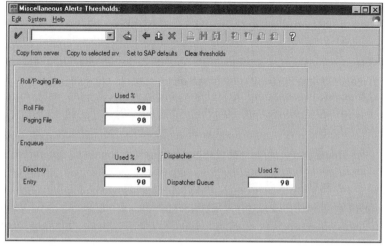

Figure 12-7:
Check your
other alerts
thresholds
here.

These values give you the percentages above which SAP returns a yellow or red alert.

The roll file primarily contains user context information. Some examples include pointers to ABAP programs, parameter values, and authorizations. When a user switches from one work process to another, this information is *rolled out.* When the user picks up another work process, the information is *rolled in.* The ratio is calculated (used space/total space).

The paging file contains data that the user is working with. These types of information may include an array of data, internal tables, and report lists. The ratio is calculated (used space/total space).

Versions of SAP more recent than 3.0 have greatly reduced rolling and paging, primarily through using extended memory. Rather than copying back and forth, the new work process maps to the area in extended memory. However, some data is still rolled and paged.

The same monitoring is done for enqueue (SAP's object lock mechanism) and the dispatcher. The enqueue monitor checks the used and total used percentages. The dispatcher monitor looks for utilization of six different work processes: dialog, update, update2, enqueue, spool, and batch. Above the threshold, an alert occurs.

Monitoring Performance

Setting the alert thresholds is all right, but the real satisfaction comes from tuning actual performance. After you get the thresholds right, you can get into the real action by monitoring performance.

Performance monitoring with CCMS, as you may expect, is really, really thorough. Any true nerd worthy of the name can have a field day with these performance monitors. By the way, performance monitoring also has a graphical view, which helps you see the health of your system.

To access the Performance Monitoring screen, choose Tools⇨ Administration⇨Computing Center⇨Management System⇨Control⇨ Performance Menu from the main menu or enter transaction code **STUN** via the command field.

From here you can start looking at different aspects of the system:

- ✔ Operating system
- ✔ Network
- ✔ Database
- ✔ SAP R/3

Monitoring the operating system

The operating system is a basic piece of the SAP puzzle, so it's a good place to start monitoring. From the Performance Monitoring screen, choose Operating System⇨Local⇨Activity or enter transaction code **OS06** in the command field. You can see the operating system monitoring screen in Figure 12-8. This view is divided into CPU, Memory, Swap, and Disk summary statistics.

The SAPOSCOL program collects statistics on the operating system. (Get the name? As in SAP OS COLlect?) SAPOSCOL runs independent of the SAP instance. As a matter of fact, it collects data even when SAP is stopped. The background job SAP_COLLECTOR_FOR_PERF-MONITOR takes the data out of shared memory and stores it.

If you double-click on a statistic like CPU Utilization Idle Percentage, the system returns a comparison for the last 24 hours. You can perform these analyses for all the statistics shown in OS06. See Figure 12-9 for idle CPU utilization for the last 24 hours.

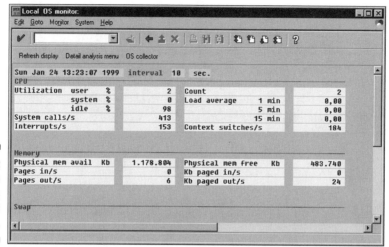

Figure 12-8:
Monitor the operating system here.

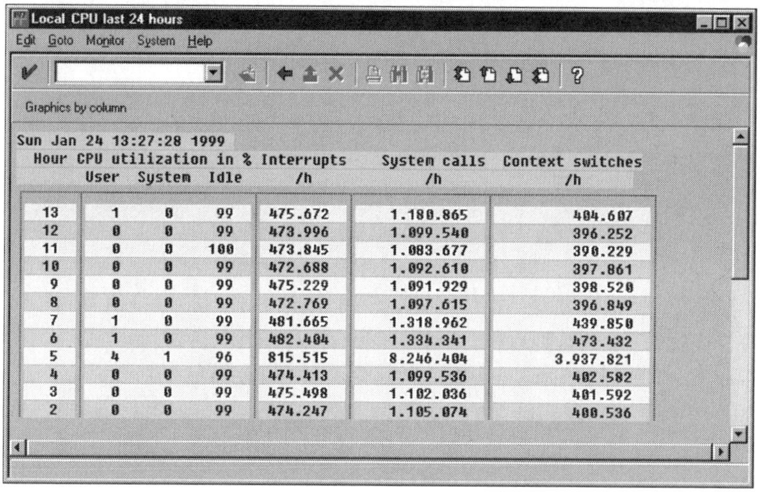

Figure 12-9:
You can check out idle CPU Utilization for the last 24 hours.

To see a graphical representation, click the Graphics by Column button. You can also see other graphical views depending on the button selected on the right-hand side of the graphical monitor. Figure 12-10 shows idle CPU utilization, in graphic form.

Another way of looking at the OS06 view is by clicking the Detail Analysis menu button from OS06. You then go to the Analyze Operating System screen. The transaction code is ST06. The options available from ST06 and OS06 are essentially the same; the difference is in presentation. Figure 12-11 shows the screen for analyzing the operating system. Notice that the buttons displayed are the same statistics shown in OS06.

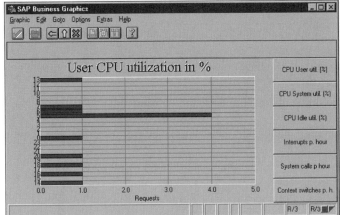

Figure 12-10:
Here's a
graphic of
the Idle CPU
Utilization.

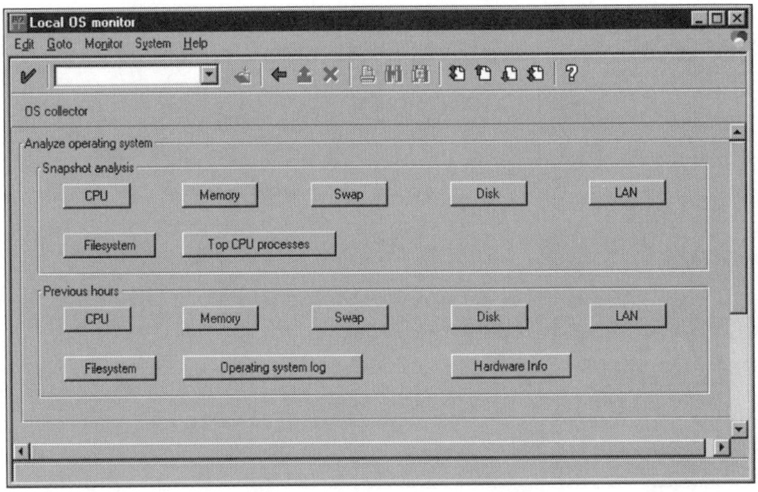

Figure 12-11:
Analyze
operating
system
detail here.

Utilizing the thresholds defined in the previous section, you can also monitor the alerts. From the OS06 screen, choose Goto➪Current Data➪Alert Monitor. This command brings up the graphical monitoring tool shown in Figure 12-12.

You can update this monitor every ten seconds if the Monitor On button is pushed in. This tool is great for monitoring the system.

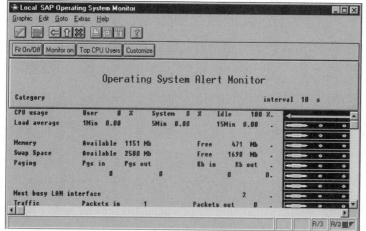

Figure 12-12:
Here
you can
graphically
monitor the
operating
system
alerts.

Checking out the network

The tool for monitoring the operating system may be great, but the network-monitoring tool is fairly feeble. The network isn't so much a direct SAP specialty, we guess. Other third-party software packages provide more functionality for monitoring the network. SAP R/3 has an interface for HP's LanProbe, for example.

The tools available in the Network Monitor menu work only with HP-UX with additional hardware and software. You get to Network Monitor from transaction code STUN by choosing Operating System⇨Network⇨Network Monitor.

The basic tool available uses the TCP/IP protocol's "ping" utility to do analysis. From transaction code STUN, choose Operating System⇨Network⇨Lan Check with ping or enter transaction code **OS01** in the command field. Figure 12-13 shows the results.

The data shows you the available servers connected to the SAP system — the database server and all application and presentation servers. From here, SAP R/3 can ping the servers to see the echo and calculate some statistics.

For a kick, why not ping a presentation server now? Here's how:

1. **From the LAN Check by PING screen, click the Presentation Server button.**

   You see a list of all attached presentation servers. See Figure 12-14 to see one presentation server attached.

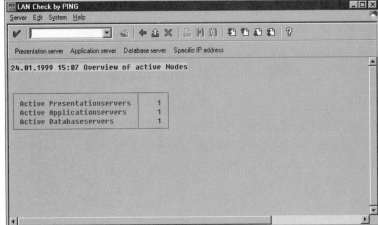

Figure 12-13:
You can
use the
TCP/IP
"ping" to
check
on your
network.

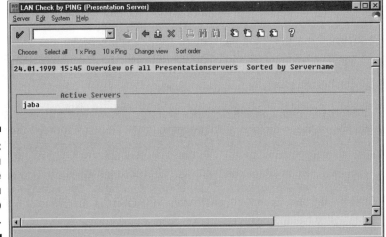

Figure 12-14:
Here you
see the
servers you
may want to
ping.

2. **Double-click the server you want to ping to select it and then click the button 10 x Ping.**

   The system then pings the server ten times and collects the response echo from the server you are logged in to. See Figure 12-15 for an example of a 10 x Ping.

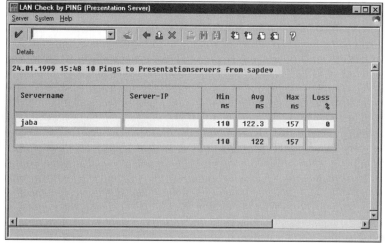

Figure 12-15:
Here are
the results
of your
10 x ping.

3. **To get the actual ping echo, click the Details button on the LAN Check by PING screen.**

To see some other network statistics, from transaction code STUN choose Operating System⇨Local⇨Activity⇨Goto⇨Current Data⇨Snapshot⇨LAN detail. The LAN interface snapshot screen shows current network statistics from the server, shown in Figure 12-16.

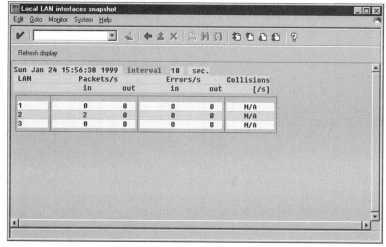

Figure 12-16:
You can
check out
network
statistics.

If you want to compare activity within a 24-hour period, follow the menu path Operating System⇨Local⇨Activity⇨Goto⇨Current Data⇨Previous hours⇨LANs. See Figure 12-17.

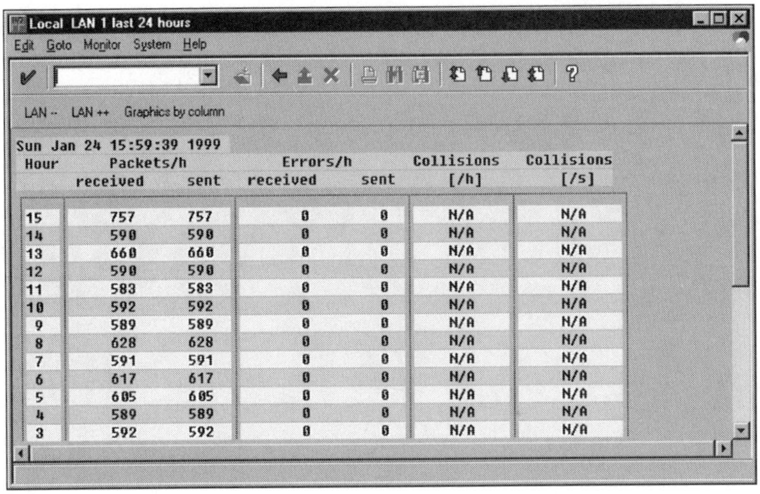

Figure 12-17:
You can compare activity within a 24-hour period.

You can also present the data in a graphical format. Just click the Graphics by Column button.

Scrutinizing the database

The performance-monitoring tool for the database works like the one for the operating system. From transaction code STUN, choose Database⇨Activity or enter **ST04** in the command field. See Figure 12-18 and Figure 12-19 for the output of **ST04** for Oracle 7.3.

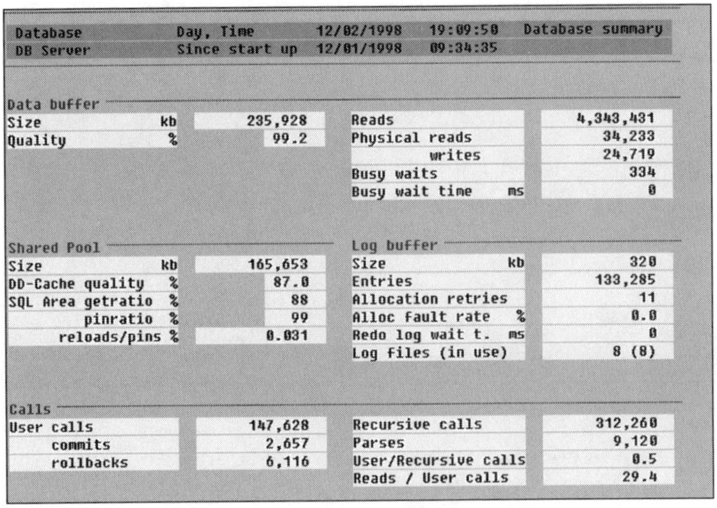

Figure 12-18:
You can monitor the database here.

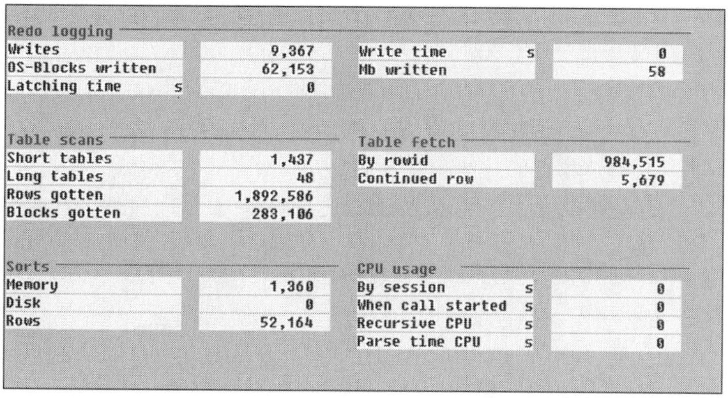

Redo logging			
Writes	9,367	Write time s	0
OS-Blocks written	62,153	Mb written	58
Latching time s	0		

Table scans		Table fetch	
Short tables	1,437	By rowid	984,515
Long tables	48	Continued row	5,679
Rows gotten	1,892,586		
Blocks gotten	283,106		

Sorts		CPU usage	
Memory	1,360	By session s	0
Disk	0	When call started s	0
Rows	52,164	Recursive CPU s	0
		Parse time CPU s	0

Figure 12-19:
Here's more
stuff on the
database.

Transaction code ST04 provides many database-specific performance metrics. Because not all the SAP R/3 databases have the same architecture, the exact performance measurement and evaluation is database-specific. However, you can observe some basic statistics in each database. The cache quality allows you to see how much of the information was stored in the buffer. If the cache quality falls lower than 90 percent, you just may want to go in and find out why.

You can get to other statistics from the main ST04 transaction code, too. Here's how:

1. **Click the Detail Analysis Menu button.**

   You see more views, each of which is database-specific. See Figure 12-20 for the options for Oracle 7.3.

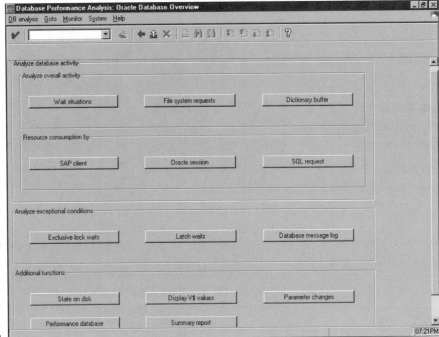

Figure 12-20:
Analyze
database
perfor-
mance here.

2. **From transaction code STUN, choose Database⊅Tables/Indexes or enter DB02 in the command field.**

   The specific view also depends on the database used. Figure 12-21 shows information on tables and indexes.

   From here you can analyze space statistics for the data and logs. In fact, the Tables/Indexes view is obviously an important tool for analyzing space statistics, and it's an SAP feature available for all databases.

3. **From the Database Performance: Tables and Indexes screen, click the Missing Indexes button.**

   From the database allocation screen, you can quickly see whether any indexes in the database or unknown indexes in the ABAP dictionary are missing. The numbers on the left-hand side represent the total number of missing indexes.

If indexes are missing, click the Create in DB button to fix the problem.

Most database manufacturers have performance-monitoring utilities. SQL Server 6.5 has the tool Enterprise Manager. Oracle uses its own Oracle Enterprise Manager. You probably use a whole string of tools to best monitor the database, but SAP's own tool is a good one to include.

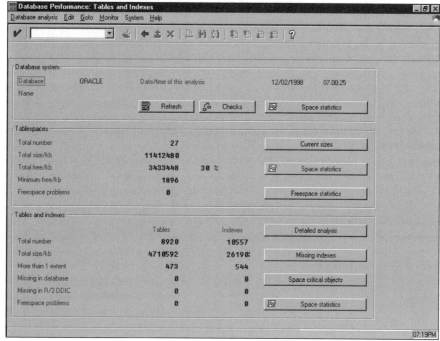

Figure 12-21:
Database
perfor-
mance:
tables/index.

Inspecting SAP R/3 itself

The CCMS for the SAP R/3 system itself is quite extensive. It gives the statistics for buffer analysis and workload analysis. SAP utilizes buffers (based on the asynchronous reading and writing) to minimize the time to access and write data. By thus saving time, SAP buffers are very important for performance. Workload analysis shows how the work processes are acting in the system. It gives response times for the work processes performing different tasks.

Checking SAP application server buffers

Buffer analysis and tuning are critical to response time and performance. You can now see actual numbers relating to the thresholds you configure for CCMS. To access the buffer analysis statistics, either

- ✔ Start at transaction code STUN and choose Setup/Buffers➪Buffers
- ✔ Enter transaction code **ST02** in the command field.

Figure 12-22 shows the Tune Summary.

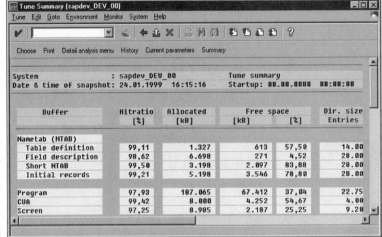

Figure 12-22:
See the
results of
your
"tuning."

The screen has eight columns:

- ✔ Buffer (buffer name)

- ✔ Hitratio (buffer reads/total logical requests)

- ✔ Allocated (amount of memory dedicated to the buffer, in KB)

- ✔ Free space (free space in buffer, shown in KB and in percentage)

- ✔ Dir. size Entries (represents the total number of entries in the table that stores the buffered information)

- ✔ Free Directory Entries (free directories entries in amount and percentage)

- ✔ Swaps (number of swaps)

- ✔ Database access (number of times needed to go to database for the object)

You can drill down into more cool information on any one of these statistics. Double-click on a particular item, and you see a more detailed analysis. Double-click on the screen buffer, and you see further detail. Figure 12-23 shows detail on the screen buffer.

To get a historical comparison with the past days (shown in Figure 12-24), right-click with the mouse and select History or press Shift+F6.

When you first start SAP, the hit ratios may be a little low. You should shoot for hit ratios of greater than 95 percent. The system needs to adjust to the types of usage on the system The optimum buffer may need a couple of days of user interaction to fill the buffers with good data.

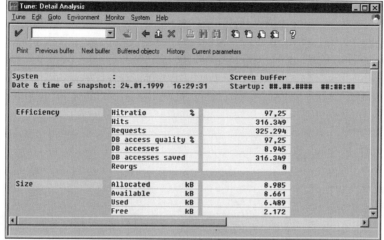

Figure 12-23:
You can get information on screen buffers.

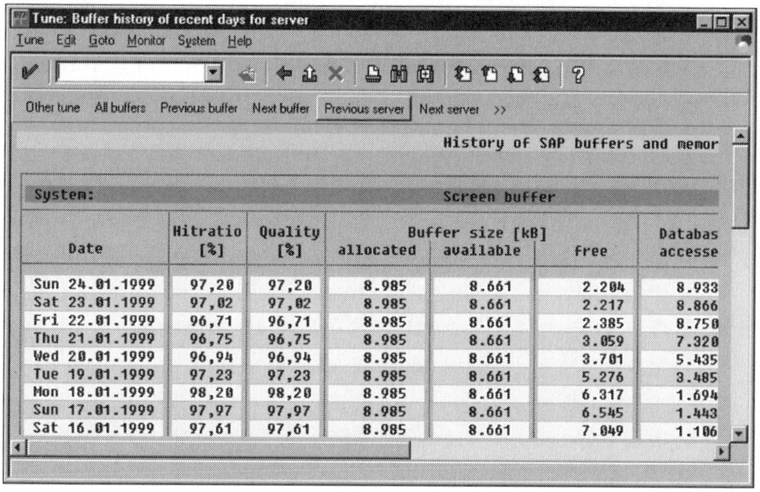

Figure 12-24:
You can get an historical comparison with past days.

Analyzing R/3 workload

Now that you have checked out the tools to monitor and analyze the other pieces like the database, operating system, and the network, you can look into the tools to monitor SAP.

Choose Tools⇨Administration⇨Computing Center⇨Management System⇨Control⇨Performance Menu⇨Workload⇨Analysis or enter **ST03** in the command field. Figure 12-25 shows the SAP Workload Analysis screen.

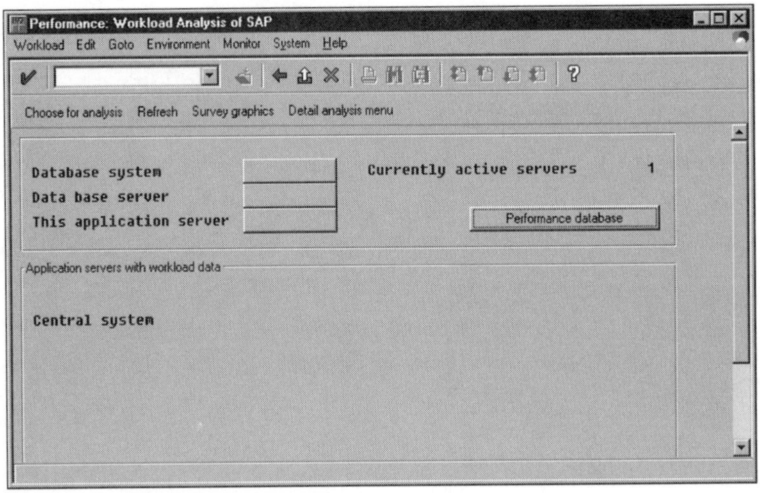

Figure 12-25:
Start here to make sure your workloads are right.

From here, you begin your investigation into workload analysis, daily statistics, and comparative statistics. Notice that the screen contains buttons for the different types of servers in your SAP R/3 system: database and application servers. Whether you have a distributed or non-distributed system, these options appear. Logically, in a non-distributed system, the performance statistics come from one computer host. Now you can go into the detailed analysis. Click the Detail Analysis Menu button to get a more detailed view of the workload in your system, shown in Figure 12-26.

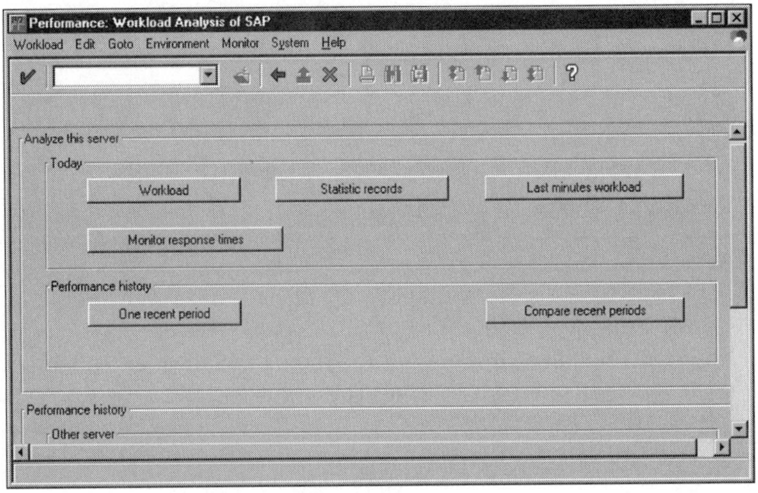

Figure 12-26:
Start here to get real details on SAP workload.

The major divisions in this screen are for analysis on one server or for a comparative analysis. Go straight to the workload analysis screen to see what is going on in the system. Click the button Workload in the Analyze This Server

Today subsection — the top-left button on your screen. The screen shown in Figure 12-27 appears.

Here you see important data about your system. The screen allows you to analyze either the dialog or update work processes. It also allows you to see analysis based on both the statistics. You can change the view by pressing one of the two buttons at the bottom of the screen. Press the appropriate button, Dialog, Background, or Total to see the different statistics. You can see which view you have by the message on the lower left-hand side of the screen.

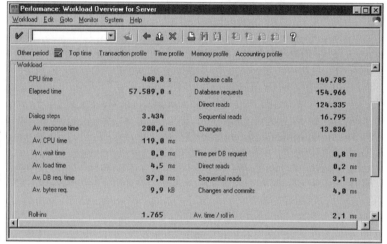

Figure 12-27: Check out the work-load for a server.

Think about what the numbers mean. You can see the averages are taken from the first and last record time entries at the top of the screen. Some key values are

- ✓ **Average Response Time:** The measurement of this metric starts when a work process gets a request from the dispatcher. This measurement does not include the response time from the presentation server to the dispatcher work process. You should target one to two seconds for dialog work processes.

- ✓ **Average CPU Time:** The amount of CPU time consumed to service the work process. This value should be about 40 percent of total response time.

- ✓ **Average DB Request Time:** The average time the database consumes to process a dialog step.

- ✓ **Average Load Time:** The amount of time needed to load and generate SAP R/3 objects such as ABAP programs, screen, and tables. You should target for 10 percent or less of average response time.

- ✓ **Average Roll-Ins:** The average time to read in data from a file or buffer.

- ✔ **Average Roll-Outs:** The average time to write out data from a file or buffer.

- ✔ **Average Wait Time:** The time a work process waits in the dispatcher queue for a free work process. You should target for about 1 percent of average response time. Anything greater may indicate the need for more work processes.

- ✔ **Database Calls:** The number of parsed requests sent to the database.

- ✔ **Database Requests:** The number of database requests made by ABAP programs. A general rule of performance is one database call to ten database requests, which makes for efficient use of the SAP buffers. You should target for 40 percent of average response time, subdivided into three categories: direct reads (10ms), sequential reads (10ms), and changes (25ms). The numbers in parentheses are suggested target times. Your values may differ because of the number of variables involved.

Take a deeper look into the actual transactions that create these response times by clicking the dialog view and then clicking the Top Time button on the tool bar. Figure 12-28 shows the screen Workload: Top 40 with Respect to Time Consumption.

The Top 40 screen gives you the top 40 in response time, sorted by response time. A great thing about this tool is that it gives a complete look at who did what and when.

Performance tuning is all about *slow is fast.* That is, make your changes slowly to get the best results quickly. Make small, incremental changes. Minimize the variables and do only one thing at a time. Remember that all the pieces are closely interrelated.

Figure 12-28:
See the transactions causing your response times.

Workload: Top 40 with Respect to Time Consumption						

Workload Edit Goto Monitor System Help

Q Top requests

Instance

SAP System	First record	00:00:30	Date 24.01.1999
Server	Last record	16:00:19	
Instance no. *	Elapsed time	15:59:49	Task type Tota

Top 40 dialog steps by response time(out of 3434)

End time	Tcode	Program	T	Scr.	Wp	User	Response time(ms)	Memory used(kB)	Wait time(ms)	CPU time(
07:02:13		RSCOLL00	B	4005	12	DDIC	81.794	974	0	27.3
00:02:19		RSCOLL00	B	1000	1	DDIC	48.017	943	0	44.4
06:02:03		RSCOLL00	B	1000	12	DDIC	38.508	943	0	21.3
14:00:43		RSCOLL00	B	1000	12	DDIC	25.133	943	0	21.9
12:01:14		RSCOLL00	B	1000	12	DDIC	24.774	943	0	21.1
08:01:23		RSCOLL00	B	1000	12	DDIC	24.455	943	0	20.8
10:00:39		RSCOLL00	B	1000	12	DDIC	24.239	943	0	20.7

Monitoring Alerts Graphically

CCMS comes with some good tools that let you monitor and see alerts graphically. The CCMS GUI tools use the same color coding scheme to address messages and alerts — you know, your basic red, green, and yellow. (The alerts, by the way, all use the thresholds you configure for CCMS, as explained earlier in this chapter in "Setting CCMS Alert Thresholds.")

Here's a more detailed look at the GUI's color convention:

✔ **Green:** Green is good. No alert was detected, based on the threshold parameters. The statistics gathered meet the okay status.

✔ **Yellow:** You probably should investigate pretty quick. The metrics gathered reveal a possible warning. Things are getting kind of critical.

✔ **Red:** Things aren't good. Check it out right away. Find the problem and fix it.

You can set the GUI to gather statistics every two minutes, but be careful that such close monitoring doesn't cause a drain on system performance.

SAP recommends continuous monitoring. Click the Timer On button in the GUI to turn it on.

Follow these steps to view your tools:

1. **From the transaction code STUN, choose <u>A</u>lerts⇨<u>G</u>lobal⇨<u>S</u>AP system.**

2. **To investigate further, click on the alert.**

   The more detailed view reveals that one of the file systems has a space problem.

3. **Investigate the problem and fix it.**

   You can get detailed information on each area by clicking on the alert.

   CCMS also has other alert monitors.

4. **From transaction code STUN, choose System.**

   Database alerts are illustrated in Figure 12-29.

   This alert monitor shows you monitors for the database.

5. **As before, click on the alert to get more detailed information.**

6. **To see the workload alert monitor, from transaction code STUN choose <u>A</u>lerts⇨<u>L</u>ocal⇨Current Workload.**

   Another important monitor is the call statistics to the database.

7. **Choose <u>A</u>lerts⇨<u>L</u>ocal⇨<u>C</u>all Statistics.**

Of course, the key to monitoring is to have some clue about what is actually happening to the system at the time of a red alert. Usually you can tell pretty easily. For example, a massive load of data may be getting entered into the database, bogging down performance.

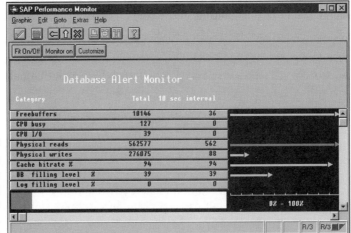

Figure 12-29:
You can check out database alerts, too.

Make changes to the system slowly, one at a time. A sure way to bring the system to its knees is to make multiple, sporadic changes. Communicate with your other Basis team members before you go off on a lone crusade to save the system.

People expect you, as administrator, to keep their systems running smoothly, prevent their systems from crashing, and stuff like that. It's a hard job. Even with CCMS, it's still a hard job, but at least CCMS provides you with gauges that show you how the operating system, network, databases, and SAP over-all are performing.

Test your SAP knowledge

What is an "alert threshold?"

A. The point at which a warning signal comes up.

B. Any threshold that is truly paying attention.

C. An 18th-century farming implement, predecessor of the thresher.

D. A modern kitchen implement, akin to the radar detector.

Where does the transaction code STUN take you?

A. To a rendezvous with extraterrestrials.

B. To downtown Los Angeles (which is like meeting extraterrestrials)

C. Nowhere really. It just knocks you out.

D. The Performance Monitoring screen, where you start most performance monitoring.

Chapter 13

Even More Monitoring

. . . .

In This Chapter

▶ Starting and stopping SAP R/3 (without hurting your database and applications)

▶ Working with SAP profiles to run SAP efficiently

▶ Managing memory to keep things running fast (relatively)

. . . .

*W*hy don't you just stop it?" you may wonder about SAP. "You know — just log out and shut the puppy down?" Well, R/3 isn't like a blender or your TV or even a little PC. It's this big thing with lots going on — particularly a database and the application using the database. People are generally sensitive about keeping the database and their application healthy and intact. If you just stop SAP, you may abruptly interrupt some important activities that you shouldn't abruptly interrupt.

SAP is more of an elephant than a mouse. That is, it can't just start, stop, and turn on a dime. In this chapter, you see good practices that you can follow to manage this elephant and keep it nicely on course. You find out how to start and stop SAP smoothly. You also find out about managing profiles and memory. Profiles aren't just some abstraction; you use them to structure what gets loaded into the system. And memory — well, memory can get overloaded, and it's important to prevent that.

Setting up profiles improperly or managing memory inefficiently in such a big system can end up having a pretty big effect. You want to manage your profiles and memory so that the system runs well, and the information you find in this chapter can help you do just that.

Starting and Stopping SAP

Starting and stopping SAP involves two tasks — starting or stopping the database and starting or stopping SAP R/3. That is, when you start SAP, you first have to start the database and then the application. Similarly, when you stop SAP, you have to stop the application and then stop the database.

Starting or stopping in CCMS

CCMS (the Computing Center Management System, described in Chapter 12) gives you nice tools to start and start R/3. Now, we have to admit, CCMS doesn't actually start or stop the database. It's good for stopping applications, though.

The CCMS start or stop tool is really only useful if you have multiple application servers within your system. If you do, you can log into one application server and stop the other application servers with CCMS. If you don't have multiple application servers (also known as a *distributed system*), stopping the system with command-line options is more practical (see the section "Starting or stopping with the command line," later in this chapter, for more information).

To start the R/3 instance from within CCMS, follow these steps:

1. **Choose Tools⇨Administration⇨Computing Center⇨Management Systems⇨Control⇨System Monitor.**

   A graphical view of your system appears, as shown in Figure 13-1.

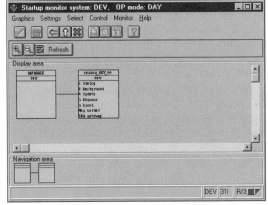

Figure 13-1:
You can monitor your systems here before starting or stopping.

The different boxes show the database server and all R/3 instances in this system. The boxes also show the SAP work processes running on each instance.

2. **After you select an SAP instance to start, choose Tools⇨ Administration⇨Computing Center⇨Management Systems⇨ Control⇨Start SAP Instance.**

If you want to stop an SAP instance, follow these steps:

1. **Choose Tools⇨Administration⇨Computing Center⇨Management Systems⇨Control⇨System Monitor.**

2. **Select the SAP instance you want to start by clicking the appropriate box with the mouse.**

3. **Choose Tools⇨Administration⇨Computing Center⇨Management Systems⇨Control⇨Control⇨Stop SAP Instance.**

Starting and stopping in CCMS works best with multiple application servers.

Prevent unauthorized personnel from starting and stopping SAP with CCMS. Only users with certain Basis profiles should have access to starting and stopping in CCMS.

Starting or stopping with the command line

You can also start and stop SAP by using the command line in Windows NT and UNIX. Command lines are more stark, daring, and nitty-gritty than menus, and command-line scripts have an added advantage over CCMS — you can use them to start or stop the database as well as the R/3 instance. The following steps outline the startup procedures of the startup scripts.

1. **Start the database.**

2. **Start/check the OS collector.**

3. **Start the SAP instance based on the start profile.**

   See "Checking out a startup profile," later in this chapter.

4. **Start the SAP instance based on default values.**

   See "Looking over a default profile," later in this chapter.

5. **Start the SAP instance based on instance profile values.**

   See "Inspecting an instance profile," later in this chapter.

At shutdown, the scripts follow these procedures:

1. **Stop SAP processes based on the** `sapstart` **program.**

2. **Stop the database.**

The way to start or stop SAP is different in Windows NT and UNIX. The procedures are the same, but the processes are a little different, as the next two sections explain.

Starting or stopping SAP on Windows NT

In Windows NT, SAP installs the SAP Service Manager GUI on the server. To use the Service Manager, follow these steps:

1. **From the Windows NT server console, go to Start⇨Programs⇨ SAP⇨SAP Service Manger.**

   The Service Manager, which you use to start and stop SAP, fires up. Figure 13-2 shows the SAP Service Manager.

Figure 13-2: In Windows NT, use the Service Manager to start and stop SAP.

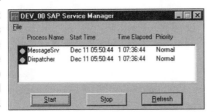

2. **To start the SAP instance, click the Start button.**

   The traffic lights go from gray to yellow to green.

3. **To stop the SAP instance, click the Stop button.**

   The traffic lights go from green to gray.

Table 13-1 shows the meaning of the traffic lights in SAP Service Manager for Windows NT.

Table 13-1	Traffic Lights in SAP Service Manager	
Color of Traffic Light	*State of Processes*	*Message*
Green	Processes are started.	The R/3 system is ready for logon.
Yellow	Processes are starting.	The R/3 system is not ready for logon.
Gray	Processes have stopped.	The R/3 system is not ready for logon.
Red	Errors occurred during startup of process.	The processes are not running. R/3 isn't ready for logon.

The inside stuff on starting and stopping: SAPSID

When the operating system starts, it also starts an SAP service called `Instance number>`. This service essentially controls the process of starting or stopping. It obtains the environmental variables from the Windows NT registry and startup variables of `START_DVEBMGS<SYS No.>_hostname.`

`SAP<SAPSID>` waits for a message from SAP Service Manager or the command `sap-start.exe` or `sapsrvkill.exe`. Depending on the message it receives, it executes the actions to start or stop the appropriate processes.

Starting and stopping on UNIX

In UNIX, a script controls the startup and shutdown process.

Here's what to do:

1. **Log onto the server as** `<sid>adm`.

2. **To start SAP, execute the** `startsap` **command.**

   `Startsap` starts the database, if needed, and then starts the R/3 instance.

   If you want to start only the R/3 instance, not the database, enter the `startsap r3` command.

3. **To stop SAP, put in the** `stopsap` **command.**

   `Stopsap` stops the R/3 instance and then shuts down the database.

The `startsap` and `stopsap` commands are aliases for `startsap_DVEB-MGS<SYS No.>_hostname` or `stopsap_DVEBMGS<SYS No.>_hostname`. The start script executes the `sapstart` process, which starts the SAP processes based on the startup profile, explained later in this chapter in the section "Checking out a startup profile." The stop script executes the `kill.sap` process, which stops SAP processes based on the `sapstart` script.

Starting and stopping the database

You can stop the database by using the database's native tools. For Oracle and Informix, SAP created an interface utility called `sapdba`. `Sapdba` allows the database administrator to start or stop the database, as well as perform other common administrative tasks. SQL Server uses SQL Enterprise Manager, and Oracle has its own tool called Server Manager to stop or start the database.

Working with SAP Profiles

In SAP, the profile has the authorizations allowed for a particular user group — the formal description of the users in the eyes of the system. See Chapter 7 for a discussion of profiles.

Three profiles control the look and feel of an SAP instance. During startup, certain parameters create the environment for the SAP instance. You define such items as the number of work processes, memory allocation to SAP, and logon language during startup. The three profiles, in their startup order, are

- ✔ Startup profile
- ✔ Default profile
- ✔ Instance profile

The profiles are actual operating system files located in the directory /USR/SAP/<SID>/SYS/PROFILE (**UNIX**) or \USR\SAP\<SID>\SYS\PRO-FILE(**NT**).

The process for changing these profile parameters is the same in UNIX or Windows NT. Here's a summary of the steps involved in changing a profile:

1. **Select the profile you want to muck around with.**

2. **Select a view, either Administration Data or Basic Maintenance, to see a logical grouping of parameters.**

3. **Select Extended Maintenance if you want to see all the configurable parameters and their values.**

    The other views are a subset of the Extended Maintenance view.

4. **After you change the values or add new values, save and activate the profile.**

As we mention previously, the configuration in the profiles affects the system, with respect to work processes, memory allocation to SAP, and logon language, when you stop and restart SAP.

SAP also helps you control versions for the profiles, so you can choose to use the latest version or an earlier version. You can see the version by the number in the Version field of the Edit Profiles screen.

In the following sections, you look over the three key profiles.

Checking out a startup profile

The startup profile (as you might guess) has the parameters that go into place when you start SAP. The `sapstart` program looks at the parameters defined in the startup profile and creates the processes it lists.

The startup profile initiates the following subordinate processes:

- Application server
- Message server
- SNA Gateway
- System log send demon
- System log receive demon

Here's how to check out the startup profile:

1. **Choose Tools⇨Administration⇨Computing Center⇨Management System⇨Configuration⇨Profile Maintenance or enter transaction code** RZ10 **in the command field.**

   The Edit Profiles screen opens, as shown in Figure 13-3.

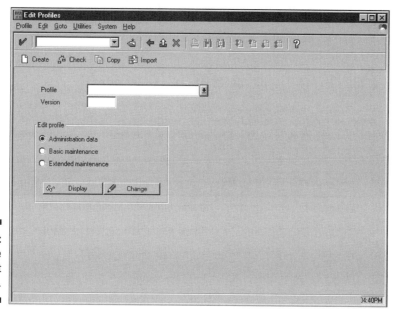

Figure 13-3:
Begin here
to check out
profiles.

2. **Click the drop-down arrow to the right of the Profile blank to make the list of startup profiles appear.**

3. **Double-click the startup profile you want to check out.**

   The naming convention is START_DVEBMGS<SYS No.>_hostname. See Figure 13-4 to see the profile.

Parameter name	Parameter value
☑ SAPSYSTEMNAME	DEU
☑ INSTANCE_NAME	DVEBMGS00
☑ SAPSYSTEM	00
☑ SAPGLOBALHOST	SAEU
☑ SAPLOCALHOST	saeu
☑ _DB	strdbs.cmd
☑ Start_Program_01	immediate $(DIR_EXECUTABLE)\$(_DB) $(SAPSYSTEMNA
☑ _MS	msg_server.exe
☑ Start_Program_02	local $(DIR_EXECUTABLE)\$(_MS) pf=$(DIR_PROFILE)
☑ _DW	disp+work.exe
☑ Start_Program_03	local $(DIR_EXECUTABLE)\$(_DW) pf=$(DIR_PROFILE)

Figure 13-4: Here's a look at one startup profile.

If you add or change any existing values, the values become active only after you stop and restart R/3.

When you first install SAP, you don't have any files on the RZ10 screen. You need to import the files from the operating system. Choose Utilities⇨Import Profiles⇨Of Active Servers. The utility reads the operating system file and creates entries in the database.

Looking over a default profile

The default profile assigns the same instance parameter values for all application servers. These values help form and develop the SAP instance. Table 13-2 lists parameters that the default profile defines.

Table 13-2	Key Parameters That the Default Profile Defines
Parameter	**Description**
SAPDBHOST	Name of the host system for the database
rdisp/vbname	Server handling updates
rdisp/enqname	Enqueue server
rdisp/btcname	Server for background jobs (see Chapter 9 for description of background jobs)
rdisp/msname	Message server

Parameter	Description
rdisp/msserv	TCP service for message server
rdisp/sna_gateway	SNA Gateway host
rdisp/sna_gw_service	TCP Service for SNA Gateway

SAP doesn't reflect any changes you make until the next time you start SAP.

Figure 13-5 shows an example of a default profile.

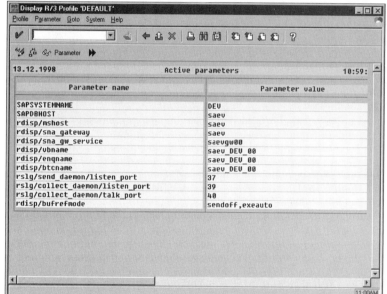

Figure 13-5:
Check out the parameters in this sample default profile.

Inspecting an instance profile

Everybody is entitled to some degree of individuality. An SAP instance gets its own personality in its instance profile, because the values in that profile are specific to a particular SAP instance. Many of the parameter values depend on the system resources available on that particular host. See Figure 13-6 for an example of an instance profile.

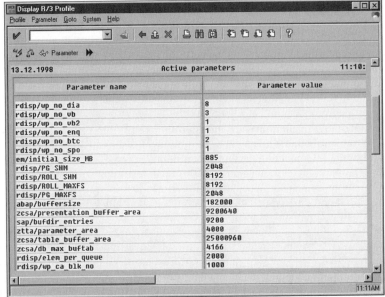

Figure 13-6:
An instance
profile sets
parameters
for a
particular
instance.

Table 13-3, Table 13-4, and Table 13-5 list configurable parameters in an instance profile.

Table 13-3	Dispatch Parameters
Parameter	*Description*
rdisp/wp_no_dia	Number of dialog work processes
rdisp/wp_no_vb	Number of update work processes
rdisp/wp_no_vb2	Number of update2 work processes
rdisp/wp_no_enq	Number of enqueue work processes; only one per system
rdisp/wp_no_spo	Number of spool work processes; only one per instance
rdisp/wp_no_btc	Number of batch work processes

Table 13-4	Login Parameters
Parameter	*Description*
login/system_client	Default login client
login/password_expiration_time	Expiration time for password in days

Table 13-5	ABAP/4 Environment Parameters
Parameter	*Description*
abap/buffersize	ABAP/4 buffer size in kilobytes
abap/heap_area_dia	Memory limits for work processes
abap/heaplimit	Maximum memory limit in bytes

Many more configurable instance parameters exist. You should be careful when making any changes to these parameters. If you over-allocate certain memory parameters, SAP may not be able to start. (Remember, too, that most configuration doesn't take effect when you enter the new parameter but after you restart SAP.)

Managing Memory

SAP and its components are big-time memory eaters. In fact, you'll probably find the memory requirements for an SAP installation higher than for other applications you currently use.

SAP memory management changed from Release 3.0*x*. If you're familiar with using the earlier version, you have some new things to get to know in Version 3.1.

You can divide a discussion of memory into two topics: buffers and user data. The following sections look at each topic.

Managing buffers

SAP relies heavily on *buffering* data — you know, stashing data here and there in temporary places. The more that SAP buffers static data, the less the system needs to go to the database to retrieve the information. SAP buffers are local to each application server. The following list presents the types of buffers in SAP:

- Table buffers
- Number range buffers
- Program buffers
- Presentation buffers (screen buffers)

  ✔ CUA buffers (menu buffers)

  ✔ Nametab buffers (ABAP/4 dictionary buffers)

When you install SAP, you set the buffers to specific sizes. You can monitor the buffer quality from within CCMS and determine whether you need to make any adjustments. Usually, you want a minimum amount of swapping in your buffers. (*Swapping* is moving stuff from one storage area to another.)

One of the first signs of a buffer bottleneck may appear in the program buffer size, especially in a development system. Make the ABAP program buffer size large enough to minimize the reloading of programs. Also observe the quality of the screen, menu, and data dictionary buffers. Make any changes gradually.

To change the buffer sizes, use the instance profile, as explained earlier in this chapter in the section "Inspecting an instance profile."

Tables are buffered in full, by generic key, or by a single record. The types of data stored in the table depend upon the application and types of users accessing information on the system. You can monitor the quality of reads on these buffers in CCMS. Poor buffer quality results in longer response times. Follow these rules for table buffering:

  ✔ Buffer only non-time-critical buffers

  ✔ Buffer static tables

  ✔ Buffer standard SAP tables only with SAP approval

Managing user data in extended memory

SAP now uses a portion of memory called *extended memory* to speed up the sharing of data among work processes. If you happen to know earlier versions of SAP, the extended memory started with release 3.0C.

An example shows how extended memory does its thing. In an SAP system, you have many front-end users accessing data. Depending on the transactions, these users switch from work process to work process. During these changes, SAP has to hand over data from one work process to another.

In earlier versions (before 3.0C), SAP used to actually transfer data from one work process to another. Boy, did that bog down the CPU and put a load on the memory!

Extended memory lessens the burden of those changes from work process to work process. During the switch from one work process to another, SAP keeps the bulk of the data in extended memory. It still rolls out a small portion of data (called *user context* data) from one work process and rolls it into another work process. But the items in the roll area are mainly just pointers to the data in extended memory, as well as pointers to programs being used and to authorizations. The pointers are much smaller than the actual data in the work processes, and they help everything to work faster and better than before.

The following steps show how SAP uses extended memory for a dialog work process:

1. The roll area is divided into two areas, `roll_first` and the rest.

2. The dialog work process consumes the space allocated to `roll_first` and then starts using extended memory.

   To minimize the amount of `roll_first` areas used, define `ztta/roll_first` as 1. `Ztta/roll_first` is the first portion of roll area allocated to a dialog work process.

3. SAP uses extended memory until it reaches the maximum allowed. The parameter `ztta/roll_extension` defines the user quota.

   The quota is nicely in place to prevent one work process from hogging all the extended memory. After all, there are lots of work processes to think about.

4. If the work process needs more memory, it uses the remaining space in its roll area.

5. If the work process needs even more memory, it uses *heap* memory.

   When the process is using heap memory, it's in *PRIV* mode. That is to say, it's private. The user is locked into the work process, which may seem a little confining, but the compensation is that no other user can utilize that dialog work process. The work process stays in PRIV mode until the transaction ends.

Table 13-6 summarizes key parameters you can use in memory management.

Table 13-6	Configurable Parameters in Memory Management
Parameter	*Effect*
`ztta/roll_first`	The first portion of roll area allocated to a dialog work process
`ztta/roll_area`	Total roll area per work process
`abap/heap_area_dia`	Heap limit per dialog work process
`abap/heap_area_nondia`	Heap limit per non-dialog work process
`abap/heap_area_total`	Heap limit, all work processes
`ztta/roll_extension`	User quota in extended memory
`em/initial_size_MB`	Fixed size of extended memory

Test your SAP knowledge

To stop SAP, you should

A. Whack it remorselessly with a log.

B. Make sure no one's looking and then push the Power Off button.

C. Ignore it for a long time. SAP will quit to get your attention.

D. In UNIX or Windows NT, use command-line scripts to start or stop the database, as well as the R/3 instance.

Use a startup profile to

A. Get your online business off the ground.

B. Jump-start yourself before you leave the house.

C. Define such items as number of work processes, memory allocation to SAP, and logon language during startup.

D. Give your resume extra sparkle.

As with all performance tuning, keep all variables to a minimum. Perform changes incrementally, and observe your result.

Part V

Being a Hero: Deployment and Troubleshooting

The 5th Wave   By Rich Tennant

BEAL & WASP DATABASE CONSULTANTS

"Your database is beyond repair, but before I tell you our backup recommendation, let me ask you a question. How many index cards do you think will fit on the walls of your computer room?"

In this part . . .

When you're operating at breakneck speed with massive systems, as you do with R/3, you have to know how to provide help and how to find advanced help for yourself. In this part, you find out how to avoid mistakes by coordinating the flow of development by using Workbench Organizer. You get instructions on putting in the patches that SAP provides to fix its own mistakes, and you try out Online Service System for getting all the latest, livest advice from people dealing with the same issues you face.

Chapter 14

Keeping Your Systems Straight with Workbench Organizer

In This Chapter

▶ Setting up the Workbench Organizer

▶ Creating change requests to identify changes

▶ Releasing change requests so that they can actually be implemented

▶ Importing change requests to put them into the new system

*A*nybody knows that in computers, small things can get confused. Files can get misnamed or put in the wrong directory. People may work on two versions of the same file and then accidentally delete the wrong one.

Maybe nobody except Basis administrators thinks so, but big things like whole SAP clients can get mixed up, too, unless you're careful. In fact, people in charge of big things like whole systems have to be much more careful than people in charge of trifling little things like individual files.

Workbench Organizer is your way to be careful with your systems. You use it to organize your landscape. (You can get a nice introduction to the landscape in Chapter 5.)

With Workbench Organizer, you can set up systems to perform certain functions like development, testing, and production. Basically, with Workbench Organizer, you implement your company's client deployment strategy (for putting your whole landscape into place). Ultimately, Workbench Organizer is your way to plan and track the transfer of objects from one system to another, so that you don't screw up.

Setting Up the Workbench Organizer

In the Workbench Organizer, you label certain systems in the SAP landscape to perform specific functions, like testing. You also create a migration path for all your customization and development. For example, suppose that your team has configured the order entry procedure in SAP. Your teammates configure the procedure in DEV (the development system). In ACP (the test system), they perform integration testing. After successfully testing the procedure in ACP (and *only* after successful testing), they can migrate the configuration to PRD (the production system). Workbench Organizer defines the routes that the configuration follows from development to production and sets up the rules it has to obey as it goes.

Setting up the Workbench Organizer is a required task that your SAP certified installer helps you complete after installation. You can check out an installed Workbench Organizer by following these steps:

1. **From the command field, enter** SE06.

   The main Set Up Workbench Organizer screen, shown in Figure 14-1, appears.

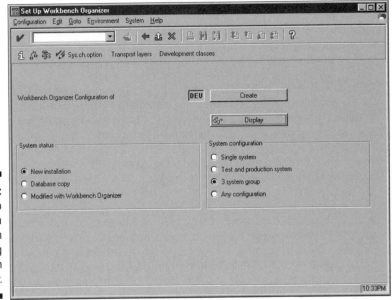

Figure 14-1:
Start here to set up a new system using Workbench Organizer.

TIP

In this example, the Workbench Organizer is already set up.

If you aren't set up, you need to make some decisions before configuring. (These decisions reflect the client deployment strategy.) You need to ask yourself these questions:

- How many systems am I using in my landscape?

- What are the purposes of these systems?

SAP recommends, at the minimum, a two-system landscape, as described in Chapter 5. In the two-system configuration, you have the integration (development) and consolidation (test) systems in one system and the delivery (production) system in a separate system. Almost all SAP Basis consultants, however, recommend a three-system landscape, with separate logical and physical systems for integration, consolidation, and delivery.

You start configuration of a newly installed system from transaction code SE06. The initial screen is divided into two sections: System Status and System Configuration. Continue with these steps:

2. **Select New Installation in the System Status frame and select 3 System Group in the System Configuration frame.**

3. **Click the Create button.**

   The system needs some information regarding your system landscape.

4. **When prompted, enter the SID (System Identification Number) for the integration, consolidation, and delivery systems.**

5. **Enter a short description for each system.**

   After you enter the appropriate data, the system generates the configuration. You see a summary after generation. Figure 14-2 shows the current configuration of a sample system.

Figure 14-2:
Check out
the current
configura-
tion of your
systems.

```
Current configuration of the Workbench Organizer


System name for Workbench Organizer and transport system: DEU

Development system:        DEU
Quality assurance system:  ACP
Production system:         PRD

System change option: All objects can be changed with Workbench Organizer

Largest request number:


Current configuration of the Workbench Organizer

Existing requests:
System  No.requests  No.objects Description

 CPI        1          640
 DEU       319         442     Development System
```

Be sure that all the systems in your system have the same configuration for
SE06. If you don't have systems set up consistently, you don't get reliable
results with Workbench Organizer.

Your system configuration settings affect four key SAP tables. Table 14-1 lists
the key tables that you configure with Workbench Organizer.

Table 14-1	Key SAP Tables You Configure with Workbench Organizer
Table	**What It Configures**
TSYST	SAP systems
DEVL	Transport layers
TWSYS	Consolidation routes
TASYS	Recipient systems

See Figure 14-3 for an example of table TSYST. Get to this screen by clicking
the System List button from the Set Up Workbench Organizer screen (refer to
Figure 14-1).

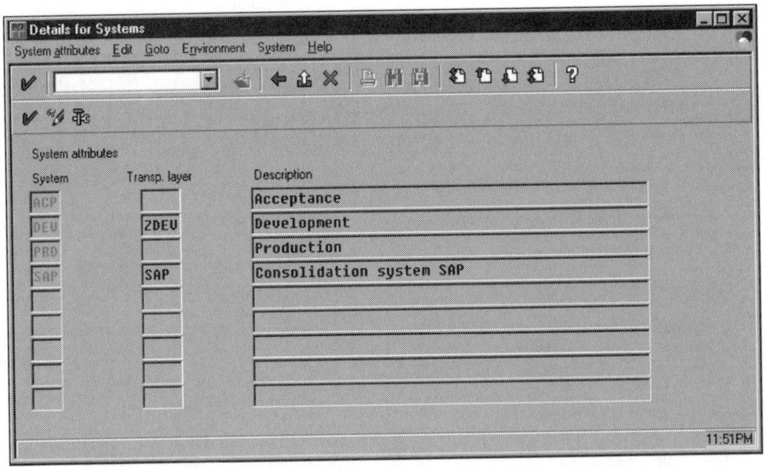

Figure 14-3:
Use TSYST
to configure
SAP
Systems.

Check out Figure 14-4 for an example of table DEVL. Get to this screen by
clicking the Transport Layers button from the Set Up Workbench Organizer
screen.

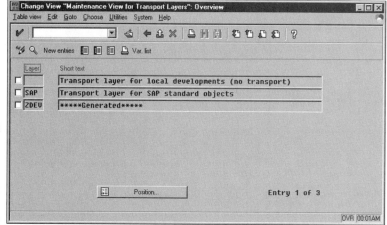

Figure 14-4:
The table
DEVL shows
Transport
layers.

Take a look at Figure 14-5 for an example of table TWSYS. Get to this screen by clicking the Consolidation Routes button from the Set Up Workbench Organizer screen.

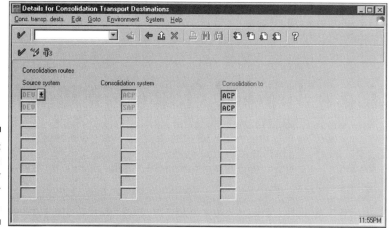

Figure 14-5:
The table
TWSYS may
be similar
to this.

Gaze upon Figure 14-6 for an example of table TASYS. Get to this screen by clicking the Deliveries button from the Set Up Workbench Organizer screen.

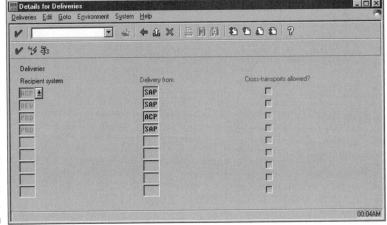

Figure 14-6:
The table
TASYS
shows
recipient
systems for
objects that
you move.

Cross-transports — transports that don't follow the migration path in your client deployment strategy — are usually a pretty dumb idea. According to the normal scenario, you create an object in DEV. Before you let it go to PRD, you make it go through the ACP system for testing. Cross-transports allow you to skip these delivery routes, which means that you might use an untested system as a production system, run into tons of bugs, and bring your company to its knees.

Creating a Manual Change Request

The change request is the vehicle for moving objects between systems. A *change request* is pretty much what it sounds like — a formal, written record of the fact that you want to change the configuration on something. Change requests are the SAP way of migrating the configuration from development to test and finally to production.

Change requests work on a *last in first out* (LIFO) concept. The latest change request applied to the target system supercedes any older configurations.

Consider an example: Your SD team configures the sales order process by flipping switch 1 and attaching it to change request number DEVK900001. Change request DEVK900001 gets imported into the test system. After testing, the team realizes that it needs to flip switch 2. So it goes back to the development system and attaches its changed configuration to change request DEVK900002. This second change request has switch 2 flipped. This new change request gets imported into the test system. Now the configuration reads `flip switch 2`. DEVK900002, which is last in, takes priority.

Change requests are logically divided into separate entities. The first is the *change request.* This change request may contain multiple types of configurations called *tasks,* in which case a one-to-many relationship exists between change requests and tasks associated with that change request.

You can create a change request in two ways:

✔ The system opens a request automatically when a change is saved.

✔ You can create an individual change request manually.

To create a change request manually, follow these steps:

1. From the command field, enter SE10.

The first screen of the Customizing Organizer appears, as shown in Figure 14-7. This main screen gives you a summary of the change request owned by you.

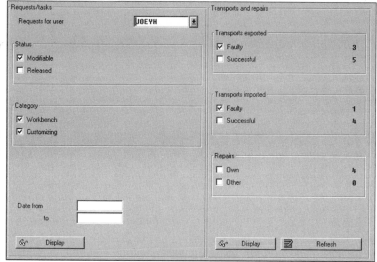

Figure 14-7:
Start at the Customizing Organizer to create a change request.

2. On the left side, select Modifiable from the Status section and Customizing from the Category section and then press Enter.

Figure 14-8 shows a list of requests for customizing in the Customizing Organizer: Requests screen.

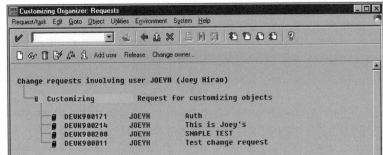

Figure 14-8:
You can see
a list of
requests for
customizing.

You can see a list of customizing requests that have not yet been released. From this screen, you can create a change request.

3. **Click the Create icon and enter a brief description of the change request.**

Figure 14-9 shows the screen for describing a change request.

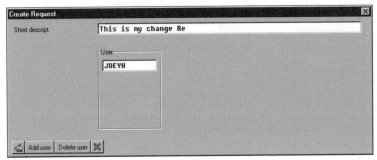

Figure 14-9:
Put in a
description
of your
change
request
here.

At this point, you can add other people who can attach tasks to the change request. Only those users who are specifically listed are able to attach any tasks to this change request.

4. **When you are finished adding other users, click the Save icon.**

5. **After you finish, click the change request tree to open it up.**

Notice that your change request, number DEVK902931, has one task attached to it, DEVK902932, as shown in Figure 14-10.

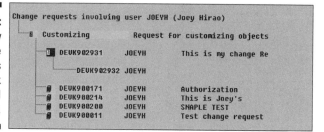

Figure 14-10:
Your new change request has one task attached to it.

TIP

The naming convention for change requests is `<SID>K<ID No.>`. That is, put the System ID of the computer, the letter *K*, and then the ID number for the request. This naming convention is the same for change requests and tasks.

Setting Up Automatic Change Requests

The other way to create change requests is to set the system change options as automatic. This technique is popular for the configuration client.

1. **To set the client for automatic recording of changes, enter** SCC4 **in the command field.**

2. **Click the Change icon and then double-click on the appropriate client.**

3. **From inside the configuration settings, select Automatic Recording of Changes.**

   Figure 14-11 shows the screen where you select automatic recording.

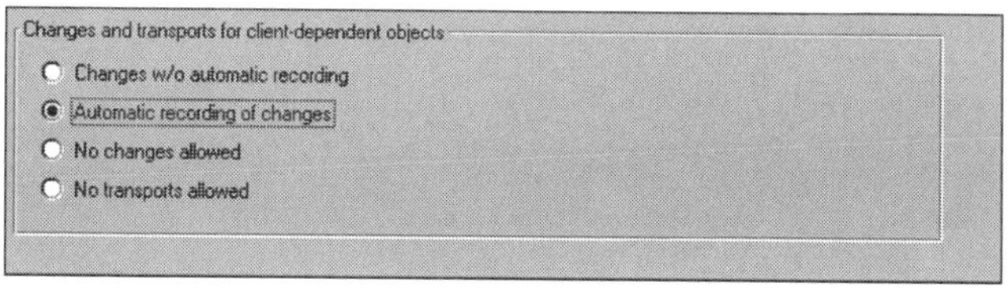

Figure 14-11:
Select Automatic Recording of Changes.

With this option set for the particular client, any changes made within the client invoke an option to attach the configuration to a change request.

TECHNICAL STUFF

A change request can have both the workbench and customizing categories associated with it. Workbench changes are usually client-independent tables and objects. Customizing is usually client-dependent customization.

Releasing a Change Request

When you are confident that the change request is complete and ready to be transported to the next system downstream, you need to release it. Follow these steps:

1. **Enter** SE10 **in the command field.**

2. **Select Status as Modifiable and Category as Customizing and then press Enter.**

3. **Enter your user name in the field at the top of the screen.**

   Refer to Figure 14-8. You return to the change request you created. But before you can release a change request, you have to release all subordinate tasks. In this case, you must release task DEVK902932.

4. **Place the cursor on the task and click once to highlight it.**

5. **Click the Release button on the toolbar, as shown in Figure 14-12.**

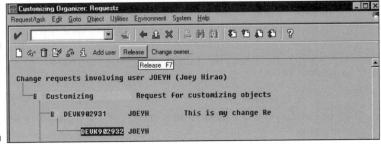

Figure 14-12:
Click the Release button on the toolbar.

After you click the Release button, you have the option of entering text about the task.

6. **Type in text to describe the task.**

   Figure 14-13 shows the text area.

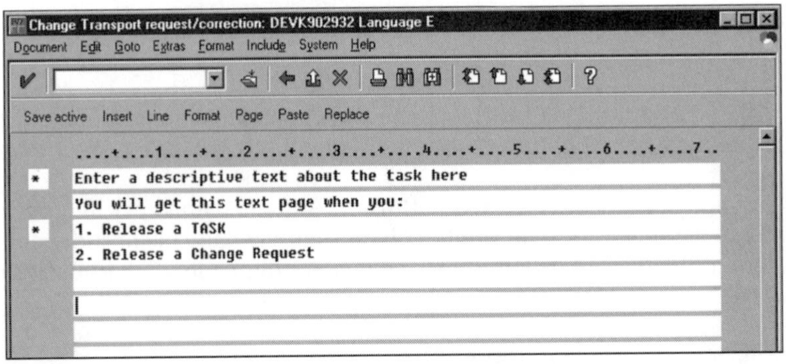

Figure 14-13:
You have the opportunity to explain your released task.

Be thorough in your documentation and enter a description of the task. You may wonder later why you released a task. Even more likely, though, other people may come across your action later, scratch their heads, and say, "Why did somebody do *this*?"

7. After you enter some descriptive text, click the Save icon and then click the green left arrow.

You have released the task. Notice that the color changes. To see a description of the different meanings for colors, press F6. Figure 14-14 shows change requests and tasks.

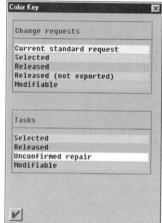

Figure 14-14:
SAP color codes change requests and tasks.

You have to release all tasks associated with a change request before SAP releases the change request itself.

The next step is to release the change request, which is similar to releasing the task. Follow these steps:

1. Select the change request and click the Release button.

You have three options for releasing the change request:

- Release the change request.
- Release the change request to another change request.
- Release the change request to a new change request.

Figure 14-15 shows the three options.

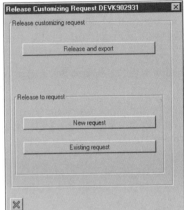

Figure 14-15:
You have
three options
when you
release a
change
request.

2. **Click the Release and Export button.**

   You export the data down to the operating system. At the same time, SAP adds the change request to the buffer of the next system, as defined by the Workbench Organizer.

If you ask us, segregating duties within the configuration/development team, with respect to change requests, is a good idea. You can have a functional team leader as the point of control for releasing change requests. That team leader has to know what's happening before releasing the request. By having one person in charge, you create a control point for allowing change requests to go downstream.

Checking the Logs on Your Change Requests

After you perform a task, you should check the written record to make sure that it has really happened. Therefore, the last step in creating a change request is to check the logs. Follow these steps:

1. **Go to Customizing Organizer: Initial Screen via transaction code SE10.**

2. **On the right side, in the Transports and Repairs section, select the check boxes for Faulty and Successful under Transports Exported.**

3. **Click Display.**

   Figure 14-16 shows the exported requests.

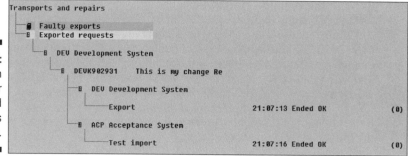

Figure 14-16:
Check on
your
exported
requests
here.

You should investigate any code above 0. Error code 4 is a warning. Error code 8 is a transport error. Anything higher than 8 indicates a problem other than the transport.

To get detailed logs, double-click on the Export or Test Import line. A *test import* means that a request was made to contact the downstream database as the basis for an import.

Importing a Change Request into the New System

In earlier examples in this chapter, the functional team members had the ability to mange the change requests. The task for importing change requests into the downstream system is purely a Basis function. You need the user name and password at the operating system to make this import happen.

Here's what to do:

1. **Log into the target system as** <sid>adm.

   Adm is SAP's administrative user at the operating system. The exact name of this user may vary with your specific platform.

2. **Go to the transport directory.**

   - In UNIX, go to CD /USR/SAP/TRANS/BIN.
   - In NT, go to DRIVE LETTER:\USR\SAP\TRANS\BIN.

Now you have two options. You can either import the change requests singularly, or en masse in the order they were exported. Either way gets the job of importing done just the same.

Because the change requests affect configuration and development in a LIFO (last in first out) manner, order is important. Here's an example to highlight the importance. Suppose that you have configuration A in change request DEVK900010, and the same type of configuration (but more accurate) in change request DEVK900020. In this example, DEVK900010 was exported first, and DEVK900020 was exported second. If you import singularly, you may inadvertently import DEVK900020 first and DEVK900010 second.

If the old configuration is present in your target system, you are at risk. How do you avoid it?

✔ Import all the change requests in the order in which they were exported.

✔ Have a flawless procedure to record the change requests release order and content.

In the scenario, if you know that DEVK900010 was the wrong configuration, you can simply choose not to import it. This technique is feasible but extremely difficult to manage.

Importing change requests one at a time

Here is how to perform a singular import of a change request:

1. **Type in this command on the command line:**

```
tp import <change request number> <target sid>
     client<target client>
```

An example using change request DEVK900010, originating from system DEV client 100 and going to ACP client 400, looks like this:

```
tp import devk900010 acp client400
```

The system processes the request and imports it into the target database. After the import, you need to check the logs.

2. **Go to Customizing Organizer via transaction code SE10.**

3. **From the Transports and Repairs section, select the checkboxes for Faulty and Successful under Transports Imported.**

4. **Click Display.**

Importing change requests all together

Here is how to perform an import of all change requests present in the target system's buffer. The buffer is populated every time a successful export occurs from the upstream system. The command line syntax is

```
tp import all <change request number> <target sid>
client<target client>
```

Consider the same example as used in the preceding section. All change requests in ACP's buffer are going to ACP client 400.

1. **Type the command at the command line:**

```
tp import all acp client400
```

2. **Check the logs, as explained in the section "Importing change requests one at a time."**

A *transport* transfers stuff from one system to another (you know, importing and exporting it). When you do a transport, you can use the tp command, and you can put a bunch of codes at the end of the command to have various effects.

Table 14-2 shows some special, unconditional code that you can use at the end of tp commands. (By the way, you probably shouldn't apply these codes without a specific purpose. You don't want to go around randomly doing stuff like that.)

Table 14-2	Codes for tp Commands	
Unconditional Code	**Import/Export**	**Command**
0	Import	Do not delete change request from target system's buffer after import
1	Import	Can be transported again
	Export	Ignore incorrect change request status
2	Import	Can overwrite original objects
3	Import	Can overwrite system objects
4	Import	Can be transported into alien system
5	Import	Can import from nonintegration system
6	Import	Can overwrite unconfirmed repair objects
8	Import	Ignore table classification
9	Import	Ignore locked transport types in target system

Chapter 15

Quick Fixes: Patches

. . . .

In This Chapter

▶ Fixing a bunch of things at once automatically

▶ Fixing errant code by hand

▶ Patching up defective executables

. . . .

I don't know that anyone, except maybe a ... *For Dummies* author, comes right out and states the obvious about the patches we talk about in this chapter. Somebody has to do it, though. Great big programs like SAP, inevitably, have tiny little bugs in them. (Bugs, of course, are defects. Problems. Faults. Limitations. *Errors.*)

Facing the problem boldly, SAP provides you with *Hot Packages* of patches to apply to the bugs. (Patches may not always be for bugs, but they usually are.)

SAP R/3 application, database, and operating system together make up a running SAP instance. A change to one could affect any of the others. Before applying any patches, research with SAP to ensure that it will not negatively affect system performance and functionality.

SAP offers three types of patches for its three components:

✔ Hot Packages, or Legal Change Patches (LCP)

✔ OSS Note fixes

✔ SAP kernel patches

Operating system and database patches are independent of SAP. Because how well SAP works depends directly on how well these other pieces work, be cautious when planning to implement any patch from independent vendors. Use your best judgment. If you are in doubt, contact SAP for advice. (But always apply patches that SAP recommends.)

Fixing Source Code Automatically: Hot Packages

Hot Packages correct known problems associated with SAP source codes — the nitty-gritty stuff.

If you are implementing the HR module, you may want to implement LCP instead of the Hot Packages. LCP contain all the fixes as Hot Packages plus HR specific fixes. As the Basis administrator, you need to discuss this with the functional leads and decide whether to implement the Hot Packages or LCPs. Usually, you implement Hot Packages when the HR module is not used and LCPs when the HR module is implemented. After you decide which one to implement, the process of applying these patches is the same.

1. **Decide on a Hot Package or LCP.**

   Set the system option for LCP if you decide to use it instead of Hot Packages.

2. **Download the files.**

3. **Apply the update with the SAP Patch Manager ("SPAM").**

4. **Apply the Hot Packages or LCP in sequential order.**

Apply your Hot Package to your test system before you apply it to your production system. Hey, if you're going to mess things up, mess up the test system.

HR Legal Change Patches are available only for maintenance levels as of 3.1H.

If you choose to apply LCP you need to set some flags in the system to set LCP as system default. Here are the steps to set those flags:

1. **Log into the customizing client in your system that allows changes.**

2. **Choose Tools⇨Business Engineering⇨Customizing.**

   You can also enter **SPRO** in the command field.

3. **Press Enter.**

   This step bypasses the initial window, First Customizing Steps.

4. **Choose Basic Functions⇨End of System Inst.**

   Follow this menu path to set LCP as system default.

5. **Choose Define Use of Component-Specific Patch Type.**

6. **Click Execute.**

7. **Click the two check buttons for LCP and then click Save.**

You have now set LCP as your default. When you download, you'll get the full LCP, with its Human Resource fixes in addition to the basic Hot Package.

Getting the repair files

To apply any of these patches, you first need to obtain them from SAP using one of the following methods:

- ✔ Download it from SAPnet.
- ✔ Extract it off disk.
- ✔ Request it from OSS.

Some files are very large. The best way to get these files is via SAPnet or the CD. Unfortunately, SAPnet is usually slower to post patches than OSS.

Downloading from SAPnet

Downloading from the Internet is often convenient. Follow these steps:

1. **Use your Internet browser to access the SAPnet site at** `https://www001.sap-ag.de`.

   You need your OSS logon name and password to get into the site.

2. **From the SAPnet home page, go to Index and follow the link to Hot Packages.**

3. **Select your version and download the patch.**

After you've downloaded the Hot Package, you have to get it ready to upload. You have to unpack (decompress) the file. Follow these steps:

1. **Log on to the SAP server as** `<sid>adm`.

2. **Go to the** `trans` **directory.**
   - `\USR\SAP\TRANS` (NT)
   - `/USR\SAP\TRANS` (UNIX)

3. **Unpack the file.**

   These commands extract the compressed CAR file into the appropriate directories. The exact form of the command depends on the operating system:
   - `CAR -xvf tmp/<ARCHIV_NAME>.CAR -V` (UNIX)
   - `CAR -xvf TMP\<ARCHIV_NAME>.CAR` (NT)

In UNIX systems, set the appropriate permissions to 775 and `owner:group` as `<sid>adm:sapsys`.

After you have your long-awaited patches, you can upload them to SAP. Here's what you do:

1. **Log into client 000.**

2. **Choose Tools⇨ABAP/4 Workbench⇨ABAP/4 Editor (button).**

   You can enter **SE38** in the command field if you prefer.

3. **Enter** RSEPSUPL **in the program field.**

4. **Click Execute.**

   This uploads the files from the operating system into R/3.

Uploading doesn't apply the patches; it just makes them available to R/3.

Downloading from CD

CDs save you the delays and intermittent access of working over an Internet connection.

1. **Access the CD for Hot Package and LCP.**

2. **From the CD directory for your system, copy the directory onto your server.**
   - `/USR/SAP/TRANS/TMP` (UNIX)
   - `\USR/SAP/TRANS/TMP` (NT)

3. **Unpack the file.**

   The exact form of the command depends on the operating system:
   - `CAR -xvf tmp/<ARCHIV_NAME>.CAR -V` (UNIX)
   - `CAR -xvf TMP\<ARCHIV_NAME>.CAR` (NT)

4. **Enter** RSEPSUPL **in the program field.**

5. **Click Execute.**

   This uploads the files from the operating system into R/3.

SAP periodically distributes updated CDs with the current patch set.

Downloading from OSS

Among OSS's many talents is that it allows you to download your patches directly from OSS itself. Here's what to do:

1. **Log on to OSS via the command field code OSS1.**
2. **Enter your user ID and password.**
3. **Click the button Services.**
4. **Click SAP Patch Service.**
5. **Choose the patch.**

    Select either Hot Packages or LCPs.

Now you're ready to actually request the patch. Follow these steps:

1. **Expand the tree view until you locate your SAP release.**
2. **Highlight the patch you want.**
3. **Click the Request Patch button.**
4. **Enter the SID for the installation you are requesting.**
5. **Click Continue.**

    You've requested the patch.

Now you can follow these steps to download the patch from your SAPGUI.

1. **With the same user logged on as before in client 000, go to transaction code SPAM and click Download.**
2. **Select the requested Hot Package and download it.**

The download may take some time, because the patch is being transferred from SAP to your server via the OSS connection. Enjoy the wait, because a useful patch is on its way.

Getting the most recent SPAM update in place

When you have the Hot Package available on SAP, you can use the SAP Patch Manager (quaintly know as SPAM) to apply the update. SAP recommends that you apply the most current SPAM update. A SPAM update is the tool to apply Hot Packages and LCPs.

Follow these steps:

1. **Log into client 000 with a user other than** SAP*.

   Ensure that this user has SAP* and SAP_NEW profiles.

   Make sure you have scheduled the job RDDIMPDP in client 000 by running the program RDDNEWPP. RDDNEWPP schedules the job RDDIMPDP to run periodically.

2. **Choose Tools⇨ABAP/4Workbench⇨Utilities⇨Maintenance⇨Patches.**

   This menu path accesses the SAP Patch Manager. You can also get to this screen by entering SPAM in the command field.

If you start with a new system, you need to first apply the SPAM update. Then you would follow the menu path Patch⇨Apply⇨SPAM Update. This process may take some time. After the process is complete, you are ready to apply the Hot Packages or LCPs.

Make sure that no other tp procedures are running. The tp program (for transports — copies between systems) is used to export and import change requests. Only one request can be processed at a time. A good way to avoid this problem is to communicate with the other Basis team members. Patches are usually applied during off-peak hours.

Now that the SPAM update is applied, you can apply the Hot Packages or LCPs to SAP itself. (Apply one or the other, not both.)

Applying the Hot Package (or LCP)

After all your preparations, you can now get the satisfaction of actually fixing your code with the patches. Here's what to do:

1. **Log on to client 000.**

2. **Choose Tools⇨ABAP/4Workbench⇨Utilities⇨Maintenance⇨Patches.**

   This shows the screen for applying the patches to SAP. You can also get to this screen by entering **SPAM** in the command field.

3. **From the drop-down menu, select the patch you want to apply.**

   Apply patches in sequence (1, 2, 3).

4. **After you select the patch, click Apply.**

   If you are in version 3.1H or greater, you have the added functionality of applying multiple patches from a *queue*. Prior to 3.1 H, you applied Hot Packages singularly in consecutive order.

   In versions 3.1H and 3.1I, you may get the message that there are no patches in the patch queue when you select the drop-down icon. The problem is with the patch queue. Fix the problem by executing the program RSSPAM11. To execute the program, choose Tools⇨ABAP/4Workbench⇨ABAP/4 Editor, or enter **SE38** in the command field. This program inserts the patches in the SPAM queue. That ought to take care of the problem.

5. **Confirm the information box that appears.**

   The default scenario is S (standard implementation of the patch). Change the setting by choosing Extras⇨Setting. Depending on the size of the file, this process may take some time.

When SAP is executing the patch, things happen automatically. Like this:

1. PROLOGUE: Checks to be sure you are authorized to apply patches.

2. CHECK_REQUIREMENTS: Checks the requirements for applying the patches.

3. DISASSEMBLE: Unpacks the files and places them into specific transport directories.

4. ADD_TO_BUFFER: Places the patch queue in your system's transport buffer.

5. TEST_IMPORT: Checks for objects in a task that is not released.

6. IMPORT_OBJECT_LIST: Object lists for the patches are imported into the system.

7. OBJECTS_LOCKED_?: Checks for objects in change requests that have not been released.

8. SCHEDULE_RDDIMPDP: Program RDDIMPDP is scheduled.

9. GENERATE_BACKUP: Backs up the objects that will be overwritten.

10. RUN_SPAU_?: Asks you to make any modification.

11. ADDON_CONFLICTS_?: Checks for conflicts between patch objects and the installed add-ons.

12. SPDD_SPAU_CHECK: Checks for necessary adjustments.

13. DDIC_IMPORT: Imports the ABAP/4 Dictionary objects.

14. DELETE_FROM_BUFFER: Deletes the buffer if the patch was applied with scenario "T."

15. AUTO_MOD_SPDD: Checks whether ABAP/4 objects can be adjusted automatically.

16. RUN_SPDD_?: Asks you to adjust your ABAP/4 objects.

17. IMPORT_PROPER: Imports ABAP/4 objects and table.

18. AUTO_MOD_SPAU: Checks for any changes that can be adjusted automatically.

19. RUN_SPAU_?: Asks whether you want to make any modification.

20. EPILOGUE: Confirms patches were implemented properly.

Checking that patching went well

After the patch is applied, check the logs. Here's how:

1. **Click Log.**

   The log file appears.

2. **If the logs look right, click Confirm.**

Fixing Source Code by Hand

Hot Packages do come out periodically to fix the problems with a specific R/3 release. However, because Hot Packages are a bundle of fixes, some time may elapse as the bundle accumulates. During the interim, SAP may recommend changes to repository objects using the somewhat innocent-sounding "OSS Note fix."

✔ A *note fix* means you have to read a text note and then put in the change by hand. You actually go into the most intimate parts of the system and change things.

✔ A *repository object* is an object the ABAP/4 Development Workbench manages.

These fixes come from SAP in the form of a OSS Note. The process is usually:

1. Identify a problem.

2. Find an OSS Note fix.

3. Apply the OSS Note fix.

Always make a copy of the original object before you start any changes. You can return it to the way it was.

Follow the notes carefully when applying the changes. The OSS Note gives you the object name to repair. Then follow these steps:

1. **Choose Tools⇨ABAP/4Workbench⇨ABAP/4 Editor.**

   You can enter **SE38** in the command field instead.

2. **Enter the object name in the program field.**

3. **Click the Source Code button and then click Display to view the source code.**

4. **Find the appropriate line to edit.**

5. **Verify that a repair is necessary.**

   Hey, maybe it's already done.

6. **If something needs fixing, click Change.**

   The system requests your developer's key.

Before you can make a change, you have to get a developer's key (a code that identifies you as a developer). Here's how to get that precious key:

1. **In OSS, click Registration and then Register Developer.**

2. **Enter your SAP username.**

3. **Select SAP object.**

4. **Enter the appropriate information from the ABAP/4 editor screen.**

5. **Click Register.**

6. **Enter the registration number in the ABAP/4 screen.**

   • You are a registered developer.

   • The repaired object is registered.

Here are some helpful techniques in applying source code changes.

✔ Create a comment at the beginning of the source code to record what is applied, when, and by whom.

  The * (asterisk) in the first position of a line denotes a comment in ABAP/4.

✔ Create a comment where the actual change takes place.

✔ Don't delete old lines, just comment them out.

Fixing Executables: Kernel Patches

An SAP kernel is a collection of its executable programs, also know as *binaries* (you know, as in *binary system,* the ones all computers use). SAP periodically makes kernel patches. It is a good idea to keep current with these patches.

To find out the kernel level, log on to the operating system as `<sid>adm` and enter **disp+work -V.**

Here's how to implement the kernel patches:

1. **Copy the kernel patch from sapservX.**

2. **Unpack the kernel patch.**

3. **Stop the SAP system.**

4. **Make a backup of the** `/USR/SAP/<SID>/SYS/EXE/RUN.`

5. **Copy the unpacked files into the RUN directory.**

6. **Start SAP.**

You can try out the actual steps:

1. **Log into SAP's server.**

   SAP has servers for regions around the world

   - sapserv4 : United States (San Francisco)
   - sapserv5 : Japan (Tokyo)
   - sapserv6 : Australia (Sydney)
   - sapserv7 : Asia (Singapore)

2. **ftp into the server.**

   Enter **ftp** as the user and **ftp** as the password.

3. **Change to the kernel patch directory.**

   Use this format for the command: `cd /general/R3server/patches/<release>/<operating system>/<hardware platform>/<database>`

   To find the contents of a directory, enter the command `ls`.

   To move up one directory level, enter the command `cd`.

4. **Enter the command bin to transfer the files in binary mode.**

5. Download the files to your local server.

Use these commands to download the files you need (in the commands, substitute the kernel patch release you need for xx):

- get dw1_xx.CAR
- get dw2_xx.CAR

After you download the files, unpack them and then copy them into the executable directory. Follow these steps:

1. Create a temporary directory.

2. Unpack the files.

Use these commands to download the files you need (in the commands, substitute the kernel patch release you need for xx):

- CAR -xvf dw1_xx.CAR
- CAR -xvf dw2_xx.CAR

3. Make a backup copy of the binary directory /USR/SAP/<SI>/SYS/EXE/RUN.

In UNIX systems, there is a symbolic link to the /SAPMNT/<SID>/EXE directory. Ensure that you maintain permission and capture all recursive paths.

4. Stop SAP completely and then copy the uncompressed files from the temporary directory into the executable directory.

The new, improved versions of executable files replace the previous ones.

5. Restart SAP and check for problems.

Chapter 16

Dumpster Diving: Error Analysis

- -

In This Chapter

▶ Looking for problems in the R/3 system log

▶ Setting up centralized logging for multiple SAP instances

▶ Viewing a dump in detail with a dump analysis

- -

*F*or most people, garbage is something you just don't want to look at. People don't even want to be reminded that refuse exists. For the Basis Administrator, though, going through the "garbage" in the R/3 system log and dump areas is a daily responsibility. A Basis Administrator has to identify and analyze problems, and the R/3 system log and the dump areas contain system messages, warnings, and errors that can help. R/3 administrators have to investigate all problems and seek resolution, or the problems could just fester and lead to disaster.

In this chapter you find out about the wealth of "dirt" you can uncover in the system log and dump analysis, and you find out about central logging of errors.

Looking into the R/3 System Log

R/3 monitors system events and records messages, warnings, and problems in the system logs. R/3 writes logs for each R/3 instance though (depending on your platform), if you have distributed SAP, logging may be centralized. (That is, centralized logging isn't available on NT or AS/400 platforms.) Let's view the R/3 log.

Follow the menu path Tools⇨Administration⇨Monitoring⇨System Log or enter **SM21** in the command field. You go to the System Log screen, which for this example has the label "System Log: Local analysis of prdnda," shown in Figure 16-1.

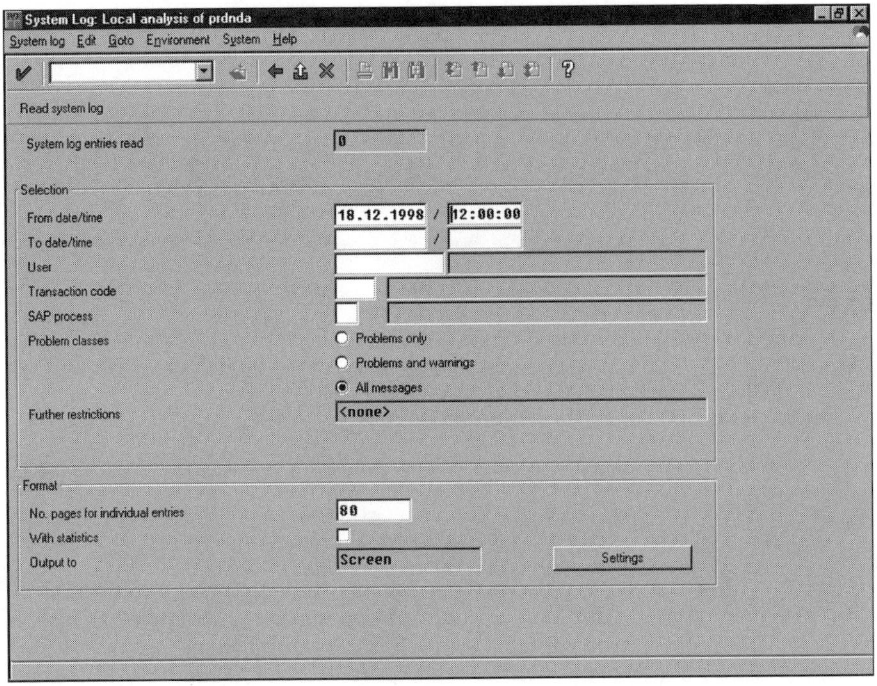

Figure 16-1:
Start here to
review the
system log.

The screen in Figure 16-1 is the main menu, from where you can view the system log. Check out the Selection view of the main screen. Table 16-1 summarizes the variables you use in the Selection view to filter your queries.

Table 16-1	Variables for Querying the System Log	
Variable	**Use**	**Explanation**
Date	Enter the "from" date and time.	Enter the full date format. If you want to see all messages for that day, leave the "time" field blank. You can also enter a "to" date, which enables you to limit your search with "from" and "to" dates.
User	Enter a username.	This is the logon name for SAP users.
Transaction Code	Enter a transaction code to search by.	

Variable	Use	Explanation
SAP Process	Enter a work process to search by.	Some of the accepted values are DP (dispatcher), VB (update), and MS (message server).
Problem Class	Click one of the options: Problems, Problems and Warnings, All Messages.	

Select the criteria for all messages for the current date and click the Read System Log button. By default, SAP sorts the results by time.

If you prefer to sort the system log by something other than time, go to menu path System Log⇨Sort. From the Sort menu, select one of the options: write sequence, time, message ID, problem class, development class, message type, instance, or program.

See Figure 16-2 for messages sorted by time.

The system log divides problems into five classes, summarized in Table 16-2.

Table 16-2	Error Classes in the System Log
Code	Function
K	System kernel messages
S	Status messages
T	Transaction messages
W	Warning messages
X	Other messages

Logging parameters for the system profile

You can add some parameters to the system profile to tailor the system log to your liking.

rslg/central/file	Central log filename, SLOGJ
rslg/central/old_file	Old central log filename, SLOGJO
rslg/local/file	Local log filename, SLOG<*System No.*>
rslg/max_diskspace/local	Length of local logfile
rslg/max_diskspace/central	Length of central logfile

To display detailed information on any line item, double-click on the item. See Figure 16-3 for an example of detailed information.

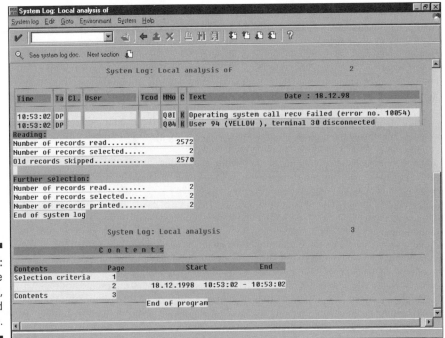

Figure 16-2:
Here's the system log, sorted by time.

```
System Log: Local analysis of                                           _ 8 X
System log  Edit  Goto  Environment  System  Help

 ✔ [              ] ◄  ← ⓐ ✕  ▤ ⋈ ⋈  ▯ ▯ ▯ ▯  ?

 See system log doc.   Next entry  ▢

 Details Page 2 Line 6 System Log: Local analysis of prdnda              1

 Time     Ta Cl. User       Tcod MNo C Text              Date : 18.12.98
 10:53:02 DP                     Q0I K Operating system call recv failed (error no. 10054)


 Details
 Recording at local and central time....................... 18.12.1998 10:53:02
 Task................    441 DP Dispatcher
 User................
 Client..............
 Terminal............
 Session............. 0
 Transaction code....
 Program name........
 Problem class....... K    SAP Basis problem
 Development class... STSK SM04,SM06,SMON

 Further details for this message type
 Module name......... ninti.c
 Line................ 0756
 Error text..........          recv10054

 No documentation for syslog message Q0 I message.

 Additional specifications for error number 10054
 ◄                                                                       ►
```

Figure 16-3:
You can see
detailed
information
on a
message.

The detailed view shows the specifics of the error or warning. Using all the information available, you can then investigate the cause of all errors.

You may also need to politely "discuss" problems (no hollering) with the user who generated these errors.

Checking Out Central Logging

You can configure R/3 to log centrally instead of on individual instances. Of course, you can only log centrally if you have at least two R/3 instances working in a distributed system. One instance gets the honor of being the central logging instance, and the other instances send the data to the central logging instance. To activate central logging, you need to set the logging parameters in the system profile, start the collector process in the central logging instance, and start the send work processes on the other instances.

You can check the system profile from the main system log screen. Follow the menu path to Environment⇨Display SAPPARAM.

Table 16-4 gives some examples of the profiles and their values.

Table 16-4	System Profile Settings for Central Logging
System Profile Settings	*Typical Values*
slg/collect_daemon/host	myhost
rslg/collect_daemon/listen_port	1200
rslg/collect_daemon/ talk_port	1300
rslg/send_daemon/listen_port	1400
rslg/send_daemon/ talk_port	1500

These values should be the same for all instances in the system. Set them in the DEFAULT.PFL system profile.

After you have set the profile parameter, you have to configure the processing for collecting and sending messages. The central logging instance does the collecting, so you configure it accordingly. Edit the startup profile to start the collect process. The following code is an example of the process of collecting for a central SAP instance with SID=DEV and SYS NO=00 running on HP-UX.

```
#----------------------------------------
# start syslog collector daemon
#----------------------------------------
_CO = co.sapDEV_DVEBMGS00
Execute_03 = local ln -s -f $(DIR_EXECUTABLE)/rslgcoll $(_CO)
Start_Program_03 = local $(_CO) -F pf=$(DIR_PROFILE)/DEV_DVEB
MGS00_myhost
```

You also have to edit the startup profiles to start the process of sending messages to the central instance. Here is an example for an SAP instance with SID=DEV and SYS NO=00 running on HP-UX.

```
#----------------------------------------
#start syslog send daemon
#----------------------------------------
_SE = se.sapDEV_DVEBMGS00
Execute_04 = local ln -s -f $(DIR_EXECUTABLE)/rslgsend $(_SE)
Start_Program_04 = local $(_SE) -F pf=$(DIR_PROFILE)/DEV_DVEB
MGS00_myhost
```

Central logging is not available in NT. Set the parameter `rslg/ collect_daemon/host` to `NONE`.

Finding Severe Terminations in the Dump Analysis

The ABAP dump analysis gives you a list of all severe ABAP terminations. (A *termination* is a transaction ended by SAP.) The system produces a dump analysis of the problem, and the detailed log in the analysis gives you a pretty good idea why the program or report ended abruptly.

Follow the menu path Tool⟶Administration⟶Monitoring⟶Dump Analysis or enter **ST22** in the command field. Figure 16-4 shows the initial Dump Analysis screen — ABAP/4 Dump Analysis.

On the Dump Analysis screen, you see a quick overview of the number of dumps created Today or Yesterday. Choose the date you want to query and press F8 to display. To select older dumps, click the Selection button in the application toolbar and enter the date of the dump. If you have daily background maintenance jobs running, SAP deletes old dumps daily (if your configuration is set up to do that). The detailed list screen shows you a list of all dumps for that particular date.

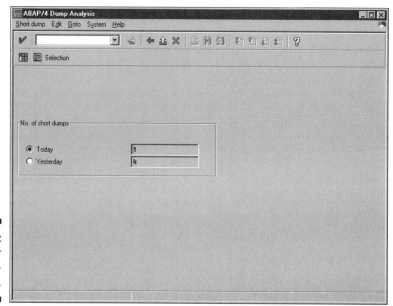

Figure 16-4:
Start your dump analy-sis here.

To obtain the specifics of a particular dump, double-click on the item. The information is divided into 19 sections. To see the overview, follow the menu path Goto➪Overview. Figure 16-5 shows the menu path to the overview.

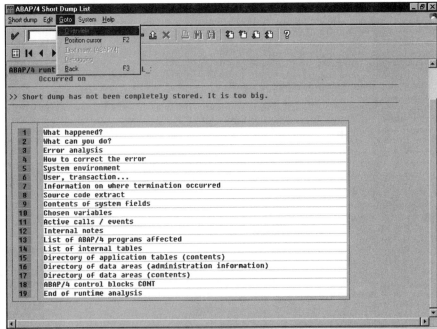

Figure 16-5:
You can see an overview for a particular dump.

To figure out what to do, take a close look at the message itself. Look at all the variables of the problem to help identify the problem. The "How to correct the error" section gives you some key words. Use these words to run searches on OSS Notes. Your problem may be an issue already identified by SAP. Be thorough in your analysis. Some other action items you might try are

  ✔ Inspect the system log

  ✔ Check the program in the ABAP editor

  ✔ Debug the program

  ✔ Perform an OSS Notes search on the problem

  ✔ Open the OSS message with SAP

  ✔ Talk to the end user

If you encounter an error in the program, contact SAP for a resolution. Don't try to correct any source code on your own. Your hasty coding could invalidate your support contract with SAP. When you do make changes, only make the ones SAP has authorized.

Of course, finding the problem isn't necessarily an end. It may be a beginning as you try to find a solution to the problem. Sometimes, it's hard to know where to start. These are the most likely reasons for dumps:

- ✔ An error in an ABAP program
- ✔ A bad configuration
- ✔ Missing configuration values
- ✔ Interface problems
- ✔ Database problems
- ✔ Operating system problems

Chapter 17

What Did Other People Do?

SAP Help, discussed in Chapter 7, is great if you're looking for a leisurely read, want some background information, don't know how to find a quick transaction code, or face any number of other trifling matters.

What do you do, though, for the strong stuff — industrial-strength problems that are the real ones users come to the R/3 Administrator about? SAP Help alone, frankly, just isn't going to be varied enough, in-depth enough, or targeted enough on the recent recurring problems of real users to get the job done. Besides, SAP Help can't talk back the way an actual SAP developer can.

For the hard-core problems and real-world needs, SAP does have a solution, though — OSS.

OSS, Online Service System, lets you search an extensive database of problems and resolutions. You can also join right in on the fun and register problems of your own. And you can get responses back from SAP developers. That's pretty interactive and hot.

In this chapter, you find out how to log a problem with SAP, how to trade mail with helpful SAP developers, and how to do a search through the OSS database.

Of course, as administrator, you don't just play with OSS. You help others play with it. Here you find out how to set up other users to take advantage of OSS, see how to set up more powerful users (developers), and see how to use the OSS connection to monitor what your people are doing.

Reading and Searching OSS Messages

The main thing you do with OSS is log in, search for notes on problems, and read the problems. The next sections tell you how to log in, register a problem, read and reply to a message, and do an OSS search.

Logging on to OSS

Logging into OSS is like logging into a remote SAP site. There are two ways to get to OSS:

- ✔ Online (through SAP)
- ✔ Offline (direct login)

Get to the offline login by selecting the Public logon selection. If you are online, go to menu path System⇨Services⇨SAP Service⇨Logon to the OSS.

SAP should have received an initial logon ID and password for your installation. When you have that, you can administer logon and ID yourself. Now you can begin using OSS.

Logging a problem with SAP

The preferred method of delivering a problem to SAP is via OSS. The following steps describe the procedures in creating and sending a message to SAP.

1. **Enter transaction code** BIBO **via the command field.**

   This step logs you onto OSS.

2. **Click Create.**

   Fill out each message section completely. The more detailed the information, the better SAP is able to help you.

3. **Enter your System type.**

4. **Enter your SAP R/3 release.**

5. **Choose the component associated with the problem.**

6. **Enter the problem priority.**

   Only system-down scenarios can be classified as Very High. All other calls need to be rated High, Medium, or Low. (SAP will downgrade a call if it does not agree with your classification.) In the Short Text area, enter a brief description of the problem. In the lines below, enter as much detail as possible.

7. **After you finish, click Save and then answer Yes to the Send message.**

    You have now logged a problem with OSS. You'll get a reply from SAP.

Reading and replying to an OSS message

SAP responds to OSS messages by phone or OSS.

Keep current with your OSS messages from SAP.

> ✔ Look for any open items in your mailboxes. If SAP needs more information, it sends you mail into the Inquiry from SAP folder.
>
> ✔ When SAP believes it has a solution for your problem, it may send back a reply in the Solution Provided folder.

To look at a message, follow these steps:

1. **Go into the appropriate folder.**

2. **Click on the folder to see the messages available in the folder.**

3. **Double-click the line item you want to check.**

    You see a complete history of that item. To see the details of the current problem, click the Long Text button.

Here's how to reply to the message:

1. **Click Display⇨Change.**

    You can then update and change the message. You may have to wait a little while before SAP allows you to update that particular item.

2. **Click Supplementary info.**

3. **Enter any additional information and then click the left green arrow.**

4. **Click Send to SAP.**

    Your response is automatically routed to SAP. When you return to the main screen, the Sent to SAP folder has an additional entry. SAP will contact you.

You can still send additional information even if you have sent the message to SAP. Here's how:

1. **Select the relevant message in the Sent to SAP folder.**

2. **Click Info to SAP.**

3. **Type your comments.**

4. **Click Send Info.**

   You then send any additional comments to SAP.

When a problem is completely resolved, click the button labeled Confirm to close out that particular problem.

Doing an OSS search

Searching is probably the most helpful OSS capability. It allows you to search the OSS database on particular issues and problems. Here's how to start the search.

1. **From the main screen, click Gen. Functions.**

2. **Click Find to start the search.**

   Start your search from broad to specific. If a particular query gives you hundreds of hits, narrow your search by SAP version, database, and so on.

All OSS Notes follow a standard format. The top portion is header information. The main text describes the issue and possible solutions. The end of the OSS Note usually gives other related OSS Note numbers.

If you want to download the text, right-click on the text. Select Download. Enter a location on your desktop to store the text. Print the text from your downloaded version. Printing directly from OSS may not be possible. OSS Notes are constantly updated using the same note number. Always get the latest Note when referring back to a particular issue.

Standard OSS Housekeeping

As administrator, you don't just get the pleasure of reading confusing solutions to perplexing problems. You have the honor of helping others do the same thing. You get to

- ✓ Establish user accounts so people can work directly with OSS.
- ✓ Register developers with SAP so they can modify SAP objects (actual program code).
- ✓ Maintain the gateway that SAP uses to access your systems.

The following sections explain each of these responsibilities.

Working with OSS users

"Hey, I want my own OSS account," people insist. Here's how to set them up.

Adding a new user

The Basis team is usually responsible for requesting new OSS user accounts.

1. **From the main screen, click Administration.**
2. **Click the User Administration button to request new OSS user accounts from SAP.**
3. **Click the Request User button to start.**
4. **Enter all required information in the request form.**

    Required fields have a "?" in the field.

Entering information isn't enough. You have to authorize your user as well. Here's how:

1. **After you enter the required data, select Authorization.**

    The screen allows you to choose the authorization for this new user.

2. **To create a new authorization, click Create or press F5.**
3. **Select an authorization you want to give to this user.**

    Select authorizations by double-clicking the item. SAP adds the selected authorization to the user.

    Table 17-1 summarizes the authorizations.

4. **Click the left green arrow.**

    This brings you back to the User request form.

Table 17-1	Authorizations for OSS Users
Authorization	*Description*
Display training schedule	See training schedule
Maintain user data	User administration
Open Service Connection	Open OSS connection to SAP
SAP message: Confirm SAP message	Mail: close messages
SAP message: Create SAP message	Mail: create messages
SAP message: Reopen SAP message	Mail: reopen closed messages
SAP message: Send to SAP	Mail: send to SAP

(continued)

Table 17-1 *(continued)*

Authorization	Description
Search for Notes	Search
Use Patchservice	Request patches
Use license key function	Get license keys from SAP
Use registration (SSCR, Customer namespaces)	Register developers and objects

Another way to add authorization is to copy from an existing user. Here's what to do:

1. **Choose User Authorizations➪Copy Reference.**

2. **Double-click the reference user.**

   SAP adds all of the reference's authorizations to your new user.

Maintaining a user

Users have a distracting habit of changing things, such as their addresses. If you don't control them enough, they'll even change their names. Here's how to update that information for an OSS user:

1. **From the main screen for user administration, click List of Requested OSS Users.**

   You see a list of users that SAP created. The names stay on this list until the user logs in. You can also see the status in the status column. You can also change any information entered in the initial data sheet.

2. **From the Main User Maintenance screen, click Address Management.**

3. **Double-click the username.**

4. **Make any changes and then save.**

You can also alter authorizations. Here's how:

1. **From the Main User Administration screen, click User Administration.**

2. **Click the username and then click Change.**

   This brings you to the same authorization screen used to create the user.

3. **Add or delete any authorizations.**

Maintaining users and their authorizations gets to be pretty routine. You can also grant privileges to developers, though, and that's a bigger responsibility because of all that developers can do to a system.

Registering developers and their objects

Objects are SAP code. When it comes to modifying objects, SAP has an extensive auditing mechanism. Before a user can create, change, or delete an object, that user must be registered as a developer with SAP. Also, you have to use a special key to modify any repository objects.

Register a developer

Everybody wants power, which means that everybody wants to be a developer. You get to decide who qualifies, and you can provide developer privileges. Here's how:

1. **From the main OSS screen, click Registration.**

2. **Select Register Developer.**

3. **Enter the user name in the blank field and then click Register.**

    The result is a long number: the user's developer's key.

The developer has to use that key to do any sort of development.

Register an object

Just as a developer needs a key, SAP objects also need keys. Here's how to create them:

1. **From the Registration screen, click Register Objects.**

2. **Enter all information and then click Register.**

    SAP generates a number — the object's registration number.

SAP put this function in place to ensure the proper tracking of all development in the customer's system. Use this generated number to do development on SAP objects.

SAP highly discourages any modification of SAP-owned objects. When doing any development, be extremely cognizant of your actions (don't screw up).

Opening the service connection

SAP utilizes the OSS connection to allow access to the customer's systems and uses the connection to probe any unusual problems and for Early Watch services. The Basis team usually monitors and maintains this gateway.

Here's how to open it:

1. **From the main OSS screen, click Service.**

2. **Click Service Connection.**

If you have not used the Service connection before, you need to do some initial setup. Follow these steps:

1. **Click Define System and then fill out all information about your installation.**

2. **After entering the initial information, click Choose System.**

3. **Expand Connections.**

4. **Place the cursor on R/3 Support. If you are opening the gateway for the first time, click the Create/Open button. If you want to change existing options, click the Change button.**

5. **Fill in all information and enter the amount of time you want the gateway to be open.**

6. **Click Save.**

   The display shows the amount of time the gateway was opened. You can close the connection by clicking the Close Connection button. Remember to close the gateway after use.

Getting connected to OSS

You have probably set up an OSS connection during installation, but maybe not. You have to set up the connection with SAP. You need

✔ A physical connection from your site to OSS (for example, an ISDN line)

✔ Official IP addresses, usually assigned by SAP

✔ Dual network interface cards (NIC) on the host server

✔ A network router (for example, an ISDN router)

✔ SAProuter application on your host

The physical connection

The first thing to figure out is your physical connection to OSS. ISDN and Frame Relay are pretty cool. If you don't know about them, then a little note in a *...For Dummies* book probably isn't the place to find out. Talk with SAP and your network administrator about it.

Official IP addresses

If you have the physical connections, you should request official IP addresses from SAP. SAP uses the direct approach of sending them directly to assure unique IP addresses to each customer site. SAP also nicely sends you a list of OSS Notes referring to OSS installation. (You can read OSS Notes even as you are setting up OSS.)

Network interface cards

After you get the IP addresses, you have to configure your hardware to use them. Specifically, you need to assign IP addresses to the NIC and the router. Often, you also need to update your routing tables to allow the proper flow of network traffic.

Configuring OSS for SAProuter

Before you continue, you should set the appropriate settings within SAP. Log in with a superuser account and enter **OSS1** in the command field. If you prefer, follow the menu path System⇨Services⇨Sap Service. Enter Parameter⇨Technical settings to configure your OSS settings.

Select Change to configure the settings. In the SAProuter field, enter the IP address and the hostname of the machine running SAProuter. Also select the appropriate SAP server by choosing the menu path SAProuter at SAP⇨City. Save your changes. After the other pieces get configured, you have access to OSS from within SAP.

Configuring SAProuter

The next step is to configure SAProuter, a service that has to run on both ends of an OSS connection. In other words, SAP has a SAProuter on its end and you have SAProuter on your end. SAProuter is software that permits and denies access to OSS. (By the way, this is by no means a true firewall, but it's okay.)

You can look at the syntax of SAProuter.

The SAProuter program is located in drive: \USR\SAP\SID\SYS\EXE\RUN on NT machines and /USR/SAP/SID/SYS/EXE/RUN on UNIX machines. SAProuter also needs a control table (saprouttab) for it to run. The table saprouttab has five columns, like the following example.

```
# This is saprouttab table
# Example
# P/D Source Host  Dest.Host Dest.Service Password
   P  172.30.3.*       *        *
   D  172.30.2.*       *        *
```

Saprouttab is a permissions table that contains routing information.

- P permits connections to be built.
- D denies connections.
- Read-only lines begin with a #.
- The default service port is 3299.
- Passwords are optional. If entered, the passwords are required for routing and connection.

SAProuter must be started to connect to OSS. Log in as <SID>ADM and start SAProuter. In UNIX, run the following command:

```
>saprouter -r -R /absolute location of saprouttab/saproutatb &
```

It is also a good idea to include the SAProuter command in the startup script for the operating system. Look at the following examples.

UNIX

Create the script in /SBIN/RC3.D as user root. This starts SAProuter at boot time.

```
#############################################################
##    /sbin/rc3.d/S920saprouter
##    Start SAProuter software for OSS Connection
            Authentication
#############################################################
su - <sid>adm -c /sapmnt/<SID>/exe/saprouter -r -R
/sapmnt/<SID>/exe/saprouttab
```

Create the script in /SBIN/RC3.D as user root. This stops SAProuter at system shutdown.

```
#############################################################
##    /sbin/rc3.d/S920saprouter
##    Stop SAProuter software for OSS Connection Authentication
#############################################################
su - <sid>adm -c /sapmnt/<SID>/exe/saprouter -s
```

Windows NT

Start by adding SAProuter as a service started during system startup. Login as <SID>ADM and execute the following command from the DOS prompt. After the command is executed successfully, a service is created. Set the service to start automatic and logon as SAPServiceSID, the SAP service user account.

```
>ntscmgr install SAProuter -b
drive:\usr\sap\<SID>\SYS\exe\run\saprouter.exe -p "service-r
-R drive:\usr\sap\<SID>\SYS\exe\run\saprouttab"
```

Log in as <SID>ADM and access SAProuter help. The following shows the
results from SAProuter-Help.

```
start router : saprouter -r
stop router  : saprouter -s
soft shutdown: saprouter -p
router info  : saprouter -l (-L)
new routtab  : saprouter -n
toggle trace : saprouter -t
cancel route : saprouter -c id
dump buffers : saprouter -d
flush    "   : saprouter -f
start router with third-party library: saprouter -a library
additional options
-R routtab : name of route-permission-file    (default
          ./saprouttab)
-G logfile   : name of log file               (default no log-
          ging)
-T tracefile : name of trace file             (default
          dev_rout)
-V tracelev  : trace level to run with        (default 1)
-H hostname  : of running saprouter           (default local-
          host)
-S service   : service-name / number          (default 3299)
-P infopass  : password for info requests
-K [myname]  : activate SNC; if given, use 'myname' as own
          sec-id
-A initstring: initialization options for third-party library
          expert options-B bufsize   : max. queuelen per
          client        (default 500000 bytes)
-Q queuesize : max. total size for all queues (default
          20000000 bytes)
-W waittime  : timeout for blocking net-calls (default 5000
          millisec)
-M min.max   : portrange for outgoing connects, like -M 1.1023

# this is a sample routtab : ————————————
D    host1               host2      serviceX
D    host3
P    *                   *          serviceX
P    155.56.*.*          155.56
```

(continued)

(continued)

```
P     155.57.1011xxxx.*
P     host4           host5      *           xxx
P     host6           localhost  3299
P     host7           host8      telnet
S     host9
PO,*  host10
KP    sncname1                   *           *
KS    *               host11     *
KT    sncname3        host11     *

# deny routes from host1 to host2 serviceX
# deny all routes from host3
# permit routes from anywhere to any host using serviceX
# permit all routes from/to addresses matching 155.56
# permit ... with 3rd byte matching 1011xxxx
# permit routes from host4 to host5 if password xxx supplied
# permit information requests from host6
# permit native-protocol-routes to non-SAP-server telnet
# permit ... excluding native-protocol-routes (SAP-servers
         only)
# permit ... if number of preceding/succeeding hops
         (saprouters) <= 0/*
# permit SNC-connection with partnerid = 'sncname1' to any
         host
# permit all SAP-SAP SNC-connections to host11
# deny all SNC-connections  with partnerid = 'sncname "abc'
# open connects to host11 with SNC enabled and partnerid =
         'sncname3'

# first match [host/sncname host service] is used
# permission is denied if no entry matches
# service wildcard (*) does not apply to native-protocolroutes
```

The TCP/IP utility PING is a great way to see whether you can hit your target from your location. If that is successful, that means that packets are being sent and received at the remote location.

Using an offline OSS connection

After completing the installation, you should have access to OSS. Access is achieved two ways: Online from SAP or offline. Complete the following steps to gain access to SAP offline.

If you are using Windows 95/98 or Windows NT, create two files and place them in C:\WINDOWS (Windows 95/98) or C:\WINNT (Windows NT).

```
File one: sapmsg.ini
[Message Server]
001=oss001.wdf.sap-ag.de
File two: saproute.ini
[Router]
sapserv4=/H/my_ip_address/H/204.79.199.2/H/
```

Start SAPlogin.exe from your desktop. From here, select the option for the SAP Router For field. Click Generate from list. At this point the SAPlogon is communicating to SAP and getting information. You should see the message "Retrieving." A few seconds later the open area is populated with SAP's login groups, Public and Japanese.

Select the Public icon and then the Add button. This process adds Public as one of the logon options to the main logon screen. When you login with public, you are logging on offline from SAP. This allows you to continue using OSS even without having SAP online.

Part VI

The Part of Tens

The 5th Wave   **By Rich Tennant**

5th Wave Power Tip: To increase application speed, punch the Command Key over and over and over as rapidly as possible. The computer will sense your impatience and move your data along quicker than if you just sat and waited. Hint: This also works on elevator buttons and crosswalk signals.

In this part . . .

Lists can be lifesavers, especially for overworked admin-
strators overwhelmed with responsibilities. Here you
find the most useful, most practical lists we can think of —
grief-saving housekeeping tasks, ways to safeguard security,
and Oracle error codes you probably want to have at your
fingertips.

Chapter 18

Ten Daily Jobs

Assume. You've heard that famous word, and you've probably heard the famous saying about it — "assume makes a fool out of u and me." (Or something like that.) People assume that all kinds of things have happened successfully as they use SAP. The only problem is that those things haven't always happened. And when they haven't — well, the hue and cry can reach the farthest walls of the corporation and beyond.

Housekeeping is never the most glamorous job in any establishment. In the case of SAP, though, it just may be the most valuable job. And as administrator, your job is to go around backing up everybody and making sure that what they think happened has really happened. Most of the time, they're right — what they wanted to happen did happen. Some of the time, though, what they thought happened didn't.

If you do your job right, you correct problems quickly, and people hardly know you exist. They're right to assume that everything went well. Ignore the ten housekeeping tasks in this chapter, though, and you end up with a mess on your hands — guaranteed.

So without further ado, here is a list of ten places where you can check on things that may or may not have happened as planned.

SM21 System Log: Analyze and Correct All Warnings and Error Messages

If SAP took it upon itself to terminate programs or transactions, you can find out about those actions in the system log, which you access through transaction code SM21. The idea of terminating programs or transactions may sound harmless enough in its abstract form, but a terminated program or transaction can have far-reaching effects. Maybe, for example, somebody is putting together a critical budget for a big client, with the entire future of the account at state, when a key transaction misfires. And then the results are wrong, confusing, and incomplete; the person who needs those results is stressed out; and suddenly the whole situation snowballs out of control.

But you can avert all those drastic results with a little simple monitoring and some corrective action. So check this system log every day. Figure 18-1 shows the screen where you check out the system log.

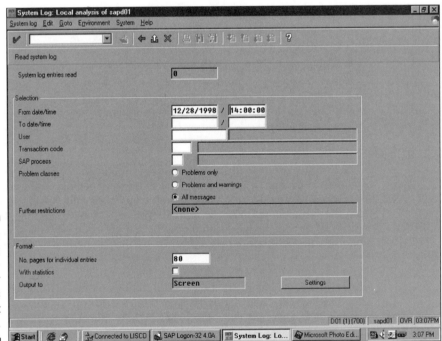

Figure 18-1:
Check here for programs or transactions that got terminated.

SM13 Update Records: Check and Analyze All Aborted Updates

If people think that they have updated their files, but actually they haven't — well, nobody likes that to happen. Suppose, for example, that your company closes a huge account, deposits $1,000,000 into the database of the company's assets, and then writes a check against it. But the check doesn't get issued because somebody else thinks the $1,000,000 doesn't exist, and then one thing leads to another, with people pointing fingers at each other and getting mad.

A file that doesn't get updated is a Very Bad Thing, especially in a production system. It's a situation that fosters confusion, hostility, purchases of Valium, firings, and general malaise. You can avert all that ugliness by using transaction code SM13 to find out whether any updates have been aborted and then following up to correct any that do occur. (If no updates have been aborted, you and everyone else can have peace of mind.)

SM50 Process Overview: Analyze and Investigate Long-Running and Terminated Work Processes

Work processes, as explained in Chapter 12 and elsewhere, are the workhorses of your system. If your people are displaying dialog boxes or doing background processes or printing, they're creating work processes. Work processes that go on too long are hogging system time — and may have something wrong with them. Processes that get terminated prematurely may have something wrong, too. In the Process Overview screen, accessed through transaction code SM50, you can tell at a glance which work processes are running and which have errors. Just a quick look on your part can help you prevent a great deal of consternation on somebody else's part. You should check the work processes periodically during the day.

SP01 Spool Request Overview: Analyze and Resolve All Warnings and Errors

You usually spool stuff when you want to print it, as we explain in Chapter 8. Other processes get spooled, too. The thing is, people sometimes drop their guard a bit when something is spooled, assuming that their documents are going to get printed or faxed or whatever. If something goes wrong in that spooling process, however, they may not know about it. By checking the Spool Request Overview screen (enter transaction code SP01 to get there) for warnings and errors, you can really help people.

ST03 Workload Analysis: Analyze and Perform Any Necessary Adjustments

As Chapter 12 of this book explains, you analyze workload to see how R3 itself is performing. You can also check out the database system and the database server. Make sure that dialog or update work processes are tuned properly, and if they aren't, tune them. People want to know that their system is running nicely, and they notice when it isn't. You can use the workload analysis to keep things running smoothly for them. Just enter transaction code ST03 to begin your workload analysis.

ST02 Buffer Analysis: Analyze Hit Ratios and Perform Any Necessary Adjustments

If the hit ratios in buffers (little storage areas in memory) begin to slip, that's just as bad as when the hit ratio slips for a batter in baseball. Buffers have to get their hits. If they don't, you're the batting instructor, and you have to make adjustments and get those buffers hitting properly again.

Figure 18-2 shows the buffer analysis screen for one system. Chapter 12 in this book is also a good place to find out about buffers.

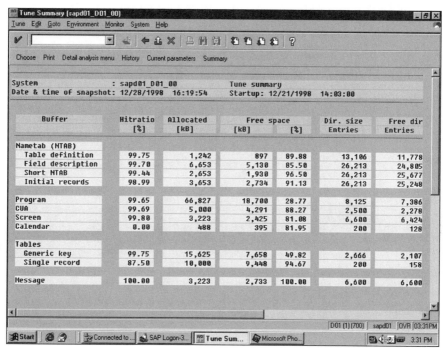

Figure 18-2:
Make sure
your hit
ratios are
okay.

OS06 OS Monitor: Analyze, Correct, and Resolve Any Issues

The operating system is the basis of everything else that's going on. A sick operating system is going to make databases and applications *look* pretty sick, even if they aren't. You can check out

- CPU utilization
- Memory
- Swap
- Disk response time

Figure 18-3 shows the OS Monitor screen. You can read about monitoring the operating system in Chapter 12.

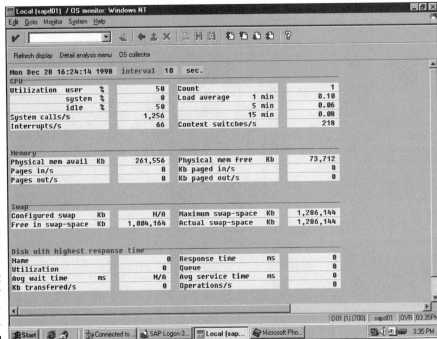

Figure 18-3:
You definitely want to monitor your operating system.

DB02 Storage Management: Monitor Database Growth and Make Any Modifications

Generally speaking, people don't use SAP for fun; they use it to get information — data. The data resides in databases, and your database consists of tables. Those tables can get oversized, or full, or become annoying in some other, unexpected way. You can help everybody a great deal if you monitor your databases and make sure that the indexes are working right.

Monitor OS and Database Error Log: Analyze Any Errors and Correct

You can also check the error logs for your operating system and database. (Checking the error logs is not the same as monitoring performance, listed earlier in this chapter.)

You can go straight to the logs for a quick listing of errors that day. When you find errors, check them out. Users are sometimes in denial about errors, refusing to accept that the error may be there. You can help make sure that those errors really aren't there, or at least not for long.

Verify Success of Nightly Backup: Check Logs of Tools Utilized

Murphy's Law applies to backups: The backup that you don't get is the one you need. Avoid consternation (and getting fired) in the future by checking your backups now.

Chapter 19

Ten Security Steps

*Y*ou may be a basically trusting person, and that's fine. You don't have to be paranoid and think that everyone is trying to break into your system and wreak havoc.

Oh, never mind. As an R/3 administrator, paranoia isn't an affliction at all. It's a healthy state of mind. You *should* go around thinking that everyone is trying to break into your system and maliciously perform all kinds of dangerous acts on it. Then when you're in the proper state of mind, you should do everything in your power to prevent said vandals (imaginary or not) from stealing information, deleting crucial data, changing privileges for naive and unsuspecting users, or otherwise messing things up.

You should protect security because it's just not worth the hassle that arises if security breaks down.

RUN Report RSUSR006 and Check for Locked Users

From a security standpoint, locked users are important. If you see certain users repeatedly locking themselves out of the system, they may be attempting to break in. (Or they may just be absent-minded, which is very possible.) Talking to these misguided souls to see what is wrong often makes the most sense. Perhaps they need more access than they currently have, or perhaps they don't know where they can access the information that they are trying to get.

- ✔ SAP* is a special user that is always available on new clients.
- ✔ DDIC is the SAP data dictionary user.

A locked DDIC user means that certain SAP functions will not run properly — including the transport process.

Follow these steps to check for locked users:

1. **From the main screen, go to the ABAP Editor by entering transaction code** SE38.
2. **Enter the report name** RSUSR006 **and execute.**

Change the Standard SAP* Password in Client 000, 001, and 066

As we explain in Chapter 11, SAP R/3 comes with three clients: 000, 001, and 066.

In a newly created client, the password is PASS. Because PASS is a *documented* password (anybody can find it, making it worth little as a password), you have to change it for security reasons. Follow these steps to change the documented password:

1. **Log in as** SAP*.
2. **Before pressing Enter, click the New Password button on the logon screen.**
3. **Enter the new password.**

Change the Standard DDIC Password in Client 000, 001, and 066

Like SAP*, the DDIC password is also well documented and therefore available to resourceful people whose intentions may not be favorable. You should change the standard DDIC password, using the same procedures as for changing the password for SAP* in the preceding section of this chapter.

Inactivate User SAP*

Because SAP* is the known superuser account, you need to secure the logon name. Protecting SAP* against unwanted users involves editing the SAP* user profile and setting a system profile parameter.

To make this work, follow these procedures:

1. **Log on to all clients and remove all profiles from SAP*.**

2. **Ensure that user SAP* exists in all clients.**

3. **To prevent unauthorized users from easily deleting SAP*, ensure that SAP* is a member of group SUPER.**

4. **Go to the User Administration screen, using transaction code SU01.**

5. **Include the following in the DEFAULT.PFL profile parameter:**
   login/no_automatic_user_sapstar to a value greater than zero.

   The line removes special properties from SAP* to be created with password PASS even if the user master record is nonexistent. By default, when user SAP* is nonexistent in the user master record, the system automatically allows logon to the client using SAP* with the password PASS. After logging in, SAP* has access to everything. The suggested line in DEFAULT.PFL, therefore, is a security precaution to prevent someone with password PASS from having access to everything.

Putting a line in DEFAULT.PFL

Here's how to put a line in DEFAULT.PFL when you deactivate user SAP*:

1. **Enter transaction code RZ10.**

2. **Select Default Profile from the profile field and Extended Maintenance from the Edit Profile options.**

3. **Click the Change button.**

4. **Click the Create icon and add in the parameter:**
   login/no_automatic_user_sapstar
   Value=1

You need to stop and restart SAP to activate your change.

Ensure That User DDIC Exists in All Clients

DDIC is a special SAP user. Certain functions, such as transport activities, utilize user DDIC during the process. If the user isn't there, the transport process trying to use it is essentially up the creek, isn't it? Powerless.

Enter Impermissible Passwords in Table USR40

Villainous users have a certain evil intelligence about them. They can figure out the obvious passwords, so you have to stay a step ahead of them. Here's how to prevent some obvious passwords from working:

1. **Enter transaction code SM30 in the command field.**

2. **Enter the table USR40 and click the Maintain button.**

3. **Enter in any passwords that you want to be impermissible and then save.**

   After you complete these steps, no user is allowed to enter the obvious passwords that you specified.

Limit Logon Attempts with the Incorrect Password

The parameters in Table 19-1 limit the number of logon attempts with an incorrect password. Enter values that make sense for your environment. Follow these steps to set up a parameter to limit logon attempts:

1. **Enter transaction code RZ10 in the command field.**

2. **Add the profile parameters listed in Table 19-1 to the DEFAULT profile.**

Table 19-1	Limiting Logon Attempts	
Parameter Name	*Description*	*Default*
`login/fails_to_session_end`	Number of invalid login attempts until session ends	3
Parameter Name	*Description*	*Default*
`login/fails_to_user_lock`	Number of invalid login attempts until user is locked	12
`login/min_password_lng`	Minimum password length	3

Set System Time Limits for Users

The system parameters in Table 19-2 set time limits for users. Enter values that make sense for your environment.

To set time limits for users, follow these steps:

1. **Enter transaction code RZ10 in the command field.**

2. **Add the profile parameters in Table 19-2 to the DEFAULT profile.**

Table 19-2	Limiting Logon Attempts	
Parameter Name	*Description*	*Default*
`login/password_expiration_time`	Number of days the current password is valid.	0 (no expiration time)
`login/system_client`	Default logon client.	000
`rdisp/gui_auto_logout`	The maximum time limit without input at SAPGUI. After this time, the session ends.	0 (unlimited)

Set Authorizations for OSS Users

Allow OSS users only those functions that are necessary for end users. You don't want your end users doing things that administrators (such as yourself) may do. You probably want to strip the end users of any administrative authorizations.

Follow these steps:

1. **From the OSS screen, choose Administration⇨Authorization Analysis.**

2. **From here, query to see different queries on OSS authorization.**

Chapter 20

Ten Oracle Error Codes

. . . .

In This Chapter

▶ Enjoying what you see when Oracle works right

▶ Identifying what's wrong

. . . .

A s if SAP itself isn't enough to worry about, you have to worry about your database system. When all else fails, people come to you to solve their problems. Everything may not be a Basis problem, but your users are likely to forget that in a crunch. Here are ten of the most common Oracle error messages.

Often, you need to change size parameters for the database or its tables. To specify parameters, you have to use the appropriate commands for your operating system (which could be NT, UNIX, or something else.) In this list of error messages, we suggest the type of commands you can use. You need the specific command for your own operating system.

ORA-00000 normal, successful completion

Wouldn't life be grand if you just saw this message each time? You can pretty much ignore it if it does come up. It's just a confirmation that an operation finished successfully. In an ideal world, you'd only see this message. Of course, because other messages do come up, you get a chance to intervene as R/3 Administrator and take care of things.

ORA-00055 maximum number of DML locks exceeded

"Oh, man," you're likely to exclaim when you see this one. "I exceeded my DML locks quota again." The DML locks specifies the maximum number of locks — one for each table changed in a transaction.

The message means that a requested database operation wanted to use resources that were already used. That is, the operation requested a number greater than the maximum number of DML locks you have designated.

An obvious way to fix the problem would be to use the commands of your operating system to increase the DML_LOCKS parameter in the initialization parameter file and restart the database. You set the number of locks with the parameter DML_LOCKS in the `init<SID>.ora` parameter file.

ORA-00107 failed to connect to network listener process

Usually, the reason that a database process couldn't connect to the network listener is that someone failed to start that listener. (The listener is the process that "listens" for requests to the database.) Consider starting the listener.

ORA-00257 archiver is stuck

This error message means that an error occurred in the ARCH process while trying to archive a redo log.

A *redo log* is a record that Oracle keeps of errors that occur during archiving. You use the log to recover your database. You know, the logs help you "redo" the database.

Often, the message means that the archive directory ran out of space. A possible correction would be to make space available in the archive directory.

ORA-01555 snapshot too old (rollback segment too small)

Old snapshots can always be a problem. Those snapshots of you and your former significant other can come back to haunt you in your present relationship. In Oracle, the snapshot refers to space you've set aside. You get this message when you haven't set aside enough of it.

To be more specific, the message usually means that your didn't have sufficient Rollback Segments available. A *rollback segment* is a place in the database where an uncommitted transaction can be rolled back if a transaction does not "commit" (doesn't finish). As with previous members of the list in this chapter, the most likely fix is to make an adjustment to parameters — in this case to the parameters of Rollback Segments.

ORA-01599 failed to acquire rollback segment "name"

In this case, the cache space is full. That is, the cache already has the number of entries you've designated for it. A possible correction would be to adjust the size parameters of Rollback Segments. Consider making a larger rollback segment.

ORA-01628 max # of extents num reached for rollback segment num

Here, too, the system has exceeded the number you have set in your parameters. Again, you can adjust the size parameters of the Rollback Segments. You might consider making a larger rollback segment.

ORA-01630 max # of extents num reached in temp segment in tablespace name

Tables, too, can run out of space in your database. You can use parameters to increase the size of the tablespace.

ORA-01650 unable to extend rollback segment name by num in tablespace name

Sometimes when you want to extend a rollback segment, Oracle won't let you do it. Here is another error your can run into when tablespace is too small. To fix the problem, use parameters to increase the size of the tablespace.

ORA-01652 unable to extend temp segment by num in tablespace name

Like Rollback Segments, Temp Segments can run into problems when the tablespace for them is too small. The probable correction is to increase the size of the tablespace.

Part VII
Appendixes

In this part . . .

As you proceed down the path of SAP, occasionally you'll find something that just looks like jibberish. Trust us. Usually, it's just a term that you don't know yet.

In this part, we've listed common SAP terminology and transaction codes in handy alphabetical order. When you're stumped, start here.

Glossary

· ·

*I*t can be quite frustrating to be reading about something, like maybe OSS, and then coming across some other term that you're not familiar with. That shouldn't have to happen.

This glossary is a quick guide to key terms in this book to keep you from being distracted by unfamiliar terms when you're trying to learn about something important.

ABAP

Advanced Business Application Programming. SAP's fourth-generation programming language, used to develop applications that run in SAP.

ABAP/4

SAP's proprietary programming language, which you can use when you need even more control than you can get from all the applications modules and third-party solutions that are already a part of SAP.

Alerts thresholds

Little "alarms" that tell you when you have a problem; used in CCMS. Alerts are available for the database, the operating system, and the network, as well as global alerts. Their coding system is red, yellow, and green, just like traffic lights.

Application server

A server that helps out the Database server a great deal by loading updates, deletions, and queries into its own cache and processing them.

Background processing

Jobs that run in the background, at a scheduled time. You don't have to be working interactively to run them (except, obviously, to schedule them in the first place).

Basis

Basis is the technical infrastructure of your R/3 implementation, including matters pertaining to the system, to databases, to functional modules, to Enterprise Resource Planning itself, and to anything else that may otherwise somehow fall through the cracks.

Basis Administrator

The nimble-footed person who has to keep your technical infrastructure working (but who shouldn't have to do everything).

Binary patch

Another name for *kernel patch* — a patch (using binary code) to replace existing executables with better ones.

Buffer

A buffer is an area set aside in memory for temporary storage. In life, it's a little safety zone that you set up, such as a friendly person who stands between you and somebody trying to attack you.

CCMS

Computing Center Management System. The place where you take charge and monitor all kinds of performance things — such as workloads, databases, and the network.

Change request

You don't just go in, change objects in SAP, and then slip away without a trace. You fill out a change request so that you can follow your progress every step of the way and other people can check on you later. A change request is pretty much what it sounds like — a formal, written record of what you do when changing the configuration.

Client

In R/3, a client is a self-contained unit that has separate master records from other clients and its own set of tables. A client is a logical system and not necessarily a separate physical system, which can be outright confusing if you're accustomed to thinking of *clients* as individual computers in a client/server network. On behalf of everyone who provides R/3 services, we apologize for the ambiguity.

Client copy

In a client copy, you bring over the master records and tables from a source client to a second, target client.

Client delete

Expunging a client, often to make way for a client refresh.

Client transport

Use it to copy between systems instead of within one system.

Clipboard

Clipboards used to be these things that reporters carried around. They didn't really have anything to do with cutting and pasting, but now they do. You probably know clipboards from Windows. The SAP clipboard holds stuff that you cut from the screen. Very handy. Useful for transferring stuff from application to application in R/3 or even from R/3 to another application.

Correction

Correction is, like, fixing things. You may correct a database, for example, by transporting a fresh instance of the database to replace one that, you know, is not acceptable for some reason.

Cross-transport

A cross-transport is a bad idea. It's importing and exporting in a sequence other than the standard one from development to testing to production (for example, by going straight from development to production).

Database Administrator

That anomaly whose mind works the way databases work and who can fix databases when they break.

Database server

The most important of the servers in the three-tier landscape, a database server is a powerful server processing zillions of requests for data.

Developer's key

Code that identifies you as a developer, used to make OSS Note Fixes. Also, any of the small metal items on a ring in the pocket or purse of your average programmer.

Early Watch

An SAP service where SAP actually logs into your system and checks it out for you using client 066. The service may sound a little "Big Brother"-ish, but you only get it if you request it, and SAP is only there to help.

ERP

Enterprise Resource Planning, a concept that SAP has made famous (and probably has made possible). ERP means drawing upon all the information from all the business systems of your company to make what you hope are singularly intelligent decisions.

Executable

Someone about to be shot. In SAP, a program that you run to do things (like word processing, business applications, things like that).

Hot Packages

Bundle of patches to correct R/3 bugs. A single Hot Package corrects bugs in multiple applications at once.

Instance

"Instance?" "Instance?" Who sits up nights thinking of terms like "object," "instance," and stuff like that to keep SAP administrators going bonkers?

If an instance were called, say, a "processor," or a "computer," or a "server," you'd know what was under discussion. Call it R/3 itself and you'd be fine, because one installed R/3 system is an "instance."

An instance is a computer or server or R/3, really, but there's a distinction because a server can have a number of different faces (to use the assigned word, "instances"). An instance is the resources like memory and work processes that go with one application server or database server. You can vary those instances as System Administrator.

Kernel patch

A very famous war officer. (Get it? Colonel Patch? Never mind.) In SAP, code to repair a bug in your executables.

Legal Change Patch (LCP)

LCPs contain all the fixes Hot Packages contain plus HR-specific fixes.

Local copy

When doing a client copy, a local copy is a copy within a single logical system. Local copies are the good ones when contrasted with remote copies, which cause too much network traffic.

Log

Not a tree stump. A fancy name for *list,* like Captain Picard's. It remembers what happens while your system runs.

Master record

Your master records are key information — for your users, they are stuff like usernames, authorizations, and other really important stuff. For vendors, the master records are addresses, phone numbers, banking information — also really useful stuff. Master records are records that are pretty permanent — categories like "address" that you aren't going to change.

Menu bar

A menu bar is probably no news to you. The menu bar is the list of names across the top of the screen that you use to do things — like the menu in about a zillion other programs. R/3 menus are neatly dynamic, changing according to your application and task.

Metadata

Metadata is data that describes other data — the kind of data definitions that you put into a data dictionary.

Open systems

Open systems, in SAP, means the ability to work across the complex lattice-work of platforms, operating systems, and databases that make up the modern corporation — the ability to go anywhere in your company data, find anything, and do anything.

OSS

OSS (Online Service System) contains error reports, notes on problems, requests for development, and stuff like that from users.

OSS Note Fix

OSS text recommending a patch you have to install by hand because a Hot Package for the fix isn't available yet.

Patch

Bug fix. You download them from SAP in the form of *Hot Packages,* then transfer them to your own system.

Presentation server

The server that meets the public. Often your desktop PC, the presentation server runs SAPGUI.

Reference client

A reliable, stable client you can then use when doing things like copying a client. 000 is a reference client prepackaged with SAP.

Remote copy

When doing a client copy, a remote copy is a copy from one SAP system (say, DEV) to another (ACP, perhaps). Remote copies aren't such a great idea because they put a real load on the network. Most of the time, use client export and import instead of remote client copy.

Report

Reports are, generally, the main thing that end users are looking for as they do business in R/3. A report is actually an ABAP/4 program that gets database information and displays it. In some cases, you can also analyze things by using reports.

SAP

SAP, in German, stands for *Systeme, Anwendungen, Produkte in der Datenverarbeitung.* Luckily, the initials carry over nicely to English, where SAP means *Systems, Applications, and Products in Data Processing.*

SAP Patch Manager

See *SPAM.*

Security Administrator

The person you blame when unauthorized people get access to stuff.

Server

A person in a restaurant who politely brings you food. In computer systems, a server is a networked computer that provides services to other computers, such as managing their common data or managing connections to the host system.

Session

A window that you open to run an additional R/3 task. You can open several such windows, even run the same task in more than one window (just like in Microsoft Windows).

SPAM

A cheap meat that some people find disgusting. In SAP, SAP Patch Manager, used to download and apply Hot Packages.

Swap

A trade between two boys in the Tom Sawyer era. Also, a flea market/bartering situation. In computers, temporarily placing material from memory onto the hard drive to aid in processing. (You can regulate swap in Computing Center Management System.)

Syslog (system log)

The system log records R/3 errors and events. You use it to find out about programs or transactions that get terminated, errors in databases, and other stuff.

System Administrator

Mr. or Ms. Techie, who understands operating systems well enough to keep them working and to keep things that depend on the operating system — like printing — working.

System landscape

Before the world of technology came along, a _landscape_ used to be "a view of the land," much as a _seascape_ is a "view of the sea." Now, though, a landscape refers to the overall design of a system, the big picture. You're no doubt used to the term anyway and probably aren't reading this.

Table

Place where you put hamburger buns, garden burgers, plates, ice cream, and a flower vase. Whoops. Wrong table. In SAP, a table is a place where you put data — an array of data, if that matters to you.

Task

What you actually do to systems when implementing a change request. Also, in life, any kind of a project or job to do.

Three-tier client/server architecture

A good architecture, where work gets distributed over a database server, an application server, and a presentation server.

Transaction code

Transaction codes are the direct route to a task that you want to perform. You type a transaction code into the command field, such as S000 to return to the main menu screen.

Transport

A transport is a transfer of important stuff (system components) from one system to another, using an export and an import.

Two-tier client/server architecture

A less-than-ideal setup, where two servers do the three functions of a database server, application server, and presentation server. Conflicts arise and processes slow down (by nanoseconds at a time).

Window

A window is the box that you see on the screen with your application in it. Click on it to make it active.

Work process

A work process is the basic unit you configure when making an operation mode.

You can have work processes for these activities:

- ✔ Administering Dialog
- ✔ Updates of change documents
- ✔ Background processing
- ✔ Spool
- ✔ Lock administration

Workbench Organizer

Workbench Organizer helps you record and control the changes that you make to systems, helping to prevent embarrassing screw-ups. Developers and administrators are just as capable as anybody else of copying something to the wrong place or changing the wrong program.

Transaction Codes

R/3 transaction codes send commands that execute the functions of SAP.
Here's what the codes do.

Transaction Code	Text
S-33	Display table
S00	Short Message
S000	System Menu
S002	Menu Administration
S@E	Debugging
SA01	Number range maintenance: ADRNR
SA02	Academic title (cent. addr. admin.)
SA03	Title (central address admin.)
SA04	Name prefixes (centr. addr. admin.)
SA05	Name suffix (centr. addr. admin.)
SA06	Address or personal data source
SA07	Address groups (centr. addr. admin.)
SA08	Person groups (centr. addr. admin.)
SA09	Internat. versions address admin.
SA10	Address admin. communication type
SA38	ABAP/4 Reporting
SA39	SA38 for Parameter Transaction
SABB	ABAP/4 Manual: Flight Booking
SAD0	Address Management call
SADC	Address: Maint. communication types
SADP	Init.scr. addr.maint.person in comp.
SADR	Address maint. - Group required!

(Continued)

Transaction Code	Text
SADV	International address versions
SADX	Directory exchange
SALE	IMG Application Link Enabling
SAMT	ABAP/4 Program Set Processing
SAR	Maintain Transaction Codes
SAR0	Display Standard Reporting Tree
SAR1	Structure of an archive object
SAR2	Definition of an archive object
SAR3	Archiving: Customizing
SAR4	Definition of the archive classes
SAR5	Assignment of archive classes
SAR6	Archive events: Generation program
SARA	Archive Management
SARL	Call of ArchiveLink Monitor
SARP	Reporting (Tree Structure): Execute
SART	Display Report Tree
SAX4	Addresses: X.400 addresses generated
SB01	Business Navigator - Component view
SB02	Business Navigator - Process flow vw
SB04	Maintain IMG activity assignment
SB05	Business Navigator - ALE View
SB06	Business Navigator - Component view
SB07	Business Navigtr - Process flow view
SB09	Business Navigtr - Process flow view
SB10	Business Navigator - Component view
SBEA	BEAC corporate flight system
SBEW	Table widget for flights

Transaction Code	Text
SBI1	Maintain enhancement to InfoSource
SBI2	Maintain enhancement to master data
SBI3	Maintain append for InfoSource
SBI4	Maintain append for master data
SBI5	Delete InfoObjects
SBPT	Administration Process Technology
SBTA	Test background processing
SBTU	Background processing for user
SC38	Start Report (Remote)
SCA1	Cannot be executed directly
SCA2	Cannot be executed directly
SCA3	Cannot be executed directly
SCAL	Factory Calendar with GUI
SCAR	Record CATT procedures
SCAT	Computer Aided Test Tool
SCC0	Client Copy
SCC1	Client Copy - Special Selections
SCC2	Client transport
SCC3	Client Copy Log
SCC4	Client Administration
SCC5	Client Delete
SCC6	Client import
SCC7	Client import - postprocessing
SCC8	Client export
SCC9	Remote client copy
SCCL	Client import - postprocessing
SCD0	Change Documents for Utilities

(Continued)

(Continued)

Transaction Code	Text
SCDN	Change Documents for Number Ranges
SCDO	Display Change Document Objects
SCMP	Comparison of Customizing
SCOA	SAPconnect: Administration
SCOM	SAPcomm: Configuration
SCON	SAPconnect: Configuration
SCPF	Generate enterprise IMG
SCT1	Logical imports - overview
SCU0	Table Analyses And Comparison
SCU1	Table Comparison - Export to Tape
SCU2	Table Comparison Against Tape
SCU3	Table History
SCUI	Communicate system status to SAP
SD11	Data Modeler
SDBE	Matchcode objects (test)
SDC1	Dictionary Nametab - Export (Compar)
SDC2	Dictionary Nametab - Comparison
SDMO	Dynamic Menu (old)
SDPI	Number Range Maint.: SD_PICKING
SDWO	ABAP/4 Development WB Initial Screen
SE01	Transport and Correction System
SE02	Environment Analyzer
SE03	Transport Utilities
SE06	Set Up Workbench Organizer
SE07	Transport System Status Display
SE09	Workbench Organizer
SE10	Customizing Organizer

Transaction Code	Text
SE11	ABAP/4 Dictionary Maintenance
SE12	ABAP/4 Dictionary Display
SE13	Maintain Technical Settings (Tables)
SE14	Utilities for Dictionary Tables
SE15	ABAP/4 Repository Information System
SE16	Data Browser
SE17	General Table Display
SE30	ABAP/4 Runtime Analysis
SE32	ABAP/4 Text Element Maintenance
SE35	ABAP/4 Dialog Modules
SE36	ABAP/4: Logical Databases
SE37	ABAP/4 Function Modules
SE38	ABAP/4 Editor
SE39	Splitscreen Editor: Program Compare
SE40	MP: Standards Maint. and Translation
SE41	Menu Painter
SE43	Maintain Area Menu
SE44	Hierarchy Display
SE48	Program Analysis: Call Hierarchy
SE49	Program Analysis: Table Manipulation
SE51	Screen Painter
SE52	Parameterized screenpainter call
SE54	Generate table view
SE55	Internal table view maintenance call
SE56	internal call: display table view
SE57	internal delete table view call
SE61	R/3 Documentation

(Continued)

(Continued)

Transaction Code	Text
SE62	Industry Utilities
SE63	Translation: Initial Screen
SE64	Terminology
SE65	R/3 Doc. Short Text Statistics
SE66	R/3 Documentation Statistics
SE68	Translation Administration
SE71	SAPscript form
SE72	SAPscript styles
SE73	SAPscript font maintenance (revised)
SE74	SAPscript format conversion
SE75	SAPscript settings
SE76	SAPscript Translation Layout Sets
SE77	SAPscript Translation Styles
SE80	ABAP/4 Development Workbench
SE81	SAP Application Hierarchy
SE82	Customer Application Hierarchy
SE84	ABAP/4 Repository Information System
SE85	ABAP/4 Repository Information System
SE86	ABAP/4 Repository Information System
SE87	Data Modeler Information System
SE88	Development Coordination Info System
SE89	Maintain Trees in Information System
SE90	Process Model Information System
SE91	Maintain Messages
SE92	Maintain System Log Messages
SE93	Maintain Transaction Codes
SE95	Customer Enhancements to AEW Objects

Transaction Code	Text
SECR	Audit Info System
SENN	Access translation
SEPS	SAP Electronic Parcel Service
SERP	Reporting: Change Tree Structure
SEU	Object Browser
SF01	Logical file names
SF02	Platform-independent file names
SF03	Platform-independent file names
SF04	Platform-independent file names
SF05	Platform-independent file names
SF06	Platform-independent file names
SF07	File Name Analysis
SFAC	Field selection maintenance
SFAW	Field Selection Maintenance
SFAX	BC Sales
SFL1	Demo example flight master synchron.
SFT1	Public Holiday maintenance
SFT2	Public Holiday Calendar maintenance
SFT3	Factory Calendar Maintenance
SH01	Online help: F1 Help server
SH02	Online help: Link tracing
SH03	Call extended help
SHD0	Transaction variant maintenance
SHD1	Internal: Variant transaction call
SHDB	Record batch input
SHDG	Heidelberg: Global values
SHDS	Internal: Save transaction variant

(Continued)

(Continued)

Transaction Code	Text
SIAC	Transport link for IAC objects
SICK	Installation Check
SIM1	EDM Menu Entry for Entity Type
SIM2	Cluster Processing
SIM3	Start EDM Graphics
SIM4	EDM Menu Entry: Data Model
SIM8	EDM Analysis
SIMC	Analyze Cluster
SIMM	EDM Information Model Master AIN
SIMO	EDM Information Model Maint. AIN
SIMT	EDM Test Translation Tool
SIN1	SAPBPT: Inbox
SINA	SAPBPT: Maintain Standard Config.
SK18	SAPcomm: Activities display
SK20	SAPcomm: System parameter
SKRT	SAPcomm: Routing test
SKTX	Translation
SL37	Software Logistics Check (SM37)
SLDB	Logical Databases (Tree Structure)
SLG0	Application Log Object Maintenance
SLG1	Analyze application log
SLGN	Number range maintenance: APPL_LOG
SLIN	ABAP/4: Extended Program Check
SLIS	FI-SL Spec.Purpose Ledg. Info.System
SLLS	Translation Statistics
SLW1	Maintain translation environment II
SLW2	Maintain translation environment

Transaction Code	Text
SLW3	WL scheduler
SLW4	Translation: Application hierarchy
SM01	Lock transactions
SM02	System Messages
SM04	User Overview
SM05	System Message Dialog Box from ABAP
SM12	Display and Delete Locks
SM13	Display Update Records
SM21	System Log
SM28	Installation Check
SM29	Model Transfer for Tables
SM30	Call View Maintenance
SM31	Table Maintenance
SM32	Maintain Table Parameter ID TAB
SM33	Display Table Parameter ID TAB
SM34	Viewcluster maintenance call
SM35	Batch Input Monitoring
SM36	Define Background Job
SM37	Background Job Overview
SM38	Queue Maintenance Transaction
SM39	Job Analysis
SM49	Execute Logical Commands
SM50	Work Process Overview
SM51	List of SAP Servers
SM54	TXCOM maintenance
SM55	THOST Maintenance
SM56	Number Range Buffer

(Continued)

(Continued)

Transaction Code	Text
SM58	Asynchronous RFC Error Log
SM59	RFC Destinations (Display/Maintain)
SM63	Display/Maintain Operating Mode Sets
SM64	Release of an Event
SM65	Background Processing Analysis Tool
SM66	Systemwide Work Process Overview
SM67	Job Scheduling
SM68	Job Administration
SM69	Display/Maintain Logical Commands
SMEN	Dynamic Menu
SMGW	Gateway Monitor
SMLG	Maintain Logon Group
SMLI	Language Import Utility
SMLT	Language Transport Utility
SMME	Output control Message Block Table
SMO1	Repository Information System: SMOD
SMO2	Repository Information System: SMOD
SMO3	Repository Information System: SMOD
SMO4	Repository Information System: SMOD
SMO5	Repository Information System: SMOD
SMOD	SAP Enhancement Management
SMPC	Translation Interface PC - R/3
SMW0	SAP Web Repository
SMW2	Test multipart MIME interface
SMX	Display Own Jobs
SNRO	Number Range Objects
SNUM	Number Range Driver

Transaction Code	Text
SO00	SAPoffice: Short Message
SO01	SAPoffice: Inbox
SO02	SAPoffice: Outbox
SO03	SAPoffice: Private Folders
SO04	SAPoffice: Shared Folders
SO05	SAPoffice: Private Trash
SO06	SAPoffice: Substitution on/off
SO07	SAPoffice: Resubmission
SO09	SAPoffice: Branch to Folder
SO10	SAPscript: Standard Texts
SO12	SAPoffice: User Master
SO13	SAPoffice: Substitute
SO15	SAPoffice: Distribution Lists
SO16	SAPoffice: Profile
SO17	SAPoffice: Delete Shared Trash
SO18	SAPoffice: Shared Trash
SO19	SAPoffice: Default Documents
SO20	SAPoffice: Private Default Document
SO21	Maintain PC Work Directory
SO22	SAPoffice: Clear Temp. PC Files
SO28	Maintain SOGR
SO30	SAPoffice: Reorg.
SO32	SAPoffice: Create All Users
SO36	Create Automatic Forwarding
SO38	SAPoffice: Synchr. of Folder Auths.
SO40	SAPoffice: Cust. Layout Set MAIL
SO41	SAPoffice: Cust. Layout Set TELEFAX

(Continued)

(Continued)

Transaction Code	Text
SO42	SAPoffice: Cust.Layout Set TELEFAX_K
SO43	SAPoffice: Cust.Layout Set TELEFAX_M
SO44	SAPoffice: Cust. Layout Set TELEX
SO51	Create Addresses for SAPoffice
SO52	Deletes Address from User Master
SO54	Download of Internet Addresses
SO60	Call R/3 Help Library
SO61	R/3 Library
SO70	Hypertext: Display/Maint. Structure
SO71	Test plan management
SO72	Maintain Hypertext Module
SO73	Import graphic into SAPfind
SO74	Hypertext Structure Editor
SO75	Getting Started with the R/3 System
SO77	Release Customizing
SO78	View List for Structure MENUS000
SO80	SAPfind: Free Text Retrieval Dialog
SO81	SAPfind: Free Text Indexing (Test)
SO82	SAPfind: Free Text Retrieval Batch
SO85	SAPfind: txt_seq_search
SO86	SAPfind: Txt_seq_search_1
SO90	SAPfind: shell folders service prog.
SO91	SAPfind SO: SAPoffice Marketing Info
SO95	Pregenerated Search Queries - Selec.
SO99	Put Information System
SOA0	ArchiveLink Workflow document types
SOA1	ArchiveLink: Early Archiving

Transaction Code	Text
SOA2	ArchiveLink: Late Archiving
SOA3	ArchiveLink settings early
SOA4	ArchiveLink settings late
SOA5	ArchiveLink Simultaneous Archiving
SOA6	ArchiveLink settings simult.
SOBJ	Attribute Maintenance Objects
SOBT	assign attributes to maint. objects
SOFF	SAPoffice: Area Menu
SOFR	Mapping of telex recipients
SOJ2	SAP Objects: Display Methods
SOJ3	SAP Objects: Display Return Values
SOLE	OLE Applications
SOLI	Load OLE type info
SOLO	OLE Object Browser
SOPA	SAPoffice: Maintain Parameter
SOPE	SAPoffice: Exclude Document Types
SOTD	SAPoffice: Maintain Object Types
SOY1	SAPoffice: Mass Maint. Users
SOY2	SAPoffice: Statistics data collect.
SOY3	SAPoffice: Statistics Evaluation
SOY4	SAPoffice: Access overview
SOY5	SAPoffice: Inbox overview
SOY6	SAPoffice: Document overview
SOY7	SAPoffice: Folder overview
SOY8	SAPoffice: Mass Archiving
SOY9	SAPoffice: Inbox Reorg.
SOYA	SAPoffice: Change folder owner

(Continued)

(Continued)

Transaction Code	Text
SP00	Spool and Related Areas
SP01	Output Controller
SP02	Display Output Requests
SP03	Spool: Load Formats
SP11	TemSe directory
SP12	TemSe Administration
SP1T	Output Control (Test)
SPAD	Spool Administration
SPAM	SAP PATCH MANAGER (SPAM)
SPAT	Spool Administration (Test)
SPAU	Display modified DE objects
SPBM	Monitoring parallel background tasks
SPBT	Test: Parallel background tasks
SPDD	Display modified DDIC objects
SPH1	Create and maintain telephony server
SPH2	Maintain outgoing number change
SPH3	Maintain incoming number change
SPH4	Activ./deactiv. telephony in system
SPH5	Define address data areas
SPH6	Server description is lang.-dep.
SPH7	Addr.data area texts are lang.-dep.
SPHA	Telephony administration
SPHC	Customizing telephone integration
SPR1	Delta Customizing for Project
SPR2	Delta Customizing for Enterprise IMG
SPR3	Upgrade Customizing for Project
SPR4	Upgrade Cust. for Enterprise IMG

Transaction Code	Text
SPR5	Transport enterprise IMG
SPR6	Transport Project: Status/Hdr.data
SPR7	Transport: Project notes
SPR8	Print WinWord IMG notes
SPR9	Display Structure: System install.
SPRA	Display structure: Ext. Refer. IMG
SPRB	IMG note editor switch
SPRM	Update settings
SPRO	Initial screen: Customizing
SPRP	Project Management
SPRQ	Start of a transaction
SPTP	Text elem. maint. for print formats
SQ00	ABAP/4 Query: Start Queries
SQ01	ABAP/4 Query: Maintain Queries
SQ02	ABAP/4 Query: Maintain Funct. Areas
SQ03	ABAP/4 Query: Maintain User Groups
SQ07	ABAP/4 Query: Language Comparison
SRCN	Delete country-specific reports
SRET	Report selection
SRFN	Rename Tool for Function Modules
SSC	SAP R/3 appointment diary (internal)
SSC0	SAP R/3 appointm.cal. (employee)
SSC1	SAP R/3 (own) appointments diary
SSCA	Appointment Diary: Administration
SSCV	Appoint. diary: VisualBasic frontend
SSM0	Menu maintenance and test
SSM1	Session manager generation call

(Continued)

(Continued)

Transaction Code	Text
SSMT	Modification 2.2 > 3.0
SST0	Project analysis selection screen
SST7	Complex Analysis
SSUC	Structure graphic: copy settings
SSUD	Structure graphic: delete settings
SSU0	Structure graphic: central settings
SSUX	SAP Structural Graphics: Model Graph
ST01	System Trace
ST02	Setups/Tune Buffers
ST03	Performance,SAP Statistics, Workload
ST04	Select DB activities
ST05	SQL Trace
ST06	Operating System Monitor
ST07	Application monitor
ST08	Network Monitor
ST09	Network Alert Monitor
ST10	Table Call Statistics
ST11	Display Developer Traces
ST12	Application Monitor
ST14	Application Analysis
ST22	ABAP/4 Runtime Error Analysis
ST4A	Database: Shared Cursor Cache (ST04)
ST62	Create industry short texts
STAT	Local transaction statistics
STDR	TADIR consistency check
STM1	Group abbreviations
STMP	Proposal pool: Selection

Transaction Code	Text
STMS	Transport Management System
STP4	Select DB activities
STT0	Test Organization
STUN	Menu Performance Monitor
STW1	Test Workbench: Test catalog
STW2	Test workbench: Test plan
STW3	Test workbench: Test package
STW4	Test Workbench: Edit test package
STW5	C maintenance table TTPLA
SU01	Maintain User
SU02	Maintain Authorization Profiles
SU03	Maintain Authorizations
SU05	Maintain Internet users
SU10	Mass Changes to User Master Records
SU12	Mass Changes to User Master Records
SU20	Maintain Authorization Fields
SU21	Maintain Authorization Objects
SU22	Auth. Object Usage in Transactions
SU23	Load Tables in TAUTL
SU24	Auth. obj. check under transactions
SU25	Copy initial defaults
SU26	Compare authorization data
SU30	Overall Authorization Checks
SU50	Maintain User Defaults
SU51	Maintain User Address
SU52	Maintain User Parameters
SU53	Display Check Values

(Continued)

(Continued)

Transaction Code	Text
SU54	Maintain User Menu
SU55	Start User Menu
SU56	Analyze User Buffer
SU80	Archive user change documents
SU81	Archive user password change doc.
SU82	Archive profile documents
SU83	Archive authorization docs.
SU84	Read archived user change documents
SU85	Read archived password change doc.
SU86	Read profile change documents
SU87	Read authorization change documents
SU96	Table maint.: Change SUKRIA
SU97	Table maint.: Display SUKRIA
SU98	Call report RSUSR008
SU99	Call report RSUSR008
SUB%	Internal call: Submit via commnd fld
SUCH	Translatability CHECKs
SUCU	Table authorizations: Customizing
SUIM	Call AUTH reporting tree (info sys.)
SUPC	Profiles for activity groups
SUPE	Integrated user maintenance
SUPF	Integrated user maintenance
SUPO	Maintain org. levels
SVGM	SAP R/3 Procedure Model
SVGS	View for activity in Procedure Model
SVMC	Start view maintenance with memory
SWDA	Settings in SAP Workflow

Transaction Code	Text
SWDC	Workflow Definition: Administration
SWDN	Number Range Maint.: SWD_WDID
SWE2	Display/Maint. of Event Type Linkage
SWE3	Display Instance Linkages
SWE4	Change event log status (on/off)
SWEC	Linkage Change Doc.->Workflow Event
SWED	Assignment chng.doc./WF object type
SWEL	Display event log
SWEN	Number Range Maintenance: SWE_EVTID
SWF1	WF: Wizard for creating T100W
SWF3	WFP: Call Pattern Repository
SWI1	Selection report for workflows
SWI2	Work item analysis (statistics)
SWI3	Workflow Outbox
SWI4	Task Analysis
SWI5	Workload Analysis
SWI6	Object links
SWI7	Workflow resubmission
SWLC	Check Tasks for Agents
SWLD	Workbench for Workflow 3.0
SWLE	Execute a work item
SWLP	Copy a Plan Version
SWLV	Maintain Work Item Views
SWLW	Workbench for Workflow 3.0
SWO1	Business Object Repository
SWO2	Business Object Repository
SWO6	Customizing Object Types

(Continued)

(Continued)

Transaction Code	Text
SWRP	Dummy for IAC Workflow Status
SWT0	Configure workflow trace
SWU0	Event Simulation
SWU1	User RFC Monitor
SWU2	Event RFC Monitor
SWU3	Consistency check: Customizing
SWU4	Consistency Test for Standard Task
SWU5	Consistency Test for Customer Task
SWU6	Consistency Test for Workflow Task
SWU7	Consistency Test for Workflow Templ.
SWU8	Technical Trace On/Off
SWU9	Display Technical Trace
SWUA	Start Verification Workflow
SWUB	Workflow RFC destination maintenance
SWUC	Customizing task (obsolete)
SWUD	Diagnostic Tools
SWUE	Initiate Event
SWUF	Workflow monitor
SWUH	Test method
SWUI	Test attributes (from Rel.4.0 onwards)
SWUJ	Test roles (from Rel.4.0 onwards)
SWUM	Create/Edit Document Template WF
SWUN	Number Range Maintenance: FORMABSENC
SWUR	Send mails for work items
SWUS	Shell for Starting Workflows
SWUW	Number Range Maint.: SWW_WIID
SWWA	Start monitoring report RSWWDHIN

Transaction Code	Text
SWWB	Restart of background job SWWDHEX
SWWD	Activate error monitoring for WIs
SWXF	Form Uses: Initial Screen
SX52	SAP-EDI: Create Subset
SXDA	SAPdxfer: Center
SXDB	SAPdxfer: Center
SYNT	Display Syntax Trace Output

Index

Notes

Notes

Notes

Notes

Discover Dummies™ Online!

The *Dummies* Web Site is your fun and friendly online resource for the latest information about *...For Dummies*® books on all your favorite topics. From cars to computers, wine to Windows, and investing to the Internet, we've got a shelf full of *...For Dummies* books waiting for you!

Ten Fun and Useful Things You Can Do at www.dummies.com

1. Register this book and win!
2. Find and buy the *...For Dummies* books you want online.
3. Get ten great *Dummies Tips*™ every week.
4. Chat with your favorite *...For Dummies* authors.
5. Subscribe free to *The Dummies Dispatch*™ newsletter.
6. Enter our sweepstakes and win cool stuff.
7. Send a free cartoon postcard to a friend.
8. Download free software.
9. Sample a book before you buy.
10. Talk to us. Make comments, ask questions, and get answers!

Jump online to these ten fun and useful things at
http://www.dummies.com/10useful

For other technology titles from IDG Books Worldwide, go to
www.idgbooks.com

Not online yet? It's easy to get started with *The Internet For Dummies*,® 5th Edition, or *Dummies 101*®: *The Internet For Windows*® *98*, available at local retailers everywhere.

Find other *...For Dummies* books on these topics:

Business • Careers • Databases • Food & Beverages • Games • Gardening • Graphics • Hardware
Health & Fitness • Internet and the World Wide Web • Networking • Office Suites
Operating Systems • Personal Finance • Pets • Programming • Recreation • Sports
Spreadsheets • Teacher Resources • Test Prep • Word Processing

IDG BOOKS WORLDWIDE
BOOK REGISTRATION

We want to hear from you!

Visit **http://my2cents.dummies.com** to register this book and tell us how you liked it!

✔ Get entered in our monthly prize giveaway.

✔ Give us feedback about this book — tell us what you like best, what you like least, or maybe what you'd like to ask the author and us to change!

✔ Let us know any other ...*For Dummies*® topics that interest you.

Your feedback helps us determine what books to publish, tells us what coverage to add as we revise our books, and lets us know whether we're meeting your needs as a ...*For Dummies* reader. You're our most valuable resource, and what you have to say is important to us!

Not on the Web yet? It's easy to get started with *Dummies 101*®: *The Internet For Windows*® *98* or *The Internet For Dummies*®, 5th Edition, at local retailers everywhere.

Or let us know what you think by sending us a letter at the following address:

...*For Dummies* Book Registration
Dummies Press
7260 Shadeland Station, Suite 100
Indianapolis, IN 46256-3917
Fax 317-596-5498

™

...FOR DUMMIES

BESTSELLING BOOK SERIES